The
Pan-American
Dream

The

Pan-American

Dream

*Do Latin America's Cultural Values
Discourage True Partnership with
the United States and Canada?*

Lawrence E. Harrison

Westview Press
A Member of the Perseus Books Group

Grateful acknowledgment is made for permission to reprint the following:

The table on page 88 from *El Sueño Pan-Americano* by Francisco Andrés Orizo. Copyright © 1991 by Francisco Andrés Orizo. Reprinted by permission of the author.

Excerpts from "The United Fruit Co." by Pablo Neruda. Copyright © 1991 by Fundacion Pablo Neruda, Regents of the University of California. From *Canto General*, edited and translated by Jack Schmitt. Reprinted by permission of the University of California Press.

Designed by Nancy Sabato

FIRST EDITION   Published by BasicBooks, A Division of HarperCollins Publishers, Inc.

Library of Congress Cataloging-in-Publication Data

Harrison, Lawrence E.
    The Pan-American dream : do Latin America's cultural values discourage true partnership with the United States and Canada? / by Lawrence E. Harrison.
        p. cm.
    Includes index.
    ISBN 0-465-08916-X (hc)   ISBN 0-8133-3470-5 (pb)
    1. Pan-Americanism. 2. Latin America—Relations—United States. 3. United States—Relations—Latin America. 4. Latin America—Relations—Canada. 5. Canada—Relations—Latin America. 6. Values—America. 7. Free trade—America. I. Title.
F1410.H26   1997
303.48'27308—dc20   96–24670
                                                                      CIP

98 99 00 RRD 10 9 8 7 6 5 4 3 2

In memory of Carlos Rangel
To whose wisdom and courage we are all indebted.

Contents

Acknowledgments

I wish to express my gratitude to the Scaife Family Foundation for its support, also the Center for International Affairs at Harvard University with which I was associated (for the third time) while working on this book. I wish to thank Kermit Hummel, publisher of Basic Books, for his encouragement and support, and the copy editor, Linda Carbone, for her unfailing good judgment and advice.

I also wish to acknowledge a number of people who provided me with helpful reactions and suggestions: Maria Lucia Victor Barbosa, Rodrigo Botero, Leon Bouvier, Charles Brayshaw, Marshall Brown, Shirley Christian, Isaac Cohen, Carlos Escudé, Mark Falcoff, Patricia Galeana, Mariano Grondona, Eileen Heaphy, Philip Heymann, David Hojman, Martín Hopenheyn, Anthony Interlandi, Mark Krikorian, Lynne Lambert, Lawrence Lederman, Ozay Mehmet, Carlos Alberto Montaner, Luis Pasos, José Osvaldo de Meira Penna, Michel Riel, Sharon Stanton Russell, George Scialabba, Peter Skerry, James Walsh, Sidney Weintraub, and Arthur Wortzel.

Finally, I wish to express my gratitude to my wife, Patricia Crane Harrison, for her patience, support, and innumerable helpful suggestions.

Introduction

Dream or Reality?

On 11 December 1994, in Miami, the Partnership for Development and Prosperity was signed by thirty-four Western Hemisphere chiefs of state, including President Bill Clinton, Prime Minister Jean Chrétien of Canada, Presidents Ernesto Zedillo of Mexico, Carlos Saúl Menem of Argentina, and Eduardo Frei of Chile, and President-elect Fernando Henrique Cardoso of Brazil. Among the goals of the Miami summit was the negotiation of a Free Trade Area of the Americas within ten years. The rhetoric of the meeting repeatedly evoked the impressive progress of Western European integration since World War II.

Thirty-three years earlier, on 17 August 1961, in Uruguay, President John F. Kennedy and the Latin American chiefs of state had signed the Charter of Punta del Este, which inaugurated the Alliance for Progress, "established on the basic principle that free men working through the institution of representative democracy can best satisfy man's aspirations ... for work, home and land, health and schools." Latin America was to be transformed—and immunized against infection from the Cuban Revolution—within ten years. But ten years later, the Alliance had lost its way in a rash of military takeovers of elected governments.[1]

Is the Partnership for Development and Prosperity—the successor to the Enterprise for the Americas Initiative George Bush announced in 1990—destined to follow the Alliance for Progress, Franklin Roosevelt's Good Neighbor Policy, and a number of less-known hemispheric initiatives, into the cemetery of frustrated good intentions, of Pan-American dreams? Can a coherent, functional, durable community that will transform the dream into reality be constructed with building blocks so different: to the north, the United States and Canada, prosperous First World countries with centuries-old democratic institutions; to the south, Latin America's poor Third World countries, whose

1

centuries-old political traditions and institutions are for the most part authoritarian and which, in most cases, are today experimenting with democratic institutions and free-market economic policies for the first time? Why are the United States and Canada so different from, so far ahead of, Latin America? Why has it taken so long for Latin America to conclude that democratic capitalism and intimate, open relationships with the United States are in its own best interests? Finally, what might be done to enhance the prospects for a genuine, dynamic community in the Hemisphere?

Those are the questions I shall try to answer in this book.

I visited Washington in January 1995, a few weeks after the Miami summit, to talk to U.S. government policy makers about the prospects for the Western Hemisphere. The incipient Mexican crisis notwithstanding, they were uniformly euphoric about the unanimity achieved at the summit and convinced that a new day had dawned for relations within the Hemisphere. And surely there were some important differences from the Alliance years: freely elected governments were in power everywhere except in Cuba and, less obviously, Mexico (although only in Costa Rica, Chile, and Uruguay did democracy go much beyond electoral forms). Latin American intellectuals and politicians who had spent most of the post–World War II period blaming the United States, "dependency," and "imperialism" for Latin America's problems were increasingly convinced that their problems were home-grown—and that their well-being depended heavily on intimate political and economic relations with the United States. And virtually all Latin American governments were pursuing free-market, internationally oriented economic policies after decades of statist or socialist experimentation and import substitution policies that avoided the "exploitation" of the world market.

The optimism of my State Department and National Security Council interlocutors reflected the new Latin American politics and economics. But the officials also repeatedly referred to the new wave of Latin American leaders, many of them educated in prestigious U.S. universities and "world-class" professionals. Frequently mentioned were Carlos Salinas de Gortari, the former Mexican president and architect of the North American Free Trade Agreement (NAFTA), who had done graduate work at Harvard; and Alberto Dahik, the vice president of Ecuador, who had studied at Princeton and was engaged in a campaign to promote transparency in government.

Shortly before my visit to Washington, the Mexican peso was devalued, triggering a crisis that not only staggered the Mexican economy and political system but also threatened the economic stability of other Latin American countries, chiefly Argentina and Brazil, and cooled the fervor of international investors for emerging markets, at least temporarily. Moreover, the crisis rendered worthless the cost-benefit calculations on which the U.S. decision to approve NAFTA was based, and the adverse trade and employment consequences of the new calculations have combined with an unpopular U.S. $20 billion bailout package to sour U.S. interest in expanding NAFTA.

Prominent economists, including Deputy Secretary of the Treasury Lawrence Summers,[2] have developed sophisticated technical explanations of what went wrong in Mexico, but such explanations address chiefly one dimension of the crisis—economic policy and its management—and they are akin, if the reader will indulge my hyperbole, to blaming the collapse of the Ottoman Empire on a clumsily managed devaluation. The Mexican crisis occurred in a much broader political, institutional, and ultimately cultural setting—authoritarian, overcentralized, opaque, inefficient, and corrupt—that Summers and others have largely ignored. The Mexican crisis compellingly reminds us that intimate trade relationships are risky in the absence of shared values and institutions. It also reminds us of the wisdom of the Europeans in insisting that new entrants into the European Union possess proven democratic credentials.

Soon after the peso's collapse, Carlos Salinas de Gortari fled Mexico, his reputation sullied not only by his considerable responsibility for the crisis but also by the alleged involvement of his brother, Raúl, in the murder of a prominent politician and subsequent revelations that Raúl had deposited upward of $100 million in secret bank accounts in Switzerland and elsewhere. Later in 1995, Alberto Dahik was accused of corruption by Ecuadoran authorities and fled to Costa Rica, where he sought asylum.

Is the Partnership for Development and Prosperity doomed to relive the disappointments and frustrations of the Alliance for Progress? Since the viability of the Partnership will inevitably depend on substantially shared values and institutions, it is impossible to address that question without addressing another, much broader issue: Why, as we approach the end of the twentieth century, are Canada and the United States, their own problems notwithstanding, a half-century or more ahead of Latin America with respect to the sturdiness of their democratic institutions, the level of prosperity enjoyed by the average citizen, and the access of the average citizen to education, health services, opportunity for advancement, and fair treatment in the legal system? What explains the Latin American traditions of authoritarianism, abuse of power, suppression of economic creativity, and social injustice?

Obviously, a number of factors—for example, resource endowment, climate, policies and institutions, history, sheer luck—are relevant. But I believe that by far the most important factor behind the divergent evolution of the northern and southern parts of the Western Hemisphere is cultural values and attitudes with respect, for example, to work, frugality, education, merit, community, and justice. Canada and the United States have been powerfully influenced by Anglo-Protestant culture, in which those and other progress-prone values are emphasized. Latin America has been powerfully influenced by Ibero-Catholic culture, which accords lower priority to those values. The profound cultural differences are palpable in a world view of people in Canada and the United States that is very different from the world view of Latin Americans. Those differences also influence the divergent policies and contrasting institutional strengths—and the divergent histories.

Culture is acquired; it is not transmitted genetically. And it changes, as we have seen in Japan in the nineteenth century, and post-Ottoman Turkey and indeed Spain itself in the twentieth. And it is changing in Latin America, driven chiefly by mass communications, above all television; higher, although still lagging, levels of education; the growing consensus that democratic capitalism is the most efficient and just way to organize human societies; and to some extent by the rapid growth of Protestantism, among other factors. And we also see cases, for example, in Chile in recent years, where new policies and institutions are influenced by culture, but culture is also influenced by new policies and institutions.

If fundamental cultural differences principally explain the North-South divergence in the Hemisphere, then *convergence* depends largely on cultural change in Latin America—the reinforcement of those values that lie behind the success of Canada, the United States, Western Europe, and now several East Asian countries.

In order to assess the prospects of the Partnership for Development and Prosperity, and indeed the future more generally of relationships in the Americas, I examine in some depth in chapter 1 the cultural divide in the Hemisphere and how that cultural divide has reflected itself in the evolution of sharply contrasting societies in the North and South. We shall look at some other possible explanations for the chasm in human well-being that separates Canada and the United States from Latin America, including natural resource endowment, climate, policies and institutions, and "dependency." And we shall review the role of culture as a negative force in Latin America's development, as perceived by Latin Americans and foreigners going back to the eighteenth century. Finally, I shall discuss ten cultural factors that operate very differently in progressive and traditional societies. They will, I hope, help the reader understand better and more concretely the relationship between culture and progress.

I dig further into the variations of Anglo-Protestant culture in chapter 2, which examines the evolution of Canada and the United States—"siblings, not twins"—and their sometimes adversarial, more often cooperative, open, and amicable relationship. That relationship constitutes a model for a Pan-American community.

Chapter 3 reviews the troubled history of relationships between Latin America and the United States, focusing particularly on the period after World War II and the decades of the "dumbbell," adversary relationship against a cold war backdrop that deterred Latin America from really engaging with the United States until the last decade of the twentieth century. Latin America has paid dearly for those decades lost to excessive nationalism, "dependency," and flirtation with socialism and the nonaligned movement.

We shall pay particular attention to the two dramatic changes that have occurred in Latin America starting in the 1980s: (1) the displacement of authoritarian governments in Argentina, Brazil, Chile, Uruguay, Paraguay, Bolivia, Peru, Ecuador, Panama, Nicaragua, El Salvador, Honduras, and Guatemala by democratically elected governments; and (2) the end of closed, import-substitution economic policies that reflect fear of the world market and "exploitation" by the advanced countries, above all the United States, and their replacement by open, export-oriented policies and an economic embrace of the United States. Taken together, these two developments appear to be transforming the North-South relationship in the Hemisphere from one of conflict and mistrust toward one of cooperation.

Are these trends likely to endure? Will democratic institutions root firmly and irreversibly, and will their functioning lead to the liberalization of Latin American societies as has occurred elsewhere, for example, in Spain? Will the new economic policies produce generalized benefits sufficiently swiftly to overcome the political pressures that inevitably arise, particularly as a consequence of the fiscal and monetary restraint necessary to achieve stabilization? And will the combination of democratic institutions and open economic policies drive these societies toward more equitable distribution of income, wealth, land, and opportunity, as has happened in Spain?

Why has Latin America taken so long to adopt the democratic-capitalist model and to seek close economic relationships with the United States? The intellectual community in the United States bears some responsibility for this costly delay by reinforcing the traditional view of many Latin American intellectuals and politicians that the United States is a greedy, irresponsible, even brutal superpower whose affluence is the result of the same "exploitation" that has caused Latin America's underdevelopment. I devote chapter 4 to the destructive role of U.S. intellectuals and reexamine the history of that archetypal symbol of "Yankee imperialism," the United Fruit Company, as a case in point.

What happens in Latin America generally, and in Latin America's relationships with the United States and Canada, will be decisively influenced by what happens in Argentina, Brazil, Chile, and Mexico, the subjects of chapters 5–8. The four countries are key actors both within Latin America and within the Western Hemisphere during these years of transition. If the movement toward democratic-capitalist modernity proves irreversible in these countries, the rest of Latin America is likely to follow.

Argentina, which was considered a developed country early in this century, has recently come out of many decades of militarism, nationalistic economic policies, high inflation, and economic stagnation and currently enjoys democratic political stability, price stability, and improved economic prospects—the "Tequila effect" of Mexico's financial collapse at the end of 1994 notwithstanding. But the opening up of the Argentine economy has been accompanied by significant deficits in the balance of trade, high levels of unemployment, and stagnation of real wages, all of which have been aggravated by the Tequila effect. The big question is whether Argentina's antidemocratic cultural tradition is changing fast enough to permit its nascent democratic institutions to withstand the short-term political pressures generated by economic reform. Carlos Saúl Menem's victory in the 1995 presidential elections, with Argentina still quivering from the Mexican economic earthquake, is an encouraging sign.

During the twentieth century, Brazil's economy has been among the fastest-growing in the world, despite chronic high inflation that has contributed to Brazil's record of extreme inequitability in distribution of income and wealth. In 1994, Fernando Henrique Cardoso, former guru of dependency theory and now a centrist who seeks closer ties with the United States, was elected president following his involvement in a successful stabilization program just before the elections. In order to maintain inflation under control, he must cut back sharply on government spending at both the national and state levels, including the privatization of inefficient state enterprises, which none of his predecessors was able to accomplish in the face of strong political pressures. But, as its performance throughout this century demonstrates, Brazil has both the resources and the entrepreneurship to sustain high growth, and it has been running a substantial trade surplus in recent years, although 1995 showed a deficit. The crucial questions are its ability (1) to exercise fiscal restraint, especially through privatization, and (2) to move toward greater equitability, at the same time preserving its democratic experiment.

Chile has led the way in the adoption of the open economic policies that have become the accepted model throughout Latin America. The policies were installed during the Pinochet regime and have been sustained through the subsequent elected governments of Christian Democrats Patricio Aylwin and Eduardo Frei Ruiz-Tagle. The Allende-Pinochet period notwithstanding, Chile's democratic tradition is stronger than that of most Latin American countries, and its resounding economic success in recent years reflects a blend of good policies with the cultural and institutional strengths that also explain that progressive tradition. But Chile has been among the most inequitable countries in the world with respect to income distribution.[3] And the extent to which its rapid growth is being accompanied by improvement in the standard of living of the working class is a crucial issue, not least of all for continued Chilean political stability.

The last two decades of the twentieth century have seen dramatic changes in the Mexican economy and Mexico's relations with the United States. But they have also underscored Mexico's political and social failures, and the failure of the 1910 Revolution and its offspring, the Partido Revolucionario Institucional (PRI), to modernize Mexico. The symbol of that failure is the torrent of poor Mexicans who migrate, often illegally, to the United States. The economic crisis that exploded shortly after Ernesto Zedillo was installed as president at the end of 1994 soon became a political crisis, one that gravely threatens the political monopoly enjoyed by the PRI for most of this century. The chapter on Mexico will examine the underlying causes of the crisis and the possibility that Mexico will emerge from it a stable, vigorous democracy within a dynamic NAFTA.

Trade, narcotics, and immigration are three prominent and controversial strands in the fabric of hemispheric relationships, and a chapter is dedicated to each.

The North American Free Trade Agreement, which opens free trade among Canada, the United States, and Mexico, is a symbol of the recent dramatic shift in Latin America's view of economic relations with the United States, particularly since it was promoted by a Mexican president, Carlos Salinas de Gortari. Three major issues attach to its future: (1) the limits on NAFTA's development that may be implicit in an organization that combines rich and poor countries—unlike the European Union, where only Greece and Portugal, accounting for 6 percent of the Union's total population, are "poor" (although the per capita GNP of both is higher than any Latin American country); (2) the impact on NAFTA of the Mexican crisis—and vice versa; and (3) accession of other Latin American and Caribbean countries in the wake of the Mexican crisis.

The narcotics industry has obvious pernicious effects for consuming countries, above all the United States, where the market involves millions of buyers, but also Canada and, increasingly, the Latin American countries themselves. While significant employment, income, and foreign exchange benefits attend production, processing, and transport of narcotics in Latin America, above all in Colombia, Bolivia, Peru, and Mexico, the industry poses a mortal threat to the fragile democratic institutions of these countries, and its corrupting influence can be felt in virtually all Latin American countries.

Particularly since 1965, when the United States substantially liberalized its immigration policies, the Hemisphere has witnessed a vast flow of legal and illegal immigrants—perhaps upwards of 10 million—from South to North, Mexico being by far the principal source.[4] In recent years, Canada's immigration policy has been the most liberal of the advanced countries, with about 1 percent—about 275,000—of Canada's total population being admitted annually. (One percent of the U.S. population would amount to about 2.5 million immigrants annually, roughly double the current flow of legal and illegal immigrants into the United States.) Immigration has become a hot political issue in both countries.

Its consequences for the receiving countries are both positive and negative, but at least in the United States, a consensus appears to be emerging that uneducated, unskilled immigrants compete with poor citizens for jobs and social services, and they depress wage levels at the lower end. Obviously, the sending countries benefit from the outflow of unskilled persons, in part because they are unable to generate employment for them, in part because they benefit from the remittances the emigrants send to relatives back home.

Of particular concern to me is the extent to which Latin American immigrants, of which Mexicans constitute by far the largest proportion, are acculturating to the American value system. If Latin America's problems reflect Ibero-Catholic culture, then a perpetuation of that culture in immigrants will lead to below-average economic performance and consequent social problems that will aggravate the already worrisome problems of poverty and divisiveness in the United States.

The concluding chapter will recapitulate the answers to the questions posed in the introduction. It will also draw together the several threads of the preceding chapters into what I hope will be a sufficiently substantial and coherent fabric to permit some generalizations about where "the Hemisphere idea" may be going and at what velocity, and what might be done both in Latin America and in the United States to enhance the chances that the Pan-American dream will, ultimately, become a reality.

1

The Roots of the Divergence: Anglo-Protestant versus Ibero-Catholic Culture

In the five centuries since Columbus stumbled upon the New World in his quest for a western sea route to Asia, the colonies and subsequent countries of the Western Hemisphere have followed very different paths that have led to striking contrasts in their circumstances at the end of the twentieth century. The United States and Canada, where democratic institutions and capitalism tracking back to the colonial period have been refined and blended to promote high levels of national progress, have evolved from remote, dependent colonies of Britain or France into the dominant of the three contemporary regional poles of world power: North America, Western Europe, and East Asia. The United States and Canada have their problems, of course, but many stem from success, and they seem almost trivial by comparison with the problems Latin America confronts.

Spain's and Portugal's former colonies, which had a century's head start and are half again more populous than the United States and Canada, are today roughly half a century behind them with respect to the maturity and stability of their political institutions, prosperity, and social justice. It is only in recent years that democratically elected governments have predominated in Latin America, and many of the democratic experiments are precarious. The standard of living is roughly one-tenth that of the United States and Canada. Distribution of land, income, wealth, and opportunity is highly inequitable by the standards of the advanced democracies.

Contrasts in progress have reinforced colonial origins—British versus Iberian—in defining the nature of relationships in the Hemisphere. The United States and Canada, both affluent, behave essentially like members of a family—some ideological, institutional, and psychological differences notwithstanding—occasional spats and all. Citizens feel at home in each other's countries and cross the border frequently, and with remarkably little hassle, to visit. They trust each other substantially, a trust born of shared values and similar institutions; the greatest volume of trade between any two countries in the world; an intricate web of relationships that include private enterprises, social and professional organizations, the arts, and sports; and a tradition of intimate cooperation in defense matters. The foregoing applies particularly to anglophone Canada, but it is also substantially true of francophone Quebec Province.

Relationships among the Latin American countries are facilitated by common culture, including language. But those relationships are less comprehensive, less open, less trusting than that between the United States and Canada, and border disputes that sometimes erupt into threats or even violence are common—for example, between Honduras and El Salvador, Venezuela and Colombia, Peru and Ecuador, Chile and Argentina.

At the root of the troubled relationship between the United States and Latin America during the past century is the imbalance in progress and power between them. (Canada has been substantially exempt from the North-South tension because its population is one-tenth that of the United States; its projection of power and influence into the world is correspondingly smaller; and it is geographically more remote from Latin America and the Caribbean.) The imbalance is reflected, in the extreme, in repeated U.S. interventions in the Caribbean Basin, motivated chiefly by fear that chronic instability, particularly in Nicaragua, Haiti, the Dominican Republic, and Cuba, would be exploited by adversaries—Germany at the time of World War I, the Soviet Union and Cuba during the cold war. The imbalance is more generally reflected in the tone of post–World War II relationships, at least until the past few years: often mistrustful and adversarial, and commonly referred to in government and academic circles as "the dumbbell"—the United States at one end, Latin America at the other.

THE SPECIAL CASE OF THE ENGLISH-SPEAKING CARIBBEAN

The English-speaking Caribbean countries, all former British slave colonies, are, with about 6 million people, tiny by comparison with the rest of the Hemisphere.[1] (Latin America has about 425 million people, the United States about 260 million, Canada about 30 million.) They have been generally more successful than Latin America in building democratic institutions and social justice, modestly more successful in economic development. All gained independence from Britain after World War II. With the exception of Belize and Guyana, all are islands.

Relationships between the United States and the English-speaking Caribbean have benefited from a common language and the common British heritage. But the vast discrepancy in power and economic progress as well as racial issues and the cold war have produced episodes of tension and conflict: the excesses of Black Power, particularly directed against tourists in the 1970s; the first term of Michael Manley in Jamaica in the mid–1970s, when he tilted toward Fidel Castro; the invasion of Grenada in 1983. These episodes notwithstanding, relations between the United States and the English-speaking Caribbean countries have generally been warmer and more open than those between the United States and Latin America. The relationship is even warmer between Canada and the English-speaking Caribbean, fellow members of the British Commonwealth. The level of development of the Caribbean countries places them closer statistically to Latin America than to the United States and Canada. But common language and institutions make for easier communication with North America.*

To be sure, the English-speaking Caribbean preserves strong ties with the United Kingdom, including preferential trade access to Europe under the Lomé Convention.

Some interesting questions related to culture arise in the context of the English-speaking Caribbean, particularly with respect to the political and economic diversity among the various countries. The political stability of Barbados is not representative: the bounds of democratic conduct have frequently been overstepped, for example, in Trinidad, Guyana, Grenada, and Antigua. Nor is Barbados's prosperity ($6,540 GNP per capita in 1992) representative: in the same year, the per capita GNP of Guyana was $330 and of Jamaica $1,340; that of neighboring St. Vincent and the Grenadines was $1,990, and Belize, Grenada, and

*I appreciate that "North America" embraces Mexico, Belize, the five Central American countries, and Panama—and by some definitions the Caribbean islands—as well as the United States and Canada. In Spanish, *Norteamérica* is often used to mean either the United States alone or the U.S. and Canada. I ask the reader's indulgence in such narrower uses in this book. Which countries are intended should be apparent from the context.

Dominica were only slightly higher. I argued in *Underdevelopment Is a State of Mind* that extensive acculturation to British values, attitudes, and institutions explains Barbados's political and economic success. The quite different conditions in, for example, neighboring St. Vincent and Grenada and distant Jamaica suggest a less complete degree of acculturation, the reasons for which would be well worth investigating.

But the English-speaking Caribbean is not a major actor in the Western Hemisphere, and its continuing ties to the U.K. and Europe are underscored by a comment a U.S. government official made to me early in 1995: "The English-speaking Caribbean doesn't see itself as a member of the Western Hemisphere community." Nor have its own efforts at economic and political integration through the Caribbean Community (CARICOM) been particularly successful. To be sure, many people from the English-speaking Caribbean have migrated to the United States. The flow from Jamaica, in particular, has been so substantial that Caribbean expert Anthony Maingot has labeled it a "binational" society, along with Haiti and the Dominican Republic.[2] And the area also plays a role in narcotics trafficking (see chapter 10).

But the English-speaking Caribbean is peripheral to the central question this book addresses—the possibility of a genuine community that embraces the more than 700 million people of Latin America, the United States, and Canada—and, except as the English-speaking countries may play a role in issues like immigration and narcotics, they will not be addressed further here.

NEW MEANING TO THE WESTERN HEMISPHERE IDEA

What is sometimes referred to as the "Western Hemisphere idea" was first articulated by President James Monroe at the time the former Spanish colonies to the south were gaining their independence. But the Monroe Doctrine, enunciated in 1823, was not so much a vision of a hemispheric community as a warning to European powers to stay out of the Hemisphere. It has been interpreted by the Mexican intellectual and politician Adolfo Aguilar Zinser as a declaration of hegemony (see chapter 8). But, in fact, the United States repeatedly shied away from association with Latin America for much of the nineteenth century.

It was not until 1889 that the U.S. committed itself to a concrete expression of the Western Hemisphere idea, joining with the Latin

American republics to create an organization known first as the International Union of American Republics. The Union's trade orientation was apparent from the name of its executive organization: the Commercial Bureau of the American Republics. The name of the Bureau was changed to the Pan American Union in 1910. In 1948, the role of the organization was expanded to incorporate a collective security treaty and to strengthen the mechanism for peaceful settlement of disputes, and the name was changed to the Organization of American States.

Within a few decades of that first hemispheric meeting, and particularly in the wake of U.S. involvement in Cuba during and after the Spanish-American War and the interventions in Nicaragua, Haiti, and the Dominican Republic at the time of World War I, Latin America's chief security concern had shifted from European interventionism to Yankee interventionism. Through the years of Franklin Roosevelt's Good Neighbor Policy, World War II, the cold war and the Cuban Revolution, John Kennedy's Alliance for Progress, and the malaise of the 1970s and 1980s, the Western Hemisphere idea translated for Latin America into a blend of respect, cooperation, resentment, mistrust, and hostility that has often been referred to as "the love-hate relationship" with the United States.[3]

While the relationship between Latin America and the United States was born in amity (to be sure, a passive amity on the part of the U.S.), the relationship between Canada and the United States was born in hostility. Nova Scotia, the Eastern Townships of Quebec, and what would become Ontario and New Brunswick were largely populated by colonials who sided with Britain during the American[*] Revolution and who fled northward from what would become the United States. The hostility persisted through the War of 1812, one of the American objectives in which was the expulsion of the British from, and annexation of, Canada. Thereafter, relations steadily improved between the United States and "the British provinces of North America," and in the 1850s, following Britain's repeal of the Corn Laws at the expense of Canada's trade preferences, the Canadians considered severing the link to Britain and joining the United States.

*I appreciate that the words *America* and *American* can also be applied to the entire Hemisphere, not just the United States. In some contexts it is very awkward to use *United States*, and I ask the reader's indulgence in occasional narrow uses of *America* and *American* in this book. What is intended should be apparent from the context.

Liberalization of British policies led in 1867 to Canada's Dominion status. By 1876, the United States had displaced Britain as Canada's principal source of imports; by 1920, the United States had displaced Britain as Canada's principal market; Canada subsequently became the principal market of the U.S. and the principal source of its imports.

The two countries were allies during World Wars I and II and the cold war, and in 1988 they took a major step toward merging their economies by signing the Canada-U.S. Free Trade Agreement (CUFTA), which became the North American Free Trade Agreement (NAFTA) with the accession of Mexico in 1994. After decades of avoidance of the OAS, mostly because of presumed U.S. domination of it, Canada finally signed up in 1989.

In recent years, and particularly since the collapse of communism—the alternative to democratic capitalism favored by many Latin American intellectuals and politicians—the Western Hemisphere idea has taken on new significance. Mexico's joining with the United States and Canada in NAFTA is the most dramatic evidence of the shift. But there are several other developments that add substance to what was heretofore far more rhetorical than real.

Pressures are growing from other Latin American countries to join NAFTA, and it is U.S. policy to encourage those aspirations, in part as a hedge against regional trading blocs in Europe and East Asia, particularly should the worldwide trading system embodied in the new World Trade Organization falter. (At the 1994 Miami summit, Chile was designated the next candidate for NAFTA membership.) Latin America's new eagerness to engage the United States in trade and investment relationships is a startling departure from a decades-long—and extremely costly—strategy of avoiding "dependency" and "economic imperialism" by avoiding the world market, a departure that symbolizes a huge rethinking of ideology and policy. As recently as the 1980s, Mexico's NAFTA initiative would have been viewed throughout Latin America—and particularly in Mexico, the foundation of whose foreign policy for decades was anti-Americanism—as akin to thrusting one's head into the mouth of the lion.

The wave of democratization in Latin America of the last fifteen years, given impetus by the collapse of communism, adds substance to the Western Hemisphere idea, as does the rejection of nationalistic and statist economic policies, which have universally been displaced by free-market, open economic policies—except in Cuba. So does growing awareness of environmental problems and the realization that they do not stop at national borders, as we were reminded by the highlighting of environmental issues in the NAFTA negotiations with Mexico. The massive flow of immigrants, legal and illegal, from Latin America and the Caribbean to the United States and Canada poses major questions of economic, social, and cultural absorption in the receiving countries, at the same time increasing the human and economic ties between the sending and receiving countries. The vast narcotics trade is a tragic, destructive bond between the South and the North in the Hemisphere, one that threatens the social fabric of the consuming countries and the democracy and stability of the producing countries.

For good or bad, cultural diffusion has intensified in both directions. Television and the movies in Latin America and Canada are often the creations of Hollywood and New York, but Spanish-language radio and television stations are increasingly numerous in the United States. Popular music and food fads move freely in both directions, as do literature and the arts. Baseball remains the dominant sport linking the United States, Canada, and the Caribbean Basin. But soccer, the national pastime in most Latin American countries, has caught on in the United States, particularly after it hosted the 1994 World Cup competition. Canadian football is very similar to American football, and most of the players in the Canadian Football League are Americans. American football is popular in Mexico. And it may not be too many years before there are major league baseball, National Football League, National Hockey League, and National Basketball Association teams both south and north of the border.*

THE POWER OF CULTURE

How far will the expanding web of trade, business, family, cultural, and other relationships go? Is it possible that the resentment, mistrust, disrespect, and hostility that have often characterized relationships between the United States and Latin America for more than a century

*There are already, of course, two Canadian major league baseball teams (Toronto and Montreal) and seven NHL teams (Montreal, Ottawa, Toronto, Winnipeg, Calgary, Edmonton, and Vancouver); in 1995, four U.S. teams—Baltimore, Shreveport, Sacramento, and Las Vegas—played in the Canadian Football League. In 1996, Toronto and Vancouver entered the NBA.

will pass into history to be replaced by the attitudes one associates with good friends, or even family, as in the relationship between the United States and Canada? Is it conceivable that the idea of community as we have seen it evolve in Western Europe will one day apply to all of the Western Hemisphere? And, more concretely and immediately, how are relationships within the Hemisphere likely to unfold as we move into the first decades of the twenty-first century?

Much will depend on the extent to which values and attitudes, and the institutions that both reflect and reinforce them, converge, and that means above all the reinforcement of more progressive values and attitudes in Latin America. I believe that there is no other satisfactory way to explain the sharply contrasting evolution of the North and the South in the Hemisphere than culture—the strikingly different values, attitudes, and institutions that have flowed from the Anglo-Protestant and Ibero-Catholic traditions. Other factors—for example, resource endowment, climate, and policy choices—may be relevant, but in the sweep of history they are overwhelmed by the power of culture.

I have already noted Ibero-America's head start. The first permanent Spanish settlement was established in 1493 on Hispaniola near what is today Puerto Plata in the Dominican Republic. The first Portuguese settlements in Brazil followed within a few years. The first permanent British colony was established more than a century later, in 1607, at Jamestown in what was to become Virginia. The head start gave Ibero-America a lead that lasted until the eighteenth century. The Venezuelan writer Carlos Rangel, who in the mid-1970s incurred the wrath of the Latin American intellectual and political establishments with a book that said that Latin Americans and their Iberian cultural inheritance were responsible for Latin America's condition, notes: "As late as 1700, the Spanish American empire still gave the impression of being incomparably richer (which it was!), much more powerful, and more likely to succeed than the British colonies of North America."[4]

As we approach the end of the twentieth century, Latin America is, as I have noted, roughly fifty years behind Canada and the United States in terms of the prosperity of its citizens[5] and the solidity of its democratic institutions. What explains this striking historical flip-flop? Why is Latin America today an area of extreme social inequality, as evidenced by World Bank income distribution data?[6] Why has Latin America been so slow in adopting the democratic capitalist model, particularly open economic policies that integrate Latin America into the dynamic world market?[7]

The contrast between the United States, an exceptionally dynamic and successful society, at least until recent decades, and Latin America may be unfair. But a strikingly similar contrast has been illuminated by a study of a century of Scandinavian and Latin American economic development, which makes little mention of culture and views the divergence as essentially a policy and institutional phenomenonen.[8] But if one asks with respect to any number of policy or institutional issues, "Why did the Scandinavians choose the right path while the Latin Americans chose the wrong one?" the answer inevitably gravitates toward fundamental cultural differences.

Natural Resources? Climate? Dependency?

The roots of the discrepant evolution of the United States and Canada on one hand and Latin America on the other are centuries deep. Can they be explained by natural resource endowment? Canada and the United States are blessed with vast extensions of arable land, but so are Argentina and Brazil, the latter of which is now among the world's largest exporters of soybeans. There is no clear advantage with respect to minerals. Canada and the United States have an advantage in navigable waterways, especially the Great Lakes, and the terrain of Mexico and the Central American and Andean countries is more severely interrupted by mountain ranges.

On balance, Canada and the United States may enjoy a somewhat more bountiful natural resource endowment, but Latin America is also very well off in this regard. Even if a rich resource endowment were a precondition of rapid development—an assumption challenged by successful resource-poor countries like Japan, Taiwan, South Korea, Switzerland, and Israel—the difference in resource endowment between the North and the South in the Hemisphere is insufficient to explain the gap. And the gap, after all, is not just in economic development. It is comparably vast with respect to democratic institutions and social justice. Yet Costa Rica demonstrates that you don't have to be rich to be democratic.[9] Tocqueville correctly concluded, "Physical causes do not therefore affect the destiny of nations so much as has been supposed."[10]

Climate has to be considered as well. Early in this century, Ellsworth Huntington, like Montesquieu two centuries before him,[11] argued that the differences between the temperate and tropical zones principally explain variations in human progress.[12] The early inhabitants of the temperate zones had to work harder in the shorter growing season to put something aside for the winter. They enjoyed a more bracing, energy-inducing climate. Their shelters had to be substantial, and fuel had to be found to protect against the cold. This placed a premium on work and saving, and may also have encouraged cooperation. Those who lived in the tropics enjoyed the luxury of growing crops (or picking food that grew naturally) year-round. And shelters needed only protect against the rain. But that same ease of feeding and sheltering oneself nurtured indolence, as did the enervating climate. And the fecund environment also nurtured disease.

I have no doubt that climate has played a role in the diverse evolution of the North and the South in the Western Hemisphere, just as it has in the Eastern. Around the world, the vast majority of poor countries are found in the tropical zone, almost all rich countries in the temperate zones. But there are exceptions: all the countries of the former Soviet Union are in the temperate zone, but the World Bank lists all—including Russia—as lower-middle-income economies except Belarus, which is listed as an upper-middle-income country. Hong Kong and Singapore are both in the tropics and are both listed as high-income economies with a higher GNP per capita than Ireland, New Zealand, Israel, and Spain.

Moreover, all of Uruguay, almost all of Argentina, most of Chile, and much of Mexico and Paraguay are in the temperate zones. And many Latin Americans who live in "tropical" countries enjoy temperate climates because of the region's many elevated plateaus, as is the case with the capitals of Mexico, Guatemala, Honduras, El Salvador, Costa Rica, Colombia, Venezuela, Ecuador, Bolivia, and Brazil.

From the 1960s through the 1980s, the conventional explanation for Latin America's underdevelopment in academic circles in Latin America, North America, and Europe was "dependency." The advanced countries, above all the United States, the *dependencistas* argued, have exploited Latin America by paying low prices for Latin America's primary exports, charging inflated prices for their own manufactured exports, reaping windfall profits from investments and conspiring with Latin American oligarchies and military institutions to perpetuate oppressive political systems congenial to foreign exploitation. Fidel Castro, Che Guevara, Salvador Allende, the Nicaraguan Sandinistas, and the FMLN revolutionaries in El Salvador were all obsessed by this "foreign devil" explanation of Latin America's condition. It evoked a book that swept Latin America early in this century, *Ariel*, by the Uruguayan writer José Enrique Rodó.[13] He used two of Shakespeare's characters from *The Tempest* to allegorize Latin America and the United States: the comely, spiritual, artistic, moral Ariel contrasted with the ugly, vulgar, pragmatic, money-grubbing Caliban.

Hemispheric realities, as we approach the end of the twentieth century, make a mockery of *Ariel*. "Caliban" has produced a society that offers the large majority of citizens security, opportunity, self-expression, and justice, while "Ariel" has perpetuated societies where most citizens have experienced just the opposite, a phenomenon confirmed by the massive migration from south to north.

Dependency theory lost most of its supporters following (1) the demise of communism in Eastern Europe (Marx and, particularly, Lenin were prominent among the progenitors of the theory of imperialism on which dependency theory rests); (2) the continuing spectacular success of the East Asian countries, now including China, in the world market; (3) the overwhelming defeat of the Sandinistas in the 1990 Nicaraguan elections; and (4) the collapse of the Cuban economy after Russia cut off the vast Soviet subsidies. Latin America, which kept the United States at arm's length economically from the 1950s through the 1980s, today ardently seeks an embrace.

In retrospect, "dependency" looks very much like a myth that is "demeaning and despairing," to use political scientist Lucian Pye's adjectives.[14]

Policies? Institutions?

If there is not much to choose from between the natural resource endowment of the United States and Canada on the one hand and Latin America on the other; if climate is a relevant but not decisive factor, and one, moreover, that is likely to express itself in cultural variations; and if Latin America's underdevelopment is not the consequence of North America's prosperity, as the *dependencistas* argued, then how can we explain the stunning differences in progress between the two regions? Some may point to the fact that the United States and Canada have chosen better policies, particularly economic policies that have brought political and social progress in their train. Others may point to the building of institutions in the North that have promoted progress, and the weakness or absence of such institutions in the South.

The institutional/policy argument is framed by Nobel Laureate Douglass North, an economic historian who defines institutions as the rules of the game in a given society: "a guide to human interaction [including] formal constraints—such as rules that human beings devise—and informal constraints—such as conventions and codes of behavior."[15] In addressing the historical contrasts within the Western Hemisphere, North notes, "The evolution of North America and of Latin America differed radically right from the beginning, reflecting the imposition of the institutional patterns from the mother country upon the colonies and the radically divergent ideological constructs that shape the perceptions of the actors."[16]

North ignores Alexis de Tocqueville's overarching conclusion, on which I will elaborate, that "laws" (roughly North's "institutions," at least his "formal constraints") are far less important than "customs," or culture. But North *does* recognize the significance of culture when he refers to "ideological constructs," which could be interpreted as "culture." And it is clear from his discussion of culture that he sees it at the root of "informal" constraints.

North perceives formal constraints—"political (and judicial) rules, economic rules, and contracts"—as essentially the outcome of the interplay of competitive forces operating in a market environment within a society. Tocqueville—and Weber—would say that the structure of the "market" and the nature of the competing forces are both decisively influenced by culture.

An example that illuminates the cultural foundation of institutional development is the contrasting fundamental structures of government in Canada and the United States on the one hand and Latin America on the other: federalism, with states and provinces retaining substantial powers, in North America, centralized power in Latin America. Keith Rosenn, a professor of comparative law at the University of Miami, who has undertaken numerous comparative studies of legal systems, observes:

Canada and the U.S. were colonized by Great Britain, which allowed its colonies substantial freedom in governing themselves. In both countries, federalism was perceived as a useful technique for integrating substantially autonomous colonies into a single nation. Latin America, on the other hand, was colonized by Spain and Portugal, whose heavily centralized regimes permitted their colonies little freedom to govern their own affairs. . . . Both the U.S. and Canada, with the exception of Quebec, were products of colonizations that synthesized Protestantism, Locke's social compact theory, and the natural rights of Englishmen. This North American inheritance of theology and political theory was far more conducive to the structured dispersal of power among many regional centers than Latin America's inheritance of the centralized hierarchical organization of Roman Catholicism and Bourbon absolutism. It should not be surprising, therefore, that power in all the Latin American countries is far more centralized than in Canada or the United States.[17]

The policy/institutional explanation for Latin America's problems is clearly relevant to the contrasting north-south performance within the Hemisphere, and it offers a useful analytical tool. But, divorced from a cultural context, it leaves a huge question unanswered: Why did Latin American politicians, bureaucrats, and intellectuals consistently come up with the wrong institutional and policy answers for more than 150 years, in the face of overwhelming evidence that they were not moving in the right direction? And why did Spanish and Portuguese leaders come up with the same wrong answers until recent decades?

The better policies and institutions of the United States and Canada evolved over centuries, there for everyone to see. Fifteen years after Japan was exposed to them for the first time with the appearance of Commodore Perry's flotilla in Tokyo Bay in 1853, the Meiji leadership had begun a concerted program to adapt those policies and institutions, which were correctly viewed as crucial to the modern Japan they envisioned. Latin America substantially rejected the successful policies and failed to build viable institutions like those of the United States and Canada—and Western Europe, Australia, New Zealand, and, more recently, East Asia. That rejection cannot reasonably be interpreted as an error in judgment. That "error" persisted for the almost two centuries of Latin America's independence. It had to be driven by a force far more fundamental and credible than the uniformly poor judgment of thousands of nineteenth- and twentieth-century Latin American political and intellectual leaders.

Latin America's chronically poor policies and weak institutions—and what may appear as persistent poor judgment—are principally a cultural phenomenon flowing from the traditional Ibero-Catholic system of values and attitudes. That culture focuses on the present and the past at the expense of the future; it focuses on the individual and the family at the expense of the broader society; it nurtures authoritarianism; it propagates a flexible ethical code; it enshrines orthodoxy; and it is disdainful of work, creativity, and saving. It is that culture that chiefly explains why, as we approach the end of the twentieth century, Latin America lags so far behind the United States and Canada. And it is the very different Anglo-Protestant system of values, attitudes, and institutions that chiefly explains the success of those two countries.[18]

Tocqueville on Culture

Tocqueville's *Democracy in America* is filled with wisdom that extends beyond his incisive analysis of American democracy that, for example, anticipated some of Gunnar Myrdal's analysis a century later of the racial dilemma in the United States.[19] In a discussion of the relationship between religion and progress, Tocqueville foreshadowed Max Weber's analysis of Protestantism some seventy years later: "British America was peopled by men who, after having shaken off the authority of the Pope . . . brought with them into the New World a form of Christianity which I cannot better describe than by styling it a democratic and republican religion. This contributed powerfully to the establishment of a republic and a democracy in public affairs."[20] But few are aware that the transcendental message Tocqueville wished to communicate to his readers was the overriding importance of culture in shaping societies:

> The customs of the Americans of the United States are, then, the peculiar cause which renders that people the only one of the American nations that is able to support a democratic government. . . . Thus the effect which the geographical position of a country may have upon the duration of democratic institutions is exaggerated in Europe. Too much importance is attributed to leg-

islation, too little to customs. These three great causes [geography, laws, customs] serve, no doubt, to regulate and direct American democracy; but if they were to be classed in their proper order, I should say that physical circumstances are less efficient than laws, and the laws infinitely less so than the customs of the people. I am convinced that the most advantageous situation and the best possible laws cannot maintain a constitution in spite of the customs of a country; while the latter may turn to some advantage the most unfavorable positions and the worst laws. The importance of customs is a common truth to which study and experience incessantly direct our attention. It may be regarded as a central point in the range of observation, and the common termination of all my inquiries. . . . [I]f I have hitherto failed in making the reader feel the important influence of the practical experience, the habits, the opinions, in short, of the customs of the Americans upon the maintenance of their institutions, I have failed in the principal object of my work.[21]

Tocqueville is very clear about what he means by "customs," and it is essentially what I mean by "culture." He says:

I here use the word customs with the meaning which the ancients attached to the word mores; for I apply it not only to manners properly so called—that is, to what might be termed the habits of the heart—but to the various notions and opinions current among men and to the mass of those ideas which constitute their character of mind. I comprise under this term, therefore, the whole moral and intellectual condition of a people.[22]

While Tocqueville focused his attention on the United States, he was not oblivious to conditions in Latin America:

If the welfare of nations depended on their being placed in a remote position, with an unbounded space of habitable territory before them, the Spaniards of South America would have no reason to complain of their fate. And although they might enjoy less prosperity than the inhabitants of the United States, their lot might still be such as to excite the envy of some nations in Europe. There are no nations upon the face of the earth, however, more miserable than those of South America. . . . [23] The inhabitants of that fair portion of the western Hemisphere seem obstinately bent on the work of destroying one another.[24]

Most people think of Max Weber, for whom the study of religion opened new avenues for understanding human economic behavior, as the architect of culturalism—the belief that cultural values and attitudes powerfully influence the evolution of nations and ethnic and religious groups. Tocqueville made the case seventy years before Weber, and he made it more broadly. But the bulk of *Democracy in America* analyzes—brilliantly—the American experiment, and that is what Tocqueville is principally remembered for. In any event, many writers since Tocqueville and Weber have elaborated on the cultural foundation they constructed, and, in the wake of the collapse of Marxist-Leninist economic determinism, culturalism has new impetus.

Cultural Interpretations by Latin Americans, New and Old

When one speaks of "Latin American culture," voices are always heard that argue, "You can't generalize about countries as different as Brazil and El Salvador, Chile and Honduras, Argentina and Bolivia." And surely, there are striking differences within this vast region. But a Brazilian who travels to El Salvador, a Chilean who visits Honduras, and an Argentine who visits Bolivia will all recognize the truth of anthropologist George Foster's assertion that Iberian culture has shaped Latin America and that the similarities among Hispanic American countries are more important than the differences:

> Although following separation from Spain, a series of independent
> nations emerged, each with peculiar geographical, economic, and
> social characteristics and with local traditions and histories, the
> supranational resemblances even today, a century and a half later,
> are so pronounced that, in anthropological concept, all countries
> together constitute a single culture area.[25]

I might add that a foreigner who has lived in one or more Latin American countries for an extended period will have the same sense of recognition, of similarity, when visiting other Latin American countries.

In any event, many Latin American writers have no problem generalizing about the region. Twenty years ago, Carlos Rangel was one of the few Latin American intellectuals with the wisdom and courage to point to cultural factors as the principal reason why "the history of Latin America . . . is a story of failure."[26] At that time, most Latin

American intellectuals, for example, the Colombian novelist Gabriel García Márquez, the Chilean poet Pablo Neruda, the Uruguayan writer Eduardo Galeano, Mexico's Carlos Fuentes, and Guatemala's Miguel Angel Asturias, followed in the tradition of Rodó, blaming Yankee imperialism for Latin America's problems. Some of them cast Latin America in a magical, spiritual light that has won them celebrity not only in Latin America but in the United States, Canada, and Europe. Isaac Cohen Orantes of the UN's Economic Commission for Latin America and the Caribbean (ECLAC) believes that these Latin American writers have performed a disservice by their discouragement of self-criticism: "They see a mess and say, 'How beautiful!'"[27]

Today, the list of Latin Americans convinced that the Ibero-Catholic cultural heritage is a major obstacle to progress is long, and getting longer. In addition to Rangel and Claudio Véliz, whose recent book examines the profound differences between Anglo-Protestant and Ibero-Catholic culture, among others who share the view that values and attitudes are crucial are the prize-winning novelist Mario Vargas Llosa; the influential Cuban exile columnist and politician Carlos Alberto Montaner; and the Argentine intellectual and media personality Mariano Grondona. Vargas Llosa speaks for them, and many other Latin American intellectuals, when he says that the economic, educational, and judicial reforms indispensable to Latin America's modernization cannot be effected

> unless they are preceded or accompanied by a reform of our customs and ideas, of the whole complex system of habits, knowledge, images and forms that we understand by "culture." The culture within which we live and act today in Latin America is neither liberal nor is it altogether democratic. We have democratic governments, but our institutions, our reflexes and our *mentalidades* are very far from being democratic. They remain populist and oligarchic, or absolutist, collectivist or dogmatic, flawed by social and racial prejudices, immensely intolerant with respect to political adversaries, and devoted to the worst monopoly of all, that of the truth.[28]

In the context of the politically correct, cultural relativist late twentieth century, these contemporary Latin Americans are courageous pioneers. But in the sweep of history, they are the intellectual heirs of some prominent eighteenth-, nineteenth-, and early-twentieth-century

Latin Americans who understood very well the burden of their Ibero-Catholic inheritance.

Francisco de Miranda was a *criollo*—a Spaniard born in the New World (in 1750)—who fought on the winning sides of the American and French revolutions and the wars for Latin American independence. Miranda visited the fledgling United States in 1783–84 and kept a detailed and revealing diary of the visit. He was struck by the democratic spirit of the Americans ("[at a barbecue] . . . the very first magistrates and people of note ate and drank with the common folk, passing the plate around, and drinking out of the same glass") and by the fairness of the judicial system ("I cannot express the satisfaction I felt watching the workings of the admirable system of the British Constitution. God forgive me: but what a contrast to the system now current in Spain!"). He marveled at the industry and creativity of the Americans (of an agricultural area in Massachusetts: "The soil seems poor and is poor. But such is the industrious spirit with which freedom fills these people that a small plot of land allows them to feed their large families, pay heavy taxes, and live well and pleasantly, a thousand times happier than the slave-owning landlords of rich mines in Mexico, Peru, Buenos Aires, Caracas, and all the Spanish American world").[29]

Simón Bolívar, born in Caracas like Miranda, also had a strong sense of the significance of culture, the virtues of Anglo-Protestant culture, and the grave problems the Ibero-Catholic inheritance posed for the former Spanish colonies of South America—a view, by the way, that was shared by Thomas Jefferson:

> What Bolivar called "the habit of obedience, a commerce of interests and of religion . . . in short, all our hopes" had been dictated by Spain and had, in consequence, made his fellow countrymen indifferent to "honour and national prosperity." They had, therefore, none of the political equipment, above all none of the consciousness of "being present in the universe" or . . . of being members of a self-governing community, which were required to transform the remains of the Spanish Empire into a federation of quasi-autonomous states on the North American model. Any attempt to export the constitution of that "Republic of Saints" to Venezuela would, he observed drily, be like trying to export the English constitution to Spain.
>
> The belief that their past history and their spiritual (and hence ideological) enslavement to regal Catholicism made the

Spanish Americans unsuited for representative, federal government was also shared by the North Americans; which, in part, explains their reluctance to provide the revolutionaries with the military support they requested. "Our southern brethren," priest-ridden and unlettered, wrote Jefferson to Lafayette in 1817, were not yet ready for independence, for "ignorance and bigotry, like other inanities, are incapable of self-government." If suddenly released from the Spanish yoke they would, he warned [presciently], "fall under military despotism and become the murderous tools of the ambitions of their respective Bonapartes." It was a vision of the future that, in the last decade of his life, would haunt Bolivar also.[30]

In 1830, the year of his death, the beleaguered and embittered Bolívar wrote a chilling testament:

I was in command for twenty years, and during that time came to only a few definite conclusions: (1) I consider that, for us, [Latin] America is ungovernable; (2) whosoever works for a revolution is plowing the sea; (3) the most sensible action to take . . . is to emigrate; (4) this country [Great Colombia, later to fragment into Colombia, Venezuela, and Ecuador]* will ineluctably fall into the hands of a mob gone wild, later again to fall under the domination of obscure small tyrants of every color and race; (5) though decimated by every kind of crime and exhausted by our cruel excesses, we shall still not be tempting to Europeans for a reconquest; (6) if any part of the world were to return to a primeval chaos, such would be the last avatar of [Latin] America.[31]

The statesman, writer, and educator Domingo Faustino Sarmiento served as Argentina's ambassador in Washington from 1864 to 1868, following which he was elected president of Argentina. His comment, "We must be the United States!" derived from his appreciation of the progress made by the United States, apparent even during the troubled times of his ambassadorial service. In 1845, Sarmiento had published the classic *Facundo: Civilization and Barbarity*, a powerful indictment of the lesser-known caudillo Facundo Quiroga that was really aimed at Juan Manuel de Rosas, the dictator who dominated Argentina between

---

*At about the same time, "The United Provinces of Central America" dissolved into the component nations of Guatemala, El Salvador, Honduras, Nicaragua, and Costa Rica.

1829 and 1852. Behind "We must be the United States!" was his appreciation of the destructive currents of Iberian culture:

> Terror is a sickness that infects people like cholera, smallpox, or scarlet fever. And after you have worked for ten years to inoculate against it, the vaccine fails to work. Don't laugh, people of Hispanic America, when you see such degradation! Remember that you are Spanish, and that is how the Inquisition educated Spain. Be careful, then![32]

The Nicaraguan writer Salvador Mendieta, a champion of Central American unification, was born in 1879, five years after Sarmiento completed his term as president of Argentina. He died in 1958, three years after Juan Domingo Perón was forced into exile. Mendieta wrote his three-tome analysis of Central America's pathology, *The Sickness of Central America*, in 1906–7. He had little use for the growing influence of the United States in Central America. But when it came to pinning the blame for Central America's (excepting Costa Rica) failure to produce enduring democratic institutions, prosperity, and social justice, he ignored the United States and focused squarely on Ibero-Catholic culture as the root cause:

> While Europe in the midst of the cruelest sufferings caused by continuing wars was giving birth to religious freedom and was thereby renewing the spirituality of the world, Spain was blinding itself in fierce intolerance, and the Inquisition, the Jesuits, and the monks, in the closest alliance with increasingly despotic royal power, were chloroforming the energetic Spanish people, forcing their minds to close, paralyzing their will, and snatching away their liberties to the point of converting them into a drowsy, weak bunch of paupers. . . . [As Spain's decay progressed] the kings, in their struggle to keep themselves afloat financially, trafficked in—and degraded—everything: justice, jobs, decorations, military ranks.[33]

Mendieta's third volume, *Therapy*, is a 678-page prescription for a cultural revolution that focuses on child rearing as the crucial period of transmission of values and attitudes.

All of these observers, from the Venezuelan Miranda, born in the eighteenth century, to the Peruvian Vargas Llosa, born in the twentieth, reach essentially the same conclusion: Latin America's underdevelopment, as well as its chronically poor policies and weak institutions—

and what may appear as persistent poor judgment by its leaders—are principally a cultural phenomenon flowing from the traditional Ibero-Catholic system of values and attitudes.

Ten Key Cultural Factors

We now must ask: What are the cultural factors that influence human progress and that explain why some countries or ethnic groups do better than others?

First, a few definitions. For my purposes, *culture* is a set of values and attitudes that guide the actions of individuals and the interaction of people within a society. *Values* are ideas or norms of behavior to which a society attaches importance. *Attitudes* are ways in which people learn to respond to facts, circumstances, and issues. As Talcott Parsons observed, culture is learned, transmitted, and shared within a society.[34] As far as we know, genetics are not relevant to culture.

Obviously, we are addressing a question of enormous complexity that has been a long-standing focus of intellectual inquiry. At the highest level of generalization, that inquiry starts with "world views," or broad categories of cultures. Some examples:

• Max Weber's differentiation of cultures according to religious teaching in which he links the rational/ascetic/ethical features of Calvinist Protestantism to capitalism and economic prosperity and explains the less prosperous condition of followers of Catholicism, Buddhism, Taoism, and Hinduism as the consequence of a fatalistic, irrational, other-worldly view of life.[35]

• Talcott Parsons's elaboration of the Weberian thesis, breaking down cultures according to factors such as the extent to which the culture reinforces the bonds of kinship or weakens them through emphasis on universal values; the extent to which status is determined by achievement in contrast to family or class considerations; and the extent to which the goals of the collectivity override individual goals.[36]

• Florence Kluckhohn's five fundamental factors: how a culture views (1) the character of innate human nature (good, bad, or improvable); (2) the relation of man to nature (adapt to it or manipulate it); (3) time (focus on the past, the present, or the future); (4) human activity (being or doing); (5) human relationships (hierarchy versus equality, individual versus group).[37]

• George Foster's thesis of a universal peasant culture in which values and attitudes are profoundly influenced by a zero-sum view of the world—"all the desired things in life exist in finite quantity and are always in short supply"[38]—as in the southern Italian town of "Montegrano" in Edward Banfield's classic *The Moral Basis of a Backward Society*.[39]

In my two previous books, I discussed five fundamental factors (one is a cluster of factors) that shape the evolution of societies: (1) time orientation—societies with an orientation toward the future tend to be more progressive than those that focus on the present or past; (2) the radius of identification and trust—the farther beyond the family that radius extends, the more prone to pluralistic politics, fair play, and social justice is a society likely to be; (3) the rigor of the ethical system—the more rigor, the greater the trust and social cohesiveness; (4) attitudes about authority, which influence the proneness to horizontal/cooperative or vertical/ authoritarian relationships; and (5) attitudes about work, education, creativity, and dissent, which are crucial to economic progress and are often stigmatized in traditional societies.

I present here a structure that derives from the foregoing works and my own practical experience in Latin America and examines the divergent ways in which *progress-prone* and *progress-resistant* cultures treat ten key ideas or issues. This dual structure owes much to the work of Mariano Grondona, whose model for the progress-resistant culture is Argentina and, by implication, Latin America.[40] But it is relevant to the Third World in general, as is apparent from books like Daniel Etounga-Manguelle's *L'Afrique—A-t-Elle Besoin d'un Programme d'Ajustement Culturel? (Does Africa Need a Cultural Adjustment Program?)*[41]

The ten factors are:

1. Time Focus
2. Work
3. Frugality
4. Education
5. Merit
6. Sense of Community
7. Ethics
8. Justice
9. Authority
10. Secularism

In terms of the broad categories developed by Weber, Parsons, Kluckhohn, and Foster, the progress-prone society is rational, ascetic, ethical, universalist, achievement-oriented, activist, future-oriented, and egalitarian; seeks a balance between group and individual interests; and sees life as a positive-sum game. The progress-resistant society is fatalistic, particularistic, ascriptive, passive, individualistic and familistic, past- or present-oriented, and hierarchical, and sees life as a zero-sum game.

The progress-prone value system is exclusive neither to Protestantism nor Western Europe and North America. It also embraces the blend of Confucianism, Taoism, and ancestor worship substantially shared by China, Taiwan, Korea, Japan, Hong Kong, Singapore, and East Asian immigrants in the United States, Southeast Asia, Brazil, and elsewhere. The progress-prone value system also operates for several successful religious or ethnic groups, for example: Jews, Quakers, Mormons; India's Sikhs, Parsis, and Jains; and Pakistan's Memons. I consequently refer to the progress-prone value system as "universal progress culture," which contrasts with the static, zero-sum world of Foster's "universal peasant culture."

Let's now look at the different ways that progress-prone and progress-resistant cultures view the ten factors. I want to stress that what follows are broad generalizations that in the real world obviously vary in degree. I also want to stress that culture is not static. It changes, as recent World Values Survey data for Argentina and Mexico suggest (see chapters 5 and 8), albeit slowly.

Time Focus

Progressive cultures focus on the future; traditional societies, including those of Latin America, focus on the past or the present—the future is often in the other world. The idea of the future is implicit in the Calvinist frugality that Weber, who labeled it "asceticism," viewed as the engine of capitalism. The future is etched in the mind of the East Asian to an important extent because ancestor worship dictates a responsibility of the individual to five generations in the past but also five generations in the future. And "Judaism clings to the idea of Progress. The Golden Age of Humanity is not in the past, but in the future."[42]

Work

Work is central to the good life in progressive societies, a source of satisfaction and self-respect, the foundation of the structure of daily life, and an obligation of the individual to the broader society. Work is viewed as noble and indispensable in the Protestant, Jewish, and Confucian ethics; in many Third World cultures, including the Ibero-Catholic, work is viewed as a necessary evil, and real satisfaction and pleasure are attainable only outside the workplace. Attitudes about work are, of course, intimately linked to achievement and entrepreneurship, on which economic development depends.

Frugality

Frugality conserves the fruit (the two words share a Latin root) of work for investment or subsequent consumption. I have already noted its key role—labeled as asceticism—in Weber's interpretation of capitalism. It is also a prominent value in East Asia—witness the extraordinarily high levels of savings—although its source is Taoism rather than Confucianism. The legendary, often stereotyped, Jewish frugality may have its roots in the extreme insecurity that Jews have encountered in their precarious post-Diaspora circumstances as a persecuted minority. As Foster stresses, the traditional society sees what one gains (or saves) as at the expense of others, thus the elaborate ceremonies and fiestas where savings are redistributed. Latin American countries save about half of what East Asian countries save; yet, like other aspects of development, savings rates are susceptible to significant change through policies, as Chile's experience demonstrates (see chapter 7).

Education

Education is the key to progress in dynamic societies. In contrast to traditional Catholicism, which interposes the priest as the interpreter of God's scripture to the faithful, both Protestantism and Judaism stress the importance of literacy so that each follower can read the Bible. And education is also central to Confucianism, as evidenced by the high level of Japan's literacy relative to Western Europe in the nineteenth century, even prior to the Meiji Restoration. In traditional societies, education is seen as a frill by the masses, an entitlement of the elites. Substantial illiteracy still exists in Latin America, and in many

Latin American countries, half or more of high school–age children do not attend secondary school.

Merit

Merit as the basis for personal advancement is a substantial reality in progressive societies. It is intimately linked to achievement, the drive for which David McClelland has analyzed in *The Achieving Society*.[43] The Calvinist concept of election—the belief that God has blessed a chosen few whose state of grace is apparent from their prosperity—promotes the idea of achievement and merit. Merit is a central Confucian value, symbolized by the nationwide examinations that are common to China, Japan, Korea, and Singapore. Jewish achievement and emphasis on merit is probably driven by some of the same psychological factors that have promoted frugality, but with the additional "I'm going to show them" attitude of a persecuted minority. (I am reminded of the movie *Chariots of Fire*, in which the Presbyterian Scot Eric Liddell, running for his God, won the 400 meters race at the 1924 Olympics, and his United Kingdom teammate, the Jewish Harold Abrahams, running to prove himself as good as—if not better than—anybody else, won the 100 meters.)

In traditional societies, and particularly in Latin America, merit often goes unrecognized. Family, friends, *patrones*, and connections—*amiguismo*—are what count.

Sense of Community

The sense of community extends beyond the family to the broader society in the progressive culture. The sense of community—a wide radius of identification and trust—nourishes the ethical code and the sense of justice as it is nourished by them. In Robert Putnam's recent study of contemporary Italy, *Making Democracy Work*, the sense of community translates into the horizontal "patterns of associationism, trust, and cooperation that facilitate good governance and economic prosperity."[44] Putnam's work contains many echoes of Banfield's book, which underscored the costly consequences in terms of poverty and injustice of a vertical world view, of the absence of a sense of community, in Italy's south. More recently, Francis Fukuyama's *Trust—The Social Virtues and the Creation of Prosperity*[45] emphasized the economic benefits of spontaneous association—the sense of community and trust—in societies like Japan, Germany, and the United States.

In traditional societies, including Latin America, identification and trust are largely confined to the family. Those outside the family are inconsequential, possibly hostile, and certainly outside a felt "community." The absence of sense of community—the sense of responsibility for other persons in the society—contributes to the "invertebrate, particularist" qualities in Hispanic societies that José Ortega y Gasset has noted.[46] The absence of sense of community nurtures authoritarianism and is also linked to nepotism, corruption, tax evasion, the widespread littering so common in Latin America, lack of concern about punctuality, and the absence of traditions of philanthropy.

I want to emphasize that while the sense of community is an important factor in human progress, it is but one of several cultural factors that explain why some societies do better than others. The problem I have with Fukuyama's *Trust* is that several countries—for example, China, Taiwan, South Korea, Singapore—with relatively low propensities for spontaneous association when compared with Japan, Germany, and the United States—have grown very rapidly indeed, and at least in the cases of Taiwan, South Korea, and Singapore, that growth has been accompanied by progress toward democratic institutions. Their economic miracles are largely the consequence of other cultural factors like work ethic/entrepreneurship, education, frugality, and merit.

Nor can a highly developed sense of community assure economic dynamism and prosperity. Costa Rica, a country with a strong sense of community by comparison with the rest of Latin America and particularly Central America, enjoys democratic stability. But it is a poor country by comparison with the First World and even Argentina, Chile, and Barbados, its economic growth heavily dependent on foreign and immigrant entrepreneurship. Nor does its highly developed sense of community and independent judiciary—rare in Latin America—insulate it from typical Latin American corruption, which several Costa Rican presidents in recent decades are widely believed to have engaged in.

Ethics

The rigor of the ethical code influences political and economic performance. Weber believed that the Roman Catholic emphasis on the afterlife and, particularly, what he perceived as a more flexible ethical system, put Catholics at a disadvantage to Protestants in this life. "The God of Calvinism demanded of his believers not single good works, but a life of good works combined into a unified system. There was no room for the very human Catholic cycle of sin, repentance, atonement, release, followed by renewed sin."[47]

An anecdote will help make the point. The limits culture places on institutions, in this case legal institutions, are apparent from a conversation Professor Keith Rosenn of the University of Miami Law School recently had with an Argentine lawyer. Since the nineteenth century, the Argentine constitution has authorized trial by jury and the use of oral testimony by witnesses. But no jury trial has ever taken place. Instead, a cumbersome system of written depositions has prevailed, with the verdicts the responsibility of judges. Rosenn asked the Argentine lawyer why this was so. The latter replied, "We are a Catholic country, and everybody knows that it would be easy for a witness to lie, confess to a priest a few days later, and be absolved."[48]

A rigorous ethical code is likely to increase levels of trust, so important to political pluralism and economic efficiency. Clearly, the rigor of the ethical code influences and is influenced by the sense of community. Some traditional religions ignore ethical questions and focus on the propitiation of spirits as the essence of life. Voodoo in Haiti is a case in point: it is an important source of the acute cultural pathology of that benighted country.

Justice

The idea of justice and fair play is nurtured by both the sense of community and a rigorous ethical code. Where these are not prominent in the culture, as in Latin America, justice is a highly theoretical concept and in practice a rare commodity that is often undermined by money, influence, politics, and kinship. In Latin America, only Costa Rica, Chile, and Uruguay meet world standards for independence of the judiciary.

Authority

How authority is understood and exercised in a society presents us with a complicated cultural issue. In theory, highly authoritarian, vertical cultures like those of Latin America should not only encounter major difficulties in forging pluralistic political institutions; they should also experience slow economic growth because authoritarianism can be expected to stifle criticism and dissent, creativity, and entrepreneurship and ignore merit. This formulation characterizes Latin America's evolution as well as, until recent decades, Spain's and Portugal's. More pluralistic, horizontal cultures in which authority is diffused should gravitate naturally toward democracy, and they should nurture economic creativity. The striking differences Putnam analyzes between prosperous, communitarian northern Italy and poor, authoritarian southern Italy stand as further evidence of the political and economic costs of untrammeled authority.

But authoritarianism, linked to filial piety, is central to the Confucian ethic, and it has clearly not represented an obstacle to economic growth in Japan, at least starting with the Meiji Restoration; in South Korea, Taiwan, Hong Kong, and Singapore after World War II; or in China after the passing of Mao. Nor have Germany's authoritarian traditions, which help to explain its slower movement toward democracy than most of its European Union partners, impeded economic growth. In *Asian Power and Politics—The Cultural Dimensions of Authority*, Lucian Pye examines the political intrusion of traditional antibusiness Confucian authoritarianism into the economic sphere, which he believes explains the relative economic backwardness of the East Asian countries prior to their takeoffs. Correspondingly, the takeoffs were triggered by the disengagement of politicians from the economic sphere and their recognition of the abilities—the merit—of specialists; or their active facilitation of economic development in partnership with the technocrats. That disengagement, or even facilitation, in effect released the powerful Protestant ethic–like Confucian/Tao values of work, frugality, education, and merit of creativity. The power of those values also has a lot to do with Germany's economic success, its authoritarian traditions notwithstanding.

Secularism

Finally, religion is largely confined to the spiritual sphere in progressive societies; in traditional societies it often intrudes into worldly concerns, including politics and economics. As we can appreciate from the differences between northern and southern Italy, the link between secularism and development is strong, as Putnam notes in *Making Democracy Work*. As he says, "Organized religion, at least in Catholic

Italy, is an alternative to the civic community, not a part of it."[49] A comparably striking contrast is the dynamic, democratic, literate, and secular Turkey that has evolved from Atatürk's vision and that contrasts so strikingly with most other Islamic countries—in the extreme case, Iran—where the influence of the mullahs is still strong.

Although the role of the Roman Catholic Church was central to Latin American politics—and violence—in the nineteenth century, today all the countries are substantially secularized. The secularization is underscored by the dynamic competition of Protestantism. But the influence of the Church still reaches into the civic domain. When I visited Chile in 1995, I was told that the person considered by many to be the country's most distinguished educator, José Joaquín Brunner, cannot be named Minister of Education because of his secular views and the opposition of the Church.*

In this book, it is these ten factors that I have in mind when I use the word *culture*. They are, in my view, prominent among Tocqueville's "various notions and opinions current among men and . . . the mass of those ideas which constitute their character of mind . . . the whole moral and intellectual condition of a people" that powerfully influence how people behave as individuals and as a society.

A Prism Through Which to View the Hemisphere's Future

I appreciate that neither Tocqueville, nor Weber, nor the many other writers who have emphasized culture are going to convince skeptics, particularly two groups: those who are wedded to cultural relativism— the notion that all cultures are essentially equal and that cross-cultural value judgments are taboo, an article of faith for most anthropologists; and those, mostly economists, who believe that the problems of underdevelopment can be solved by getting the economic policies right.

If we measure the worth of societies by the way human beings are treated; by the opportunity they offer for self-expression, self-

*Brunner's association with the generally anticlerical Allende government may also be relevant, although it has not prevented his being appointed to high government position since the end of the Pinochet dictatorship.

improvement, and the pursuit of happiness; and by the degree to which justice and fair play are realities, then it is apparent that some cultures do better than others. If there's any doubt, look at the societies people emigrate from and those they emigrate to. Those who believe that people are the same everywhere when it comes to economic behavior must be prepared to explain why, in multicultural countries like Thailand, Indonesia, Malaysia, and the United States, where everyone operates with the same economic signals, some ethnic groups (the Chinese in the four countries just listed) do better than others.

And how else can the divergent evolution of the United States and Canada from that of Latin America be explained?

The principal aim of this book is not to convince skeptics. Perhaps it will at least give pause to those wedded to other explanations. As others who have written on culture have learned, often painfully, the cultural explanation of why human societies develop differently touches sensitive emotional and intellectual nerves and is sometimes confused with racism. Moreover, cultural interpretations are difficult to document. And while culture, as Putnam concludes, may be the only satisfactory predictor of the performance of societies over the long run—say, decades or centuries—in the shorter run, policy and institutional changes can deflect underlying cultural forces and may even precipitate enduring cultural change. Daniel Patrick Moynihan was quite right when he observed, "The central conservative truth is that it is culture, not politics, that determines the success of a society. The central liberal truth is that politics can change a culture and save it from itself."[50]

In the chapters that follow, a variety of evidence of the power of culture—some data, some historical comparisons and inferences, some anecdotal material, and the judgment of others—will be presented, enough, I hope, in their totality, at least to give pause to the skeptical reader. But my principal aim is to examine the likely evolution of the societies of the Western Hemisphere and their relationships with one another at a moment of apparent cultural change—and convergence. If their historic divergence and conflicts are an important consequence of cultural differences, then culture should offer a helpful prism through which to view the future.

GENES VERSUS CULTURE

A word on the genes-versus-culture, nature-versus-nurture, debate. It is obvious that some people are born with a native intelligence superior to that of others, including within families. I think it is possible that some ethnic groups have evolved gene pools that produce a higher incidence of intelligence than other groups, although I am far from convinced of that. I am particularly skeptical of the link between genes and group IQ computations, mindful of the data Thomas Sowell has cited that show a subnormal group IQ level for Russian Jews conscripted for World War I.[51] Richard Herrnstein and Charles Murray note in *The Bell Curve* that Ashkenazi Jews—a category into which Russian Jews fall—"test higher [for IQ] than any other ethnic group."[52] I might add that I share the view of those who believe that IQ is far from the only determinant of achievement and success in life.

Culture is, in my view, a much more powerful force for success or failure than any putative genetic endowment when it comes to group performance. The histories of Haiti and Barbados bear that out. The black slaves the French imported into Saint Domingue, as the French called their colony on Hispaniola, to work the sugar plantations came from the same Dahomey region of West Africa—and presumably the same gene pool—as the slaves the British imported into Barbados to work their sugar plantations. The Saint Domingue slaves revolted and established a republic, Haiti, in 1804. Once the richest colony in the Caribbean, Haiti is today by far the poorest country in the Hemisphere, largely because of the perpetuation of traditional African culture, including the Voodoo religion, and the persistence of the cultural wounds of slavery, both phenomena facilitated by Haiti's isolation. Barbados remained a British colony until 1966, by which time it had been acculturated to British values and attitudes, and liberal British political institutions now under the control of the descendants of slaves were firmly in place. Its per capita income ($6,540 in 1992) was higher than that of Argentina, Latin America's most affluent country.

If, in fact, some racial or ethnic gene pools produce higher average IQs than others, a hypothesis about which I am skeptical, the Haiti-Barbados comparison demonstrates that the power of culture can overwhelm any such genetic presumption.

2

Canada and the United States:
Siblings, Not Twins

Brethren dwelling together in unity. Children of a common mother.
—THE WORDS ON THE TWO SIDES OF THE PEACE ARCH AT THE CANADIAN-U.S. BORDER SOUTH OF VANCOUVER

Canada and the United States may enjoy better relations than any other two bordering countries in the world. They trade more with each other than any other two countries. The flow of their citizens across the border is vast—100 million people annually; a person crossing the border in either direction is typically asked one or two perfunctory questions by an official of the country being entered. Canadian Foreign Ministry officials working in Washington enjoy unusual access to U.S. government agencies and high-level officials, likewise with State Department diplomats in Ottawa. The special relationship between Canada and the United States was captured in a National Public Radio interview of the late former CIA Director William Colby following revelations that the CIA had spied electronically on Japanese officials during the mid-1995 U.S.-Japan trade negotiations. Colby acknowledged that such things happen in the spying business, but added that there were limits. "One would be insane to spy on Canada," he said.[1]

The Canada-U.S. relationship is not problem-free, and it never will be. Trade, resource, and environment disputes are constantly cropping up. In recent years, wheat, lumber, fisheries, and acid rain have been particularly prickly issues. Many problems flow from the asymmetry in the relationship of a country—the most powerful in the world—of 260 million people with a neighboring country of 30 million. The asymmetry is reflected in an American tendency to take Canada for granted, in a Canadian tendency to be obsessed with the United States.

42

Canada's repeated efforts to limit American media penetration are root-ed in this asymmetry.

U.S. inattention to Canada is troubling, particularly in light of Canada's overwhelming importance to us as a trading and investing partner—which is not widely appreciated in the United States—and as a military ally in the defense of North America. Symptomatic of that neglect was a visit I paid to a Cambridge, Massachusetts, bookstore in 1995 in search of some books on Canada. With the help of a clerk, I was able to find three books that didn't relate to travel and tourism. The same store has a Latin American section that offers hundreds of books. Yet Canada is more important to us in trade, investment, and defense than all of Latin America taken together.

Differences between Canada and the United States rooted in the asymmetry in population and power tend to magnify differences rooted in the differing histories of the two countries, particularly during the late eighteenth and nineteenth centuries. For many observers, mostly Canadians but also some Americans, the differences overwhelm the similarities. Indeed, for some Canadian intellectuals, national identity is defined by the contrasts with the United States, and some—political scientists John Herd Thompson, an American, and Stephen J. Randall, a Canadian, among them—have even noted a tendency for Canadians to feel better about themselves in the light of America's problems.[2] But as someone who has lived in Canada for six months, traveled exten-sively within it,* and read a good deal about it, I come to a quite differ-ent conclusion, one that is also influenced by my having lived for thir-teen years in Latin America, where the contrasts with the United States are vast.

CONTINENTAL DIVIDE?

In his fascinating book *Continental Divide*, Seymour Martin Lipset cata-logs a weighty list of cultural and ideological differences between the two societies that might lead the reader to conclude that they are more different than they are similar—although I don't think that is necessar-

*My wife and I lived in Ottawa in late 1993 and early 1994 while she attended the Cordon Bleu School of Cuisine. We explored a good part of Quebec and Ontario during those six months and drove through parts of Quebec, Ontario, Manitoba, Saskatchewan, Alberta, and British Columbia in the fall of 1995.

ily what he intended.[3] Those differences notwithstanding, and mindful
of the special case of Quebec, I believe that what Canada and the
United States share as offspring of Britain is far greater than the differences that separate them. They are clearly not twins, but they are just
as clearly "children of a common mother." That intimate relationship,
and the shared values and attitudes it implies, is the basis of the community that the two have enjoyed for so long.

Lipset traces one of the most significant differences—Canada's
parliamentary system and the presidential system of the United
States—to the quite different births of the two nations. Canada
emerged naturally and tranquilly from colonial to Dominion status in
1867, almost a century after the United States tore itself away violent-
ly from Britain. Lipset describes Canada's arrival at nationhood as "a
long struggle to preserve a historical source of legitimacy: government's
deriving its title-to-rule from a monarchy linked to church establishment."[4] By contrast, the United States "celebrates the overthrow of an
oppressive state, the triumph of the people, a successful effort to create
a type of government never seen before."[5] The result of these sharply
contrasting births: "Government power is feared in the south; uninhib-
ited popular sovereignty has been a concern in the north."[6]

The contrasting genesis of the two nations is reinforced by the fact
that the Americans were the winners of their revolution against the
crown while the Canadians—including upward of forty thousand loyalists who migrated from the American colonies to the Canadian colonies
during the Revolutionary War[7]—sided with the losers. The winner-
loser psychological divide is reflected in the American pantheon of revolutionary heroes—Washington, Jefferson, Madison, Paine, John Paul
Jones, for example—and the absence of any comparable Canadian figures. That divide may also be reflected in the relative optimism of the
American national character, the relative pessimism of the Canadian.

To continue the sibling metaphor, the two nations display personality differences linked to their political origins and the resulting differences in their political systems, as Lipset notes. But the differences are
easily exaggerated. Canadians tend to be more respectful of authority,
more supportive of state intervention, more concerned with order, more
cautious, more conscious of group interests in contrast to individual
interests.[8] But as I argued in *Who Prospers?*[9] a strong current of group-
ness, of association, is also apparent in American culture and history.

Francis Fukuyama makes the same point in his recent book, *Trust*, with respect to the American tendency toward "spontaneous sociability."

The Canadian judicial system places somewhat more emphasis on crime control, somewhat less emphasis on due process, than does the American system, although both goals are clearly present in both systems. Canadians are at once more egalitarian, reflected in their mistrust of unbridled individualism, and more class-conscious, reflecting a British influence that persisted well into the twentieth century—in sharp contrast with the anti-aristocratic American Revolution. One consequence is the existence of a Canadian social-democratic party, the New Democrats. Another is the far greater relative strength of the labor movement in Canada, the decisive role Samuel Gompers played in organizing labor in both countries notwithstanding. (Gompers once said, "We are more than neighbors; we are kin . . . our labor problem with all its ideals, aspirations, and ambitions is alike for both of us.")[10] Yet another is the substantially greater scope of social programs (although that divergence is a phenomenon of recent decades). By contrast, as Lipset observes, "[t]he United States has one of the weakest sets of welfare provisions in the developed world."[11]

In part because of the large francophone population that Canada inherited after the British victory over the French at the Plains of Abraham in Quebec City in 1759, and the ensuing British decision not to impose the English language and British institutions on the French settlers, Canada has tended to view itself as intrinsically a multicultural country; many Canadian intellectuals and politicians deny the existence of a national culture. The question of multiculturalism versus the melting pot is an increasingly hot political issue in the United States, above all with respect to black-white relations and the burgeoning Hispanic population, which demographers forecast will overtake blacks early in the next century.

But anglophone Canada is not really multicultural. Its bedrock is the same Anglo-Protestant system of values and attitudes that is the cultural foundation of the United States, and it is to this system that successful immigrants in Canada, be they Eastern European Slavs, Chinese and East Indians, or Caribbean blacks, acculturate. I met with several representatives of the social science faculties of the University of Calgary in September 1995, and, as in other discussions with Canadian scholars and politicians, Canadian multiculturalism— embracing not only francophone Quebec and the indigenous Indian and Eskimo peoples but also immigrants from all over the world—was asserted as an axiom. But after a conversation in which I stressed the cultural and institutional similarities between Canada and the United States, particularly in contrast with the sharp differences between Canada and the United States on the one hand and Latin America on the other, my Canadian interlocutors acknowledged the Anglo-Protestant bedrock. To be sure, the conversation took place shortly before the 30 October 1995 Quebec sovereignty referendum that traumatized Canadians to the potential consequences of unbridled multiculturalism.

Canadians and Americans thus substantially share, albeit with some variation of degree, a fundamental belief in human progress (the future), the work ethic, frugality (recent evidence of its erosion in both countries notwithstanding), education, merit, community, ethics, fair play, diffused authority, and secularism—the universal progress values. This cultural coincidence is documented by the recent research of Ronald Inglehart, Miguel Basáñez, and Neil Nevitte on value and attitude patterns in Canada, the United States, and Mexico. Their data show Canada and the United States very close to each other (and quite different from Mexico) with respect, for example, to attitudes about capitalism, the balance between human and materialist values, sexual behavior, the balance between autonomy and obedience in child rearing, the balance between the individual and the family, public morality, and political participation. (One of the few sharp divergences: Americans are much more attached to religion than are Canadians.)[12]

Our shared Anglo-Protestant culture, including the English language spoken with similar accents, and our shared North American geography thus unmistakably label us as siblings, more like each other than like our Australian and New Zealander cousins. The contrasting circumstances of our births differentiate us. And like siblings everywhere, we have developed different personality traits, traits that reflect, above all, differences in size and strength, but also the different paths taken to nationhood. The Canadian may be more reflective and cautious, and somewhat intimidated by his bigger sibling, of whose conduct he is prone to be at once envious and critical. The American may be more gregarious and, at least until recent years, confident and optimistic, still substantially imbued with the idea that there is no problem beyond the reach of Yankee ingenuity. His personality, as well as his size and strength, involve him in other relationships that lead to the neglect of his smaller sibling, thereby intensifying the latter's resentment.

But when push comes to shove, the two siblings usually work out their differences within the give-and-take framework of the pluralist, fair-play, community values they share, although the solution may be preceded by a fair amount of squabbling. That neither consistently gets the upper hand is suggested by conversations I had with two prominent Canadians in the fall of 1995. I posed the same question to both: "Can you conceive of circumstances where the relationship between Canada and the United States deteriorates to one of sustained hostility?" One, a journalist, responded, "Not so long as Canada continues to be pliant to the United States." The other, a diplomat, said, "Well, you know, we are tough negotiators and so are the Americans. But if it looks as though an issue may threaten the special relationship, the Americans cave." I might add that, from the point of view of several American diplomats with whom I spoke, the net of the dispute settlements favors neither Canada nor the United States.

CANADIAN-U.S. RELATIONS:
FROM HOSTILITY TO COMMUNITY

"Special relationship" is, of course, another way of saying "community." However strong and stable that community may be today, it has not always been thus. In fact, for more than a century following American independence, the relationship was fundamentally one of mistrust and hostility. During that period, Canadians feared that the principal objective of the United States vis-à-vis Canada was annexation. The fear was not unfounded: among the American leaders who promoted that goal were Thomas Jefferson, Samuel Adams, Lincoln's secretary of state William Seward, and the editors of the *Chicago Tribune*.[13] They were motivated in part by the belief that geography and culture conspired for one great nation in North America, in part by the conviction that the only guarantee of deterring British designs against the United States was the departure of the British from Canada.

Adversaries (1775–1867)

The onset of hostility between the British colony of Quebec and the British American colonies dates from the decision of the British commander General Guy Carleton, following the British defeat of the French in 1763, to frame a policy that would confirm continuation of the French language, French culture, aristocratic government, French civil law, and the Roman Catholic religion for the French inhabitants who formed the large majority of the population of Quebec. That fateful "multicultural" policy became a sword of Damocles that hangs over the Canadian nation to this day. It was, moreover, viewed as a provocation by the American colonists, who had resisted French incursions into the Ohio Valley and had fought the French in the French and Indian War (1754–63). The intensity of the American colonists' feelings about the French at the time can be measured by the fact that the first act of the Continental Congress in 1775 was not to declare independence but to invade Canada (unsuccessfully).

I have already noted the flow to Canada of, initially, some forty thousand American colonists who were loyal to the crown and were treated as traitors by the revolutionary Americans in a climate of mutual hatred. Other "late Loyalists" would arrive after the American Revolutionary War. The substantial new British population in Quebec forced reconsideration of the Carleton policy by the British government. In 1791, Quebec was divided into two new provinces, Lower Canada (today Quebec) and Upper Canada (today Ontario), both of which were governed, independently, according to the British constitutional monarchy system.

In some respects, the War of 1812 was a reprise of the Revolutionary War, precipitated in part by British harassment of American trade with French-controlled Europe and the searching of American ships for British deserters. But other factors were also in play: rivalry between Britain and the U.S. in the fur trade; uncertainties about the border between British Canada and the United States; British assistance to Indian tribes hostile to Americans; and the belief on the part of Americans that Canada should be part of the United States, the contrary views of British Canadians notwithstanding. The war ended in a stalemate but led by 1846 to a permanent clarification of the boundary line between the two countries following abortive efforts by

President James K. Polk to cut Canada off from the Pacific. The war also fortified the anti-American feelings of Canadians, particularly those who had fled the American colonies, and strengthened their sense of belonging to the British Empire.

The years following the War of 1812 saw the first examples of cooperative diplomacy between British Canada and the United States. Rebellions in Upper and Lower Canada in 1837 were motivated in part by the belief of rebellion leaders William Lyon Mackenzie and Louis-Joseph Papineau that the American democratic system was preferable to the British constitutional monarchy. While many Americans, particularly those living near the border, supported the rebellions, the U.S. government avoided involvement. When the rebellion leaders fled to the United States, President Martin Van Buren sent General Winfield Scott to New York to deter adventures by American citizens that might lead to wide-scale conflict. In 1842, one year after Lower and Upper Canada were merged into the United Province of Canada, Secretary of State Daniel Webster and the British minister to Washington defused a dispute over the boundary between Maine and New Brunswick, an area rich in timber resources.

In 1846, the British Parliament's repeal of the Corn Laws terminated preferential treatment of Canadian grain and timber exports to Britain, precipitating a rethinking by the Canadians of British domination of Canadian trade. In 1854, the U.S. Congress and the colonial legislatures of British North America endorsed a ten-year reciprocal trade agreement that authorized free trade in grain, coal, livestock, timber, and fish. The warming of relations was symbolized by the construction of a railway bridge across the Niagara River. The agreement brought measurable benefits to both.

Relations between the two countries were strained by the American Civil War. American Secretary of State William Seward attempted to secure Canadian support of the North by sending an emissary to Canada, in contravention of a British-U.S. agreement that British diplomats were to represent Canada. Confederate sympathizers mounted a raid on St. Albans, Vermont, from Canada and escaped after their return. And Canadian authorities refused to return some fifteen thousand draft dodgers and deserters. Tensions between Britain and the United States intensified when a Union Navy captain seized two Confederate envoys from a British ship off Cuba. Open war between the two countries was averted when the envoys were freed by Seward. The 1854 reciprocal trade agreement was a casualty of the Civil War, and the victory of the North left the Canadians and British anxious about Canada's security.

The creation of the Dominion of Canada in 1867 was thus a response to the American Civil War. Nova Scotia, New Brunswick, Lower Canada, and Upper Canada were the original components. Manitoba was added in 1870, British Columbia in 1871, Prince Edward Island in 1873, Saskatchewan and Alberta in 1905. Newfoundland and Labrador (one province) did not join until 1949. From 1867, Canada behaved increasingly as an autonomous nation, a reality that was confirmed when Prime Minister John MacDonald of Canada participated, along with British envoys, in negotiation of the 1871 Treaty of Washington, which, among other things, reestablished access of American fishermen to the waters of the Maritime provinces in exchange for duty-free access to the American market by Canadian fishermen. But the broad reciprocal trade agreement of 1854, abrogated by the United States toward the end of the Civil War, was not renegotiated. For the United States, perhaps the most important achievement of the Treaty of Washington was the departure of British forces from Canada, except for garrisons at the naval bases in Halifax, Nova Scotia, and Esquimalt, British Columbia. The Canadians viewed that aspect of the treaty with apprehension.

Détente (1867–1908)

Both countries focused their attention on national development for the balance of the nineteenth century. The Manifest Destiny of the United States to extend across the North American continent from the Atlantic to the Pacific was first articulated by the journalist John L. O'Sullivan in 1845 in terms that may have been disconcerting for Canada. O'Sullivan wrote of "the right of our manifest destiny to overspread and possess the whole of the continent which Providence has given us for the development of the great experiment of liberty and federated self-government entrusted to us."[14]

But the relationship between the two countries was a good deal less conflictive than it had been in the period between the American Revolution and the Civil War, although it was not without its strains:

the frustrated designs of some Americans on British Columbia and the Yukon; ambiguities about Alaska's borders that were resolved in favor of the United States in 1903; continuing disputes over fisheries; and a brief crisis between Britain and the United States in 1895 over the border between Venezuela and British Guiana that produced some saber rattling in both Canada and the United States.

Both countries followed essentially the same formula in the consolidation of their control over the vast land mass between the two great oceans: construction of transcontinental railways (completed in 1869 in the United States, 1885 in Canada); large-scale immigration from Europe; opening up of the prairie to homesteading; and foreign investment, above all from Britain. Canada's march to the Pacific was a good deal more pacific than America's: "Between 1866 and 1895, the United States Army fought 943 military engagements with native peoples; Canadian troops fought seven."[15] Canada's continuing jaundiced view of the United States was captured in a cartoon caricature, "'Brother [appropriately] Jonathan,' a skinny, avaricious version of Uncle Sam who invariably pressed his unwanted attentions on fair 'Miss Canada.'"[16] (Brother Jonathan bears a striking resemblance to Abraham Lincoln.) That view of their southern neighbor did not deter more than a million Canadians, including Calixa Lavallée, the composer of the Canadian national anthem, "O Canada," and James Naismith, who subsequently invented basketball, from emigrating to the United States.

Conservative and Liberal Canadian governments pursued reactivation of the reciprocal trade agreements after the Civil War ended, but they could not convince the Americans of the advantage of liberalized trade for the United States. The American rebuff led the Conservatives under MacDonald, who returned to power in 1878, to promote a protectionist National Policy similar to the American policy, which the Canadians concluded was principally responsible for America's surging industrialization. One consequence of the high Canadian tariff barriers was massive American investment in Canada: what the Americans could not export over those barriers they would now produce in Canada. Canada's industrialization thus received powerful impetus. But the interest of U.S. investors in Canada was not stimulated by Canadian protectionism alone. Canada's vast mineral and other natural resources attracted investor interest, and the common language and common institutions, including independent judicial systems, facilitated the investment flow. At about the turn of the century, Canada displaced Mexico as the principal object of U.S. foreign investment.

Protectionism notwithstanding, trade between the two countries expanded rapidly. In the years after the National Policy became effective, 38 percent of Canada's exports went to the United States, compared with 53 percent to Britain, while 60 percent of its imports came from the United States, compared to 24 percent from Britain.[17] By the turn of the century, the United States had displaced Britain as Canada's principal trading partner. But the Conservatives' commitment to protectionism galvanized national support for them, as free trade, supported by the Liberals, came to be viewed by many Canadians, with MacDonald's skillful manipulation of the issue, as the opening wedge of annexation by the United States.

Détente to Alliance (1908–45)

Britain's decline in the latter decades of the nineteenth and first decades of the twentieth century coincided with the burgeoning of American power, first apparent in its thrashing of Spain in 1898. (Commodore George Dewey destroyed the Spanish fleet in Manila Bay on 1 May 1898; American casualties were "eight men slightly wounded.")[18] It was against this backdrop of shifting world power that the relationship between Canada and the United States, already quite civil by the standards of the times, moved toward rapprochement, even alliance.

In 1906, the British withdrew their garrisons from Halifax and Esquimalt, leaving Canada wholly responsible for its own defense. In 1909, Canada, encouraged by Britain, established a Department of External Affairs. But perhaps the most significant development in the early years of the new century was the creation of the International Boundary Commission (the IBC), the International Waterways Commission (the IWC), and the International Fisheries Commission (IFC) in 1908. They initiated a continuing process of Canadian-American "effort to institutionalize and depoliticize the mechanisms of conflict resolution."[19] The IBC went about its business in a quiet, professional way, and was able to resolve numerous border disputes with a minimum of controversy.

An even more significant bilateral institution, the International Joint Commission (IJC), which superseded the IWC and IFC, was established in 1909. The IJC's jurisdiction included potentially volatile issues like power development, pollution, fisheries, and irrigation. While its efficacy is debated by historians, it was involved in scores of successful dispute settlements and is generally conceded to be at least symbolically significant.

The institutionalization of governmental relationships was paralleled by an increasingly rich north-south fabric of private relationships that included business enterprises and associations, labor unions, social organizations, college fraternities, and baseball leagues. As the relationship between the two countries broadened and deepened, the first rumbles of Canadian concern about Yankee cultural domination were heard.[20]

The success of the Conservative MacDonald's mobilization of nationalist sentiment against reciprocal trade agreements left the Liberals, under Wilfrid Laurier, with no alternative policy. The Liberals won four consecutive times, in 1896, 1900, 1904, and 1908. But the trade balance for Canada and the United States chronically ran against the former: Canada's exports to the United States in 1910 were valued at $97 million, while American exports to Canada totaled $242 million.[21] Thus, when William Howard Taft offered an extremely generous, even magnanimous, reciprocity package in 1910, Laurier's—and much of Canada's—initial reaction was incredulity and jubilation. Historians still argue over what motivated Taft's generosity, which was probably a combination of an evolving fundamental shift on American trade policy, domestic political calculation, and a genuine affection for Canada "nurtured by years of happy vacations and hearty meals at his summer home in Murray Bay, Quebec."[22]

But many Canadians, led by the Conservatives, viewed the Taft offer as a Trojan horse that would ultimately compromise Canada's independence, particularly after the U.S. Congress approved the reciprocal trade agreement by a lopsided margin. Playing the nationalism card, the Conservatives, under Robert Borden, swamped the Liberals in the 1911 elections. The reciprocal trade agreement was dead. Trade between the two countries for the next eighty years would generally expand within a protectionist regime.

Bitterness over the fate of the trade agreement dissipated in the wake of the signing in 1912 of a sweeping fisheries agreement, and plans were well under way for a joint Canadian-American celebration of one hundred years of peace following the end of the War of 1812 when World War I erupted in Europe in 1914. Canada, as a British colony, was in the "crusade to save democracy" from the outset, and American neutrality during the first years was a cause of intensifying friction, which reached a furor of resentment when, in 1916, a German submarine freighter landed in Baltimore to pick up a cargo of nickel mined by an American company in Canada, and a German combat submarine made a courtesy visit to Newport just prior to sinking five Allied ships. The United States entered the war on the side of the Allies in 1917, but "twenty months as comrades in arms could not reverse the resentment Canadians felt at three years of U.S. neutrality."[23] One Canadian subsequently wrote, "America counted her profits while Canada buried her dead."[24] On the other hand, a 1917 agreement between the Imperial Munitions Board and the U.S. Ordnance Department assured significant U.S. military procurement in Canada and U.S. financing of British procurement in Canada.

The two decades between the world wars continued the intensification of public and private relationships between the two countries. Canada established formal diplomatic representation, short of embassy status though independent of the British Embassy, in Washington in 1926, reciprocated by an American legation in Ottawa, directly across Wellington Street from the Canadian parliament, in 1927. Trade between the two countries continued to expand. American investment increased, particularly in mining and automobile manufacturing (the latter largely stimulated by Canadian tariff barriers), and Canadian investment in the United States mounted. Fraternal/social/business organizations like Kiwanis, the Lions, and Rotary Club ignored the border in their proliferation. Americans acquired Canadian hockey teams and competed in a binational league in Canada's national sport.

Prohibition added a new irritant to the perennial friction points of fishing and boundaries, and Canadian concerns about cultural penetration through the airways led to the creation of the publicly owned and financed Canadian Broadcast Corporation (CBC) in the 1930s. The Depression added an additional source of friction. With unemployment soaring in both countries, Canadians, who had been exempted from quotas in the U.S. Immigration Act of 1921, were now subjected to them. The Americans raised tariffs on agricultural products to protect their farm workers, further aggravating the economic hardships inflicted by the Depression. The Canadians retaliated. As trade declined and the Depression intensified, the United States turned away from the extreme protectionism symbolized by the Smoot-Hawley Act of 1930, and Canada tempered its economic nationalism. The first reciprocal trade agreement since 1854 was signed in 1935 and was followed in 1938 by an even broader agreement.

The outbreak of World War II created another period that bred Canadian resentment—albeit briefer than in World War I—while Canada fought and America remained neutral, particularly since Canada was not obliged by its Dominion status to come to the aid of Britain. But Franklin Roosevelt's "neutrality" masked a strong identity with the Allied cause and the need for time both to build a constituency for involvement among the American electorate and to reinforce America's capacity to fight. On 18 August 1940, Roosevelt and Canadian prime minister Mackenzie King signed an unprecedented agreement that effectively created a Canada-U.S. alliance. The principal instrument of the Ogdensberg Agreement was a Permanent Joint Board on Defense (PJBD). The signing followed by a few months a Gallup poll that found that 81 percent of Americans thought the U.S. should go to war to defend Canada.

The PJBD was a useful coordinating device, but the decision-making mainstream passed through London and Washington. Mostly because it was a source of uranium, Canada was invited to participate, albeit in a limited way, in the Manhattan Project, along with the Americans and the British. The Canadian diplomatic representation in Washington and its American counterpart in Ottawa were accorded full embassy status in 1944. Joint planning of production of military materiel worked well, and the exigencies of war substantially dismantled the tariff structure that had for so long impeded trade, for example, in agricultural products. The Canadian economy, like the American, surged out of the Depression.

World War II marked the end of Britain's two centuries as a world power and heralded the arrival of the United States as a superpower. Canada confronted a shift of the international center of gravity from its colonizer to its brash sibling neighbor.

The Alliance Amid Cold War Tensions (1945–84)

The rapid shift from hot war against Germany and Japan to cold war against the Soviet Union and subsequently China led, in 1947, to the Marshall Plan, of which Canada was a beneficiary in the sense that European recipients of American dollars could spend those dollars in Canada as well as the United States; and in 1949, to creation of the North Atlantic Treaty Organization, of which Canada and the United States were charter members. Canadians fought alongside Americans in Korea in the early 1950s. The North American Air Defense (NORAD) Agreement in 1957 added another dimension to the Canadian-American military alliance. Early warning radar lines were built and jointly manned in the extreme north of Canada; across Canada's mid-section; in the Atlantic Provinces of Newfoundland and Labrador, Prince Edward Island, New Brunswick, and Nova Scotia; and in Alberta.

But, as in World War II, the Canadians were junior partners to the dominant Americans and often found their views ignored. From the outset, some Canadian intellectuals and politicians expressed the view that the American hard line was in part responsible for Soviet intransigence, a view that would later harden into a theory of "moral equivalence" that asserted that both superpowers were comparably power-hungry and irresponsible. This current in Canadian thinking brought Truman's secretary of state, Dean Acheson, to the conclusion that "Canadians [were] incurably inclined to moralizing in foreign policy and utterly naive about international power politics."[25]

Although the fundamental bond of the Canada-U.S. alliance was never ruptured, the Canadian stance was quite different from the American with respect to the Berlin airlift, storage and use of nuclear weapons, disarmament, social and political unrest in the Third World in general, Cuba, the Organization of American States, and Southeast Asia. The disagreements were magnified by a post–World War II swing in Canadian domestic politics toward the left—a sort of delayed New Deal in a country that had lagged behind American social experimentation until then, particularly during the Depression.

Nobel Peace Prize laureate (for his role in the 1956 Suez crisis) Lester Pearson, a Liberal, skillfully piloted the Canadian relationship with the United States through the increasingly roiled waters of U.S. involvement in Southeast Asia between 1963 and 1968. But he was replaced by Pierre Elliot Trudeau, Liberal prime minister from 1968 to 1984 except briefly (1979–80), who became the symbol of a revived Canadian nationalism that sought, even needed, distance from the United States. In his first years in office, he considered withdrawing from NATO, cut the Canadian military establishment, publicly opposed the U.S. Vietnam policy, and diverged from Washington on its policy toward Latin America. These positions obviously did not endear him to Washington, particularly in the Nixon years. But the relationship was genuinely shaken by a series of economic measures, reflecting Canadian concerns about the prominence of American investment and popular culture in Canada, but also in response to the devaluation of the American dollar by the Nixon administration in 1971 and a 10 percent surtax on imports (from which Canada was subsequently exempted).

In the 1970s, the Canadian Development Corporation was created to mobilize domestic capital, with one of its goals being the displacement of American capital. Similar public holding companies with similar goals had sprung up in Latin America. A Foreign Investment Review Agency was created to screen foreign acquisitions of Canadian companies, also reminiscent of Latin America's concerns about foreign investment. The government set up Petro-Canada to compete in a petroleum industry dominated by U.S. investment—once again we are reminded of Latin America, for example, the state petroleum operations in Venezuela and Mexico. And a program was initiated to reduce Canadian "dependence" on trade with the U.S. by expanding trade with Europe and Asia. In 1980, Trudeau adopted a National Energy Policy whose principal objective was the reduction of the U.S. presence in the petroleum industry.

The fissure that developed between Canada and the United States during the Trudeau years, in part the consequence of ideological and personality conflicts with the Republican presidents of the time, was aggravated by Trudeau's ascription of moral equivalence to the United States and the Soviet Union. Particularly in the light of what we now know about the latter, this lends some credence to the remark of State Department official Lawrence Eagleburger that the prime minister seemed like "a leftist high on pot."[26]

The Special Relationship Reaffirmed (1984–95)

The victory of Brian Mulroney's Tories in the 1984 elections reversed the erosion of the Canadian-U.S. community that had occurred during the Trudeau years. The crowning achievement was a broad Canadian-U.S. Free Trade Agreement (CUFTA) in 1988 that ended more than a century during which the two countries danced around the reciprocal tariff reduction opportunity but, with the exception of the two partial agreements in 1935 and 1938, never could quite seize it. Canadian-American cooperation was also central to the subsequent (1992) signing of the North American Free Trade Agreement (NAFTA), which brought Mexico into a tripartite trading relationship; Canada's decision in 1989 to join the Organization of American States; and Canadian military participation in the Gulf War against Iraq. In sharp contrast with Trudeau's prickly relationship with Nixon and Reagan, Mulroney's warm and open relationship with Ronald Reagan and George Bush facilitated negotiation of CUFTA but did not lead to much progress on the problem of acid rain, the costly result of industrial emissions on both sides of the border.

U.S. interest in CUFTA flowed principally from the growing Canadian surplus in the balance of trade between the two countries— some $23 billion in 1986.[27] A combination of Canada's traditional concerns about being swallowed by the American leviathan and partisan politics confronted Mulroney with a much harder sell than Reagan, a sell that was made easier by the inclusion in the agreement of a dispute-settlement mechanism with historical antecedents going back to the 1908 International Boundary Commission. The Liberals and the left-of-center New Democratic parties opposed CUFTA, but the Tories won the 1988 election that served in part as a referendum on CUFTA, albeit with a minority of the total vote.

Table 2.1 provides data on the recent growth of trade between the two countries:

U.S. exports to Canada grew 11 percent from 1992 to 1993, 14 percent from 1993 to 1994. Canada's exports to the United States grew 12 percent from 1992 to 1993, 17 percent from 1993 to 1994.* Free

---

*Some Canadians who opposed CUFTA believe that trade would have grown comparably had there been no CUFTA.

Table 2.1

CANADA–U.S. TRADE, 1987–94
(U.S.$ billions)

	U.S. Exports to Canada		Canadian Exports to U.S.	
Year	Value	% of U.S. Total	Value	% of Canada Total
1987	$59.8	23.5%	$71.1	75.5%
1990	83.7	21.3	91.4	74.8
1992	90.6	20.2	98.6	77.3
1994	114.3	22.3	128.8	79.3

Sources: U.S. Department of Commerce, *U.S. Foreign Trade Highlights 1994*; Statistics Canada, courtesy of Canadian Embassy in Washington.

trade between Canada and the United States is now widely supported on both sides of the border, and no political party of any significance opposes it.

Some Canadians, Pierre Trudeau among them, have chafed at the size of U.S. investment in Canada, which totaled $203 billion in 1991 (more than twice as much as in all of Latin America).[28] But Canadian investment in the United States was *greater* than that of the United States in Canada ($233 billion in 1991), although obviously the profile of Canada in the United States is much lower than the profile of the United States in Canada.[29]

Canada's failure to find a constitutional solution to the Quebec problem precipitated Mulroney's resignation in 1992, and Jean Chrétien led the Liberals back to power in 1993 in an election that amounted to a vast repudiation of the Tories, who were displaced by the Bloc Québecois, committed to sovereignty for Quebec, as the chief opposition party in Parliament. Some Canadians believe that the Tory disaster reflected voter resentment against Mulroney's intimate relationship with Washington.[30] But the principal issue was the condition of the Canadian economy (unemployment exceeded 10 percent, and the federal government confronted grave financial problems), and Chrétien had soon established a relationship with Bill Clinton that was comparable in its warmth to Mulroney's relationship with Reagan and Bush.

CANADA UNDER THE QUEBEC SWORD OF DAMOCLES

A chapter focused on the relationship between Canada and the United States is not the place for a lengthy discussion of the agonizing problem of separatist sentiment in Quebec, which came to a head with the referendum that was very narrowly defeated—52,000 votes out of a total of 4.75 million—by Quebec voters on 30 October 1995. (That what happens in Quebec is indeed relevant to the Canada-U.S. relationship is underscored by the gyrations in American financial markets the day after the vote, also by a skillfully worded statement of support for the Canadian nation by President Clinton before the referendum.) But the Quebec problem operates in a cultural context that is central to the argument of this book.

Tocqueville, a Frenchman, noted the backwardness of the French in Quebec in the 1830s:

> I have met with men in New England who were on the point of leaving a country where they might have remained in easy circumstances, to seek their fortune in the wilds. Not far from that region I found a French population in Canada, closely crowded on narrow territory, although the same wilds were at hand; and while the emigrant from the United States purchased an extensive estate with the earnings of a short term of labor, the Canadian paid as much for land as he would have done in France. Thus nature offers the solitudes of the New World to Europeans also; but they do not always know how to make use of her gifts. Other inhabitants have the same physical conditions of prosperity, but without their laws and customs; and these people are miserable.[31]

Until 1960, Quebec was an underdeveloped province—"a semi-literate village society"[32]—within a developed country. The people of Quebec were isolated in a traditional society dominated even in the civic sphere by the Roman Catholic Church, the orientation of which was defined in a 1902 sermon by Bishop L. A. Paquet that included the following words:

> This religious and civilizing mission is the true vocation and the special vocation of the French race in America . . . our mission is less to handle capital than to stimulate ideas; less to light the furnaces of factories than to maintain and spread the glowing fires of religion and thought, and to help them cast their light into the distance.[33]

During the 1940s and 1950s, the province was run by Premier Maurice Duplessis more in the style of a Latin American caudillo than a democratic political leader. A group of modern young innovators, led by Liberal Premier Jean Lesage, triggered a "quiet revolution" in the early 1960s that soon transformed the province from "a backwoods society of French Canadians into a bustling, urban one of Québecois. In the rush to assert their status as *maîtres chez nous*, the Québecois tore themselves from the Church's embalming grip and plunged into an orgy of secularizing change"[34] that, among other reforms, ended the Church's control of the education system.

Quebec has today substantially caught up with the rest of Canada, and its transformation is comparable to that of Spain, or South Korea, or Taiwan, over the same three decades. But the process of modernization has intensified the Québecois sense of cultural and linguistic identity that has driven the movement for sovereignty. The threat to Canada's political, economic, and territorial integrity thus has its roots in the recommendations of General Guy Carleton to the British crown in 1763 that French culture and the French language be preserved within the new British colony.

Quebec's rapid progress in recent decades notwithstanding, many Québecois are convinced that they are still second-class Canadian citizens whose earlier backwardness was the consequence of exploitation by Anglo-Canadian bankers, businessmen, and politicians. The former leader of the Bloc Québecois in the federal parliament and current premier of Quebec, Lucien Bouchard, galvanized support for sovereignty during the weeks preceding the 1995 referendum, in part by asserting that 50 percent of Quebec is owned by outsiders.[35] In his speech following the defeat of the referendum and prior to resigning, Quebec Premier Jacques Parizeau blamed the loss on "money and the ethnic vote,"[36] words that prompted Canadian Jewish leaders to call for an apology.

This "exploited victim" dimension of Quebec nationalism reminds us of the dependency/Yankee imperialism explanation for Latin America's backwardness, also of Louis Farrakhan's view that black poverty is, at least in part, the consequence of exploitation by Jewish and Korean merchants.[37] In the case of Quebec, the answer is to assure control of the province's economy and destiny through separation and sovereignty—the "Québec Libre" that Charles de Gaulle promoted when he visited Expo 67 in Montreal. For Latin America, the answer used to be to achieve economic self-sufficiency by shunning the world market and foreign investment. For Farrakhan, the answer is resegregation, analogous to the self-sufficiency chimera that Latin American nationalists sought for several decades and today increasingly appreciate was exactly that—a chimera.

I hope the leaders of Quebec appreciate that the conditions in the province prior to the quiet revolution were chiefly the consequence of a traditional, religious culture that persisted for two centuries in substantial isolation from the progressive cultural currents that were driving the rest of Canada and the United States toward modernity. As in Latin America and the American ghetto, the outsiders who bring capital, organization, technology, and business savvy to Quebec should be viewed as valuable assets, not liabilities or exploiters.

Canada's agony over Quebec underscores three important lessons for the United States:

1. Multiculturalism without a foundation of shared values and attitudes, and without a sense of a national community, is a recipe for traumatic fragmentation.
2. The existence of more than one official language is an obstacle to the achievement of the sense of a national community.
3. Bilingual education with the goal of anything other than rapid mastery of English works against the achievement of a national community.

CANADIAN-U.S. RELATIONS: THE CONTRASTING SIBLINGS

The contrast between Ottawa and Washington, D.C., is a metaphor for the contrast between the two countries. Ottawa is a smaller city (about 300,000 people, but about 700,000 live in the metropolitan area) that is both easy and very pleasant to live in, its harsh winters notwithstanding. Its copper-spired neo-Gothic parliament buildings, reminiscent of London's, sit atop the Ottawa River and the headwaters of the Rideau River and Canal, which wind through the city southward on a hundred-odd mile journey to the St. Lawrence. Across the Ottawa River lies the smaller city of Hull, in Quebec Province, where many federal government offices are located, and beyond are the picturesque lakes and mountains of the Gatineau River region.

Ottawa's natural beauty is accentuated by the many parks, bicycle and walking paths, and flowerbeds that embellish it. In the English tradition, public and private owners of grassy areas take great pains to keep them in impeccable condition. Around the winter holiday season, trees in both Ottawa and Hull are festooned with sprays of multicolored lights that give the cities a magical quality, particularly when it snows. In winter, the Rideau Canal becomes a well-maintained ice thoroughfare on which thousands skate to and from work. The city's snow-removal capability is astonishing, and life goes on substantially without interruption even in blizzard conditions.

Despite an active cultural life, centered around the National Arts Center across Wellington from the Parliament, and its numerous ethnic communities and restaurants, many Canadians complain about Ottawa's "antiseptic" quality and prefer Toronto, Montreal, or Vancouver. To be sure, that antiseptic quality includes a crime rate that is a fraction of that of most American cities, of which Washington is among the most dangerous.

Washington, D.C., where I have also lived, is twice as populous as Ottawa, and its metropolitan area is several times more populous. Its setting, where the Potomac makes a turn to the south on its way to the Chesapeake Bay, is comparably scenic, its public buildings comparably impressive and handsome, although more evocative of Greece and Rome than Westminster. But Washington is not as well kept as Ottawa. Its much larger population means greater geographic spread, longer commutes, and more congestion in the center of the city, an excellent subway system notwithstanding.

Moreover, Washington has become a symbol of America's race problem. A majority of its citizens are black, and while America's quiet racial revolution of the past thirty years is apparent from the large number of blacks who have moved into the middle class (and into the Washington suburbs, where they outnumber those who live in the city), the ghetto's drug/crime/unwed mother/joblessness pathology of despair persists. Its ex-convict mayor, Marion Barry, often seen in African attire as he tries to solve the problems of a city administration mired in bankruptcy, has become a symbol of the color line that now so powerfully and disruptively defines "community" in the United States.

ARE CANADIANS MORE MORAL THAN AMERICANS?

In the fall of 1995, my wife and I drove across Canada, entering north of Burlington, Vermont, and exiting south of Vancouver. Not once did we encounter a gasoline station where one had to pay before pumping. It was not until we reached Dixon, California, that we had to prepay—a particularly cumbersome procedure that involved the use of tokens and required a return trip to the cashier if the amount actually purchased was less than the value of the tokens.* Most of the American gas stations at which we subsequently stopped did not require prepayment. A few did.

I don't want to overgeneralize from this anecdotal experience. But I think it *is* clear, Quebec aside, that Canada enjoys a higher degree of social integration than the United States, one that expresses itself in greater trust and civility—and lower levels of violence and crime—in human relationships. This contrast is ironic because the Canadians, at least rhetorically (and I believe self-deceptively—see my earlier description of my conversations at the University of Calgary), pride themselves on a multiculturalism that denies the existence of an integrating national culture.

Does this mean that Canadians are more moral than Americans, a common credo among Canadian intellectuals and politicians going back to the late eighteenth century and personified in the nineteenth by the sleazy "Brother Jonathan" and the fair "Miss Canada"? Is there an American moral flaw that justifies Pierre Trudeau's equation of Soviet and American foreign policy?

I think not, and if I am right that what fundamentally binds the two sibling nations together beyond their geographic proximity is the shared Anglo-Protestant value system and the kinds of institutions it breeds, then one would expect a comparable level of moral conduct in the two countries. A number of other factors explain the differences that some Canadians are prone to attribute to moral superiority.

That the population of the United States is ten times greater than that of Canada, and a good deal more diverse, has a lot to do with America's far greater social problems, including violent crime. Quebec aside, there is no numerically significant minority group in Canada, at

---

*The experience in Dixon evokes the mistrust of employees and customers betrayed by the complicated process one often encounters in stores in Latin America—see chaps. 6 and 7.

least none that compares with the American black population that is 12 percent of the national total—*roughly the size of Canada's total population*—and a Hispanic population that will soon overtake the black population. Blacks account for less than 2 percent of Canada's population, Hispanics for less than 1 percent.[38] Roughly half of violent crimes in the United States are committed by blacks, and while I am not aware of national crime statistics for Hispanics, data for the state of Colorado indicate a disproportionate Hispanic presence in the jail population.[39] I might add that, in Canada, the only two foreign-born groups that exceed the Canadian-born incarceration average of 10 per 10,000 are Latin American (14 per 10,000) and Caribbean (18 per 10,000—most are Jamaican) immigrants.[40]

Nor is the problem of racial integration in Canada burdened by the legacy of slavery and segregation that weighs so heavily on race relations in the United States. Yet white-against-black racism is far from unknown in Canada:

> Despite Canada's eagerness for farmer-settlers . . . African Americans were unwelcome. . . . When W.E.B. DuBois complained of this discrimination . . . the official response was blunt: "There is nothing in Canadian immigration law which disbars any person on the ground of color, but since colored people are not considered as a class likely to do well in this country all other regulations respecting health, money, etc., are strictly enforced, and it is quite possible that a number of your fellow countrymen may be rejected on such grounds." Had this form of restriction failed, however, Canada was ready to apply more overt racism: a federal order barring black immigrants was passed but never implemented in 1911.[41]

It is true that the level of immigration into Canada—about 250,000 people in 1994—is proportionately higher than in the United States, where legal immigration now approximates a million people per year and perhaps an additional 300,000 who enter illegally. But Canadian immigration policy places a heavier emphasis on skills and education, less on family reunification, than does the current American policy. (Interestingly, the 1995 recommendations of the Commission on Immigration Reform, chaired by the late former congresswoman Barbara Jordan, would reorient U.S. policy toward the Canadian model.) Moreover, the flow of illegal immigrants into Canada is much smaller than into the United States, in part because Canada does not border on a Third World country, in part as a consequence of the better Canadian coordination of governmental entities that makes it much more difficult for illegal immigrants to obtain employment or social benefits. We should note, in passing, that substantial popular opposition to current levels of immigration has been documented in both countries, and Canada took steps to reduce immigration by about 15 percent in 1995.[42]

Canadian social programs are more generous, and Canada's tax-financed single-payer health system assures coverage to everyone, in contrast to the chaotic American "system," with its significant gaps in coverage. But, as I already pointed out, the Canadian push on social programs is a phenomenon of recent decades; America was ahead of Canada until the 1950s. And today, with both countries confronting massive fiscal deficits, social program retrenchment appears inevitable for both.

Canadian self-imputed moral superiority is particularly apparent with respect to foreign policy divergences. The Canadian evaluation of America's conduct of foreign policy runs a spectrum from clumsiness and insensitivity through excessive pragmatism and, until recently, obsession with the cold war to, in the extreme, the total cynicism and raw power politics implied by those, including Trudeau, who believe in the "moral equivalence" of the United States and the Soviet Union.

The differences between Canadian and American foreign policy are fundamentally the consequence of the vast gap in power and responsibility of the two countries, *not* of differences in morality. To repeat, the ethical systems of the two countries are substantially similar because of the common Anglo-Protestant parentage. But the United States, as one of two superpowers until the end of the cold war and the only superpower today, not only has to take a position on virtually every international issue or conflict but also often must assume a leadership role to resolve the issue or defuse the conflict, a role that may involve the expenditure of vast financial and, in the extreme, human resources. Canada, too, takes positions. But it rarely must assume responsibility for an outcome.

Moreover, because it is intimidated by its more powerful sibling, Canada tends to define itself by its differences from that sibling. There is inevitably a strong temptation to seek the moral high ground because it doesn't cost much to do so, since little responsibility attaches to it.

Joseph Jockel, an American historian who has focused on Canadian-U.S. relations, notes a "narcissism" in this kind of moralizing, as do Thompson and Randall.[43] And there may be profit for Canadian politicians in distancing themselves from American policies, thereby exploiting "the latent anti-American sentiments among the Canadian public for electoral advantage."[44] A few examples:

• Mackenzie King's cabinet unanimously refused to permit Canadian aircraft to participate in the Berlin airlift in 1948 because they considered it a confrontational policy. But Canada did not have to assume responsibility for the loss of Berlin to the Soviets, as did the United States.

• Canadian leaders indicted the U.S. role in Vietnam as tens of thousands of American youths fled to Canada. But they did not have to assume responsibility for the possibility (which, to be sure, did not materialize beyond Laos and Cambodia) of dominoes falling all over Southeast Asia. No Canadian troops were at risk in Vietnam (except for some of the 2,700 Canadian volunteers who joined the U.S. Marines at the time).[45]

• Canada did not have to preoccupy itself with Cuban support of revolution in Nicaragua, El Salvador, and elsewhere in building an increasingly warm and profitable relationship with Fidel Castro that "continued a long diplomatic tradition characterized by mutual respect and cultural exchanges," in the words of Edgar Dosman, executive director of the Canadian Foundation for the Americas.[46] Nor has Canada needed to occupy itself unduly with human rights abuses in Cuba. As Dosman notes, "Cuba is back in the news. But the talk during 1995 has been less about politics and human rights than commercial opportunities and joint ventures by business and nongovernmental organizations."[47]

It is, in my view, much more accurate to interpret foreign policy differences between the two countries as a reflection of honest differences of interests and opinion that flow principally from differences in power. Assessing the moral content of the foreign policies of the two siblings is risky at best. I offer as a case in point Canadian and U.S. policy toward the government of Jean-Claude Duvalier in Haiti, in which I was personally involved as the director of the USAID mission to Haiti from 1977 to 1979. It became apparent to me early on that little progress was possible with so much of the budget being diverted to the Duvalier family and their friends, and the military. I consequently worked with the World Bank and the International Monetary Fund to devise a major new program conditioned on budgetary reform. Canada was an important source of assistance to Haiti, and I discussed the initiative with my Canadian counterpart in Port-au-Prince, who was supportive. But the decision had to be made in Ottawa.

So I visited Ottawa to present the proposal to senior officials of the Canadian International Development Agency. I was received politely, but it soon became apparent that they interpreted the initiative as Yankee bullying of a poor, defenseless country. They refused to participate.

A REMARKABLE RELATIONSHIP

We are more alike than we are different. Ontario and Minnesota are a good deal more alike than Minnesota and Mississippi. And what Canada and the United States share in a cultural sense is of decisive importance not only to the way we have evolved as progressive democratic-capitalist societies but also to our relationship with each other. There will always be issues between us, but the history of the relationship strongly suggests that we will usually find equitable solutions to them and that they will not be permitted to jeopardize the basic relationship.

The Canada-U.S. relationship is remarkable, particularly the breadth and depth of the integration of the two societies, above all their economies. It is also remarkable that the imbalance in population size and national power does not cause more difficulties than it does, for example, the fact that America accounts for roughly 80 percent of Canada's trade, while Canada accounts for roughly 20 percent of America's trade, the fact that it is America's principal trading partner notwithstanding.

As in all sibling relationships, there is some room for improvement in this one. Canada can help by resisting the temptation to judge the United States. The United States can help by broadening its awareness and understanding of Canada, particularly of its enormous importance to us. But even if we don't do better on these scores, the family— the community—will remain intact.

3

Latin America and the United States: Can Two So Divergent Paths Merge?

W hy has Latin America been so slow in adopting the democratic capitalist model, particularly open economic policies that integrate Latin America into the dynamic world market?[1] Against the backdrop of Latin America's troubled history, how should we interpret the modernization of political systems and economic policies that has occurred in the past fifteen years? And if it's true, as Tocqueville argues, that modernization ultimately depends on modern values and attitudes, how far has Latin America come toward universal progress culture?

In addressing these issues, I shall focus on the often negative role of intellectuals in Latin America, above all with respect to constructive relationships between Latin America and the United States. The comparably destructive role of intellectuals in the United States is the subject of the next chapter, in which I also take a second look at the bête noire of those intellectuals, the United Fruit Company. I shall also take note of and assess the economic and social progress Latin America has made in recent decades, as well as the growing influence of Protestantism. And I shall briefly examine Spain's transformation since 1960 and assess the usefulness of that experience as a predictor of Latin America's evolution in the coming decades.

LATIN AMERICA'S BELATED QUEST FOR DEMOCRATIC CAPITALISM

That Latin America has not made its peace with democratic capitalism—and the United States—until the last years of the twentieth century is principally the consequence of the incompatibility of traditional

Iberian culture with political pluralism and the free market, on the one hand, and the inevitable resentment of the successful by the unsuccessful, on the other. But some institutions and individuals in Latin America, North America, and Europe bear a direct responsibility for Latin America's hostility (until recently) to the democratic capitalist model—and to the United States—since World War II. In Latin America, those chiefly responsible are the Argentine economist Raúl Prebisch and his disciples, including Fernando Henrique Cardoso, the current president of Brazil; the Economic Commission for Latin America (ECLA—today ECLAC),* which Prebisch headed from 1948 to 1962;† and vast numbers of Latin American intellectuals and politicians who found in dependency theory either political or personal advantage and who placed their own needs for *dignidad* and external scapegoats above the search for the truth, as unpleasant and demeaning as that may have been, and above the real interests of their countries.

The irrationality and irresponsibility of Latin American intellectuals is the subject of *Manual del Perfecto Idiota Latinoamericano*[2] (*Manual of the Perfect Latin American Idiot*), a book published early in 1996 that had surged to the top of the bestseller lists in several Latin American countries and had sold one hundred thousand copies by mid-1996. The authors are Plinio Apuleyo Mendoza, a Colombian writer and journalist; Carlos Alberto Montaner, the Cuban exile writer and politician; and Alvaro Vargas Llosa, the son of writer Mario Vargas Llosa.

Important elements of the scholarly communities of the United States, Canada, and Western Europe, driven in part by misguided guilt feelings over the prosperity of their own societies, bear a comparably heavy responsibility for their destructive reinforcement of the prejudices of their Latin colleagues against capitalism, against the United States, and even, in some cases, against democracy.

Prebisch and ECLA

At the heart of Prebisch's world view was the idea that Third World underdevelopment is the consequence of a world economic sys-

---

*ECLA changed its name to the Economic Commission for Latin America and the Caribbean (ECLAC) in 1984.

†Prebisch was also secretary general of the United Nations Conference on Trade and Development (UNCTAD) from 1964 to 1969.

tem in which the advanced countries of the "hegemonic Center" exploit the underdeveloped countries of the "Periphery" through (1) monopolization of the production of "overpriced" industrial goods, while forcing the Periphery to produce "underpriced" primary products; and (2) multinational corporations, which allegedly drain poor countries of resources. The logical prescription: (1) high tariff barriers and the substitution of imported manufactured goods by domestic goods, if necessary (or even preferably) by state enterprises,[3] thereby bypassing the link of the Latin American oligarchies to the Center through the world market; and (2) discouragement of foreign investment.

One hears that Prebisch viewed import substitution as a temporary strategy; that he also promoted export strategies; and that he was concerned about "ethical" (cultural?) problems in Latin America. But at the heart of his theory and strategy was what he believed was the *dependent* condition of Latin America and of the Third World. In 1976, he published an article in the CEPAL Review (CEPAL is the Spanish acronym for ECLA) that asserted:

> If "dependence" is thought to be a better name for these phenomena of hegemony as manifested in the new forms which the evolution of capitalism has brought in its train, I have no objection whatever. Dependence is an inherent characteristic of the periphery. This concept was introduced in the earliest writings of CEPAL, and subsequently enriched with the valuable contributions on the subject made by various economists and sociologists. These contributions provided a clear idea of the real significance of the economic and technological superiority of the centres and their power to extract income from the periphery in excess of what their enterprises contributed to the production process."[4]

By 1976, it had to be apparent to Prebisch that South Korea, Taiwan, Hong Kong, and Singapore were disproving his thesis that the Third World's industrial production could not compete in a world market stacked against it. In the 1950s, the level of development of the East Asian "dragons" was comparable to that of Latin America. Mainly because of their decision to enter the world market, but also, I believe,

---

*Prebisch was not a Marxist, but note the parallel between the resources "stolen" by "the centre" from the Third World and the resources "stolen" by capitalists from workers in Marxist theory.

because of Protestant ethic–like features in Confucian Tao culture (emphasis on the future, work, frugality, education, merit),[5] these countries achieved and sustained astonishing economic growth rates: an average of 9 percent annually between 1960 and 1992. Today, the World Bank lists Hong Kong and Singapore ahead of Spain, Israel, New Zealand, and Ireland in its category of high-income economies; South Korea should appear in that category in the next few years. (Because of the insistence of the Peoples Republic of China, Taiwan does not appear in the World Bank data. If it did, it would probably be listed as a high-income country; its per capita income was estimated by economic historian Angus Maddison as 15 percent higher than South Korea's in 1987.)[6]

Australia is another country that undermines the credibility of the Prebisch/dependency thesis. It is a country at the periphery; it exports raw materials; its per capita income is high, and income distribution is about the same as in the United States; and its democratic traditions are deeply rooted.[7]

At about the same time the East Asian dragons were taking off, Brazil was demonstrating not only the possibility of Third World countries entering the world market with industrial products but also the consequences for economic growth. The value of Brazil's exports was $134 million in 1965, $36 billion in 1992. Manufactured products accounted for 9 percent of exports in 1965, 58 percent in 1992.[8] In the 1970s, Brazil's GDP grew at almost 9 percent annually.

Yet dependency theory, and the nationalistic, statist economic policies that flowed from it, prevailed in most of Latin America and the rest of the Third World until well into the 1980s. Its emotional appeal was very strong in Latin America: it fit so nicely with Rodó's immensely popular Ariel. And above all, it gave Latin politicians and intellectuals an ideal external scapegoat for Latin America's problems.

In 1962, Prebisch became the director of the ECLA-spawned Latin American Institute for Economic and Social Planning, often referred to by its Spanish acronym, ILPES. Two of his colleagues at ILPES were the Brazilian Fernando Henrique Cardoso and an Argentine, Enzo Faletto. Their book, Dependency and Development in Latin America, published in Spanish in 1971[9] and in English in 1979,[10] was must reading in Latin American and North American universities. It makes clear the powerful influence of Marxist theory on their views:

[W]e stress the socio-political nature of the economic relations of production. . . . This methodological approach, which found its highest expression in Marx, assumes that the hierarchy that exists in society is the result of established ways of organizing the production of material and spiritual life. This hierarchy also serves to assure the unequal appropriation of nature and of the results of human work by social classes and groups. So we attempt to analyze domination in its connection with economic expansion.[11]

For Cardoso and Faletto, Argentina's problems are explained by the fact that Great Britain and the United States, the "Center" countries that have had the most extensive economic relations with Argentina, are rich. But in addition to milking Argentina, the imperialist powers have insinuated themselves into a dominant economic and political position within the country through their bourgeois lackeys, "a hegemonic entrepreneurial agro-exporting sector."[12] Another pernicious instrument of imperialism and dependency is the multinational corporation.

The solution? Revolution!

It is not realistic to imagine that capitalist development will solve basic problems for the majority of the population. In the end, what has to be discussed as an alternative is not the consolidation of the state and the fulfillment of "autonomous capitalism" but how to supersede them. The important question, then, is how to construct paths toward socialism.[13]

Two decades after *Dependency and Development in Latin America* was published, Cardoso became Brazil's Minister of Finance, in which capacity he launched an orthodox stabilization program in the face of Brazil's chronic high inflation. Its success won him the presidency in the 1994 elections. The costly nonsense of his earlier views is far behind him: his presidential policies emphasize the strengthening of democratic capitalism, including privatization of state-owned industries; the improved functioning of the market in Brazil; fiscal restraint; Brazil's relationship with the United States (in April 1995 he made an official visit to Washington, where he was warmly received by President Clinton); foreign investment; and Brazilian exports to neighboring countries and the world market. One wonders whether he ever asks himself, "Where would Brazil—and Latin America—be today if these policies had been pushed forty years ago?"

The new leadership of ECLAC is a symbol of the transformation of Latin American attitudes about democracy, capitalism, and the United States. Gert Rosenthal, who did his graduate work in economics at the University of California, is a highly respected Guatemalan who has served as ECLAC's secretary general since 1988. He has for many years espoused the combination of the market and democratic governance as the correct model for Latin America. The same is true of another improbably named Guatemalan, Isaac Cohen, who directs the ECLAC office in Washington.

Many other prominent Latin American intellectuals, some connected with ECLAC, others not, were totally committed to the dependency/imperialism interpretation of Latin America's condition. An example is Julio Cotler, a Peruvian intellectual who coedited a book with Richard Fagen, who is among the American intellectuals most committed to the idea that Latin America's problems are principally the consequence of the alleged greed, irresponsibility, and ineptness of the United States.[14] I spoke in 1989 at a left-leaning think tank in Lima where Cotler was present. He was outraged at the idea that the principal responsibility for Latin America's condition rested with Latin Americans themselves and not with the United States. Yet many of that persuasion just a few years ago have dramatically different views today. A few examples:

• Jorge Castañeda, a Mexican who was for many years stridently anti-American and anti-imperialist, is today a *Newsweek* columnist highly critical of the utopian Latin American left and his own country.[15] (We'll meet him again in chapter 8.)

• Alberto Couriel, a Uruguayan, is a former ECLAC official who is today a senator from the left-leaning Frente Amplio in Uruguay. In a tract he wrote in 1974, he posed the question, "What variations do the ['great monopolistic international enterprises'] add to the existing capitalist tendencies of generating wealth and poverty, development and underdevelopment, imperialism and dependency, domination and subordination, exploitation and misery?"[16] His conclusion, as one might expect, was very unfavorable to the multinationals. But his ideology today falls within the democratic-capitalist framework. In 1995, in a conversation at his senate office in Montevideo, he told me he had come to the conclusion that Latin America's problems between 1950 and 1980 were substantially of its own making. He did blame the First World banks for the crisis of the 1980s, but when I pointed out that East Asians, even more adversely affected by the oil price shocks than the Latin Americans, had pulled in their belts and avoided borrowing, he modified his position: "Let's say that the First World banks *and* the Latin Americans are responsible for the 1980s."

• *Comandante* Jaime Wheelock—leader of the "Proletarians," one of the more radical of the three Sandinista factions—and I had a very frank and constructive relationship when I directed the USAID mission in Nicaragua during the first two years of the Sandinista revolution, 1979–81. He sheepishly inscribed for me a copy of his book, *Imperialism and Dictatorship*, an anti-American diatribe.[17] I quote from it to give some sense of the frame of mind of those committed to the dependency/imperialism view:

> The Nicaraguan society ... remains subjugated in a situation of acute dependency on North American imperialism ... the United States imposes on Nicaragua a regimen of development that forces Nicaragua to furnish raw materials, principally agricultural products, to the North American market while depending on Yankee industry for its manufactured goods.... [In the 1960s] An avalanche of capital and North American investors, in connection with the developmentalist demagoguery of the Alliance for Progress, massively infiltrates the Nicaraguan economy with the pretext of promoting industrial development. At the same time, the Central American Common Market is initiated, a field of operations for the bourgeois Central American exploiters and a mechanism par excellence of North American imperialism to guarantee its political, economic, cultural, and military domination over the Central American isthmus.[18]

Wheelock identifies the Central American Business Administration Institute, which is known by its Spanish acronym, INCAE, as one of the tentacles of the Yankee octopus: "INCAE is the realization of a project conceived in the highest imperialist circles. The Cabot Lodges appear as the initiators ... subordinated to Harvard University." In fact, Harvard Business School Professor George Lodge, who, like many Americans, sympathized with the Sandinista Revolution in its early days, was an architect of INCAE, the first campus of which was located in a bucolic setting about ten miles south of Managua.* Most of the INCAE faculty also sympathized with the revolution, at least in the early days, and when Wheelock became the Minister of Agriculture and Agrarian Reform in the Sandinista government, he made extensive use of INCAE for training the personnel of his ministry. Part of that training was financed by USAID.

A brief digression about Harvard University, that bastion of Yankee imperialism: I was at Harvard's Center for International Affairs in December 1982, writing *Underdevelopment Is a State of Mind*, when I received an invitation from the John F. Kennedy School of Government at Harvard to comment on the presentation of Francisco Fiallos, the Sandinista ambassador to the United States. Despite his rather dull, technical speech on Nicaragua's economic problems, Fiallos was given a hero's ovation by the three hundred people in attendance. My comments focused on Sandinista human rights abuses and, in particular, Sandinista reneging on commitments to political pluralism and nonalignment. I was booed and heckled repeatedly.

One week later, Fiallos defected to the contras, bringing hundreds of thousands of Sandinista dollars with him.

Another note about Harvard. *Comandante* Jaime Wheelock spent the academic year 1993–94 at the John F. Kennedy School of Government. Today, Wheelock is one of the larger landholders in Nicaragua, a *terrateniente*, to use a Sandinista word of opprobrium.

Self-Destructive Foreign Policies

The Prebisch/ECLA view of a world market stacked against the Third World was dominant in policy making in Latin America for more than three decades. High tariffs protected domestic industries that often produced for markets so small that efficiency would have been impossible even were domestic producers forced to compete with foreign producers—which the tariffs assured would not happen. The Cardoso-Faletto variant of dependency theory stressed the pernicious role of the Latin American bourgeoisie as "agents of imperialism," adding credibility to the statist inclinations of left-leaning politicians and fortifying

---

*That campus exists today, but it is secondary to the new INCAE campus that began operations in Alajuela, Costa Rica, in the 1980s.

the interest of many Latin American military leaders in manufacturing and even commercial enterprises. The military dominated politics between the mid-1960s and the early 1980s.

The principal internationalization of economic activity in Latin America was to take the form of integration schemes within the region: the Latin American Free Trade Association, which embraced Argentina, Bolivia, Brazil, Chile, Colombia, Ecuador, Mexico, Paraguay, Peru, Uruguay, and Venezuela; the Andean Group, comprised of Bolivia, Chile, Colombia, Ecuador, Peru, and Venezuela; and the Central American Common Market, formed by Costa Rica, El Salvador, Guatemala, Honduras, and Nicaragua, with Panama an associate. None of them significantly increased intraregional trade except for the Central American Common Market, which grew rapidly in the 1960s and then faltered in the 1970s. Interestingly, it started to falter *before* the political violence that shook Central America in the last years of the 1970s, as Isaac Cohen has noted.[19] MERCOSUR, an integration scheme involving the economies of Southern Cone countries Argentina, Brazil, Chile, Paraguay, and Uruguay has in its first years achieved significant trade expansion. It is, however, too early to conclude that MERCOSUR will be an enduring success.

Dependency theory was one of the forces that shaped the foreign policies of most Latin American countries. Latin America's traditional phobia about foreign investment is symbolized by the Calvo Doctrine, which requires that disputes with foreign investors be adjudicated in domestic courts, foreclosing recourse to international mediation and arbitration.* Until recently, the Calvo Doctrine was incorporated into the foreign policies of virtually all Latin American countries, and sometimes into their constitutions. It has had a chilling effect on foreign investment, particularly in the light of Latin America's history of frequent nationalizations of foreign-owned enterprises.

But as Carlos Escudé points out in a fascinating new book, *The Realism of Weak States—The Foreign Policy of the First Menem Government versus International Relations Theory*,[20] two other intellectual currents, which Escudé refers to as "Anglo-American," also influenced Latin American foreign-policy makers: the pragmatic (Escudé

---

*The doctrine is named after its architect, the Argentine jurist Carlos Calvo (1824–1906). Argentina is among the countries that has recently discarded it.

describes it as "security-obsessed")[21] model of Hans Morgenthau, modified by Kenneth Waltz and others; and the interdependence model of Robert Keohane and Joseph Nye, which argues that the ability of the advanced powers to impose their wishes on the Third World is declining, leaving Latin America with growing bargaining leverage and room to maneuver.

The Morgenthau and Keohane-Nye models have reinforced Latin American predilections to pursue foreign policies designed to promote national power (for example, Argentina's planning for war against Brazil and Chile); to consolidate domestic power (for example, the Argentine military's adventure in the Falkland Islands); to promote ideological ends (Che Guevara's adventures in Bolivia, as well as Cuba's promotion of revolution in many other countries). But, as Escudé insists, the proper focus of foreign policy for a country in the periphery should be *citizen welfare*, which has been sadly neglected by most Latin American foreign-policy makers until recent years. A foreign policy focused on citizen welfare would have led Latin American countries to far better relationships with the United States and would have promoted more open economic policies and, inevitably, democratic institutions.

Interestingly, the country in Latin America that has most purposefully and consistently pursued a citizen welfare–based foreign policy is Costa Rica, Latin America's oldest democracy and a country that has enjoyed consistently warm and constructive relationships with the United States.

The Heavy Costs

In 1950, the per capita GDP of South Korea and Taiwan was in the range of $525–550 in 1980 prices. The average of Argentina, Brazil, Chile, Colombia, Mexico, and Peru in the same year was three times higher, about $1,600. In 1987, the average of those Latin American countries was about $3,000; South Korea was over $4,100, Taiwan over $4,700.[22] World Bank data for 1993 show South Korea's per capita GNP at $7,660, more than twice the average of the six Latin American countries.[23] Toward the end of the 1950s, South Korea and Taiwan started emphasizing exports to the world market, particularly the United States, as the centerpiece of their economic policies—the same world market that Prebisch and the dependency theorists had convinced Latin America was a principal mechanism of capitalist, imperialist exploitation, and their underdevelopment.

In 1950, the combined value of South Korea's and Taiwan's exports was $96 million. Their combined population was about 28 million people. In the same year, the exports of the six Latin American countries, with a population of about 128 million people, totaled $3.9 *billion*. In 1986, the combined exports of South Korea and Taiwan, their combined population now about 61 million people, totaled $74.5 *billion*, while the total for the six Latin American countries was $57.3 billion (of which Brazil accounted for $22.4 billion). In 1986, the total population of those six countries was 309 million.[24] In 1993, South Korea's exports alone totaled $82.2 billion, more than the exports of Brazil, Mexico, and Argentina combined.[25]

I am not going to suggest that, with better policies, Latin America could have achieved the same growth rates as South Korea and Taiwan (and Hong Kong and Singapore, which now appear among the high-income economies in the World Bank's annual report). As I have argued in *Who Prospers?* an important part of the explanation for the East Asian miracles, including Japan's, resides in the Confucian Tao values of future, work, frugality, education, merit, and community, values that have received scant priority in the Ibero-Catholic scheme of things. But I do suggest that if Latin America had pursued, rather than shunned, the world market and foreign investment, it would be substantially better off today. This conclusion is corroborated by the performance of two Ibero-Catholic countries that have pursued open economic policies in recent decades: Chile and Spain. The Chilean experience is the subject of chapter 7. A brief discussion of the Spanish experience appears later in this chapter.

Prebisch, Cardoso, Faletto, and the innumerable other Latin American politicians and intellectuals who explained Latin America's problems as a consequence of imperialism and dependency all bear a heavy responsibility not only for production, income, and foreign exchange forgone, but also for technology transfer that did not occur (because multinationals were shunned); for unnecessarily conflictive relationships with the United States; and, ultimately, for postponing Latin America's experiment with democratic capitalism.

PROGRESS IN LATIN AMERICA IN RECENT DECADES

As large as the gap between it and the advanced democracies may be, Latin America is far ahead of many other Third World areas, above all Africa. It has experienced measurable progress in health and education. And it has enjoyed fairly rapid economic growth throughout this century, particularly in recent decades.

Life expectancy has increased substantially: from fifty-six years in 1960 to sixty-nine years in 1992, on the average, in Argentina, Brazil, Chile, Colombia, Mexico, and Peru, which account for about three-quarters of Latin America's population. Infant mortality was about 100 per 1,000 in 1960; in 1992 it was 35. Adult illiteracy was about 29 percent in 1960, about 12 percent in 1992. The population growth rate averaged 2.6 percent in 1960–70; in 1992–2000, the rate is expected to drop to 1.5 percent.[26]

Yet poverty has not decreased significantly. According to the Economic Commission for Latin America and the Caribbean, 45 percent of Latin Americans lived in poverty in 1970, 24 percent in extreme poverty. In 1990, the figures were 46 percent and 22 percent, respectively.[27]

Data complied by Angus Maddison in *The World Economy in the Twentieth Century* show average annual GDP growth in the six Latin American countries between 1900 and 1987 at 3.8 percent, faster than the United States (3.2 percent) and the averages of the advanced democracies (2.9 percent), nine Asian countries (3.2 percent),* and the USSR (3.3 percent). Brazil's average GDP growth rate was 4.8 percent during that eighty-seven-year period, the second fastest, after Taiwan (5.1 percent). The rate for Japan was 4.3 percent, for the United States 3.2 percent.

Between 1950 and 1987, the average annual GDP growth of the six Latin American countries, with Brazil leading the way at 6 percent, was 4.3 percent, well ahead of the United States at 3.2 percent, but well behind Taiwan (8.8 percent), South Korea (7.6 percent), and Japan (7.1 percent).

The economic performance of the six Latin American countries is much less impressive when GDP growth is calculated on a per capita basis, reflecting relatively high population growth. For the 1900–1987 period, annual per capita GDP growth was 1.7 percent, with population increasing at 2.2 percent. Per capita GDP growth in the United States

---

*The nine are Bangladesh, China, India, Indonesia, Pakistan, Philippines, South Korea, Taiwan, and Thailand.

was 1.8 percent, in Japan 3.1 percent. During 1950–87, per capita GDP grew at the rate of 1.9 percent in the six Latin American countries, 2.2 percent in the United States, 5.5 percent in South Korea, 6 percent in Japan, 6.1 percent in Taiwan.

If Latin America has been growing economically about as fast as the United States throughout this century yet is fifty or more years behind it in terms of the prosperity of its citizens, then clearly growth in Latin America lagged in the nineteenth and earlier centuries.[28] The gap, of course, is widened for most Latin Americans by the highly inequitable patterns of income distribution in Latin America. In order to close the gap, substantially higher growth rates will be necessary. As an example, World Bank data show Chile's per capita GNP at $2,730 in 1992, the United States's at $23,240.[29] If we assume that Chile grows at 4 percent per capita, implying a 5–6 percent GDP growth rate, while the United States grows at 2 percent per capita, implying a 3 percent GDP growth rate, it would not be until *the early years of the twenty-second century* that Chile would finally catch up.[30]

We can conclude that Latin America's goal should be the rapid growth rates achieved in East Asia since World War II (and in Japan starting in the last decades of the nineteenth century). That is possible only through an export-based economic strategy, as the East Asians have demonstrated. Yet if I am right that an important part of the East Asian miracle is rooted in the Confucian/Tao ethic of future-work-frugality-education-merit-community, then not only must the new open economic policies be pushed; a cultural transformation is also necessary. The Spanish "miracle," discussed shortly, suggests the difficulty Latin America confronts in achieving the astonishing growth rates of the East Asians.

THE SURGE OF PROTESTANTISM

Protestantism, principally of the evangelical and Pentecostal denominations,* has been growing rapidly in Latin America for several decades, a phenomenon Peter Berger has labeled "one of the most extraordinary

---

*Webster's *New Collegiate Dictionary* defines *evangelical* as "emphasizing salvation by faith in the atoning death of Jesus Christ through personal conversion, the authority of scripture, and the importance of preaching as contrasted with ritual." *Pentecostal* is defined as "various Christian religious bodies that emphasize revivalistic worship, baptism conferring the gift of tongues, faith healing, and premillennial teaching."

developments in the world today."[31] Berger goes on to describe the phenomenon as not yet a revolution but a "revolution-in-the-making."[32] His comments appear in *Tongues of Fire—The Explosion of Protestantism in Latin America*, a book written by David Martin, a British theologian and sociologist who studied the Protestant movement in Latin America for three years in the late 1980s.

Martin believes that the Protestant population of Brazil has reached about 30 million, 20 percent of Brazil's total, and is growing rapidly. Chile's Protestant population is comparably large, and Protestants account for more than 30 percent of Guatemala's population, 20 percent of Nicaragua's, 16 percent of Costa Rica's. And while the percentages are substantially smaller in Argentina and Mexico, the trend is rapidly upward. Martin estimates total numbers for the region at 15 million in the late 1960s, 40 million in the late 1980s. Patrick Johnstone, director of international research for WEC International, a Protestant organization, estimates the total in 1990 at 51 million.[33]

What is driving this nascent revolution? Martin's analysis echoes Rangel's: the growth of Protestantism, which is a phenomenon principally of the lower classes and above all those who have moved from rural to urban areas, reflects the relative (particularly by contrast with the Protestant United States and Canada) failure of Latin America to produce prosperity, opportunity, freedom, and security for its citizens, particularly in those countries with large Indian minorities. A good part of the stimulus for conversion has been supplied by the United States: "the Americanization that enters Latin America as one aspect of the religious traffic reflects the reality of U.S. cultural power in general."[34] Moreover, many of the early evangelical/Pentecostal missionaries were Americans, and many of the Latin American ministers have been trained in the United States. But the spread of Protestantism is now substantially self-sufficient and guided by Latin Americans.

What are the implications of the Protestant phenomenon for Latin America's future course? The spread of Protestantism in part reflects the aspirations of the lower classes for a better life. It also reflects a rejection of the traditional Ibero-Catholic values and institutions that have failed to produce progress for the poor. The Protestants generally attach higher importance to work, education, sobriety, honesty, and community responsibility—key elements of the universal progress values.[35] I believe that adoption of these values will inevitably result in prosperity and upward social mobility for them, just as it has for other ethnic groups in Latin America that are imbued with the same values: Germans, Japanese, Jews, Lebanese. And I agree with Martin that they will also serve the cause of democracy: "As the sacred canopy in Latin America is rent and the all-encompassing system cracks, evangelical Christianity pours in and by its own autonomous native power creates free social space."[36]

I shall take a further look at the Protestant phenomenon in the subsequent chapters on Argentina, Brazil, Chile, and Mexico.

THE SPANISH MIRACLE: A HARBINGER?

In 1960, Spain was governed by the Franco dictatorship, which would endure until 1975. Its level of development was roughly comparable to that of the more advanced Latin American countries at the time: Venezuela, Argentina, Uruguay, Chile, and Cuba. The per capita GNP of Venezuela and Uruguay exceeded that of Spain.[37] Venezuela's energy consumption per capita exceeded Spain's, while Argentina's was close behind Spain's. Uruguay (80 percent), Argentina (74 percent), Chile (68 percent), and Venezuela (67 percent) were substantially more urbanized than Spain (57 percent), which was only slightly more urbanized than Cuba (55 percent). Life expectancy was sixty-eight years in Spain and Uruguay, sixty-five years in Argentina, sixty-four years in Cuba. Adult illiteracy was 9 percent in Argentina (and probably about the same in Uruguay), 13 percent in Spain, 16 percent in Chile.

Spain has been a democracy for two decades; it is a member of the European Union; and the World Bank categorizes it as a high-income economy, with a 1992 per capita GNP of about $13,000—more than twice that of the most affluent Latin American country, Argentina, at about $6,000. Both the political and economic dimensions of the Spanish miracle were an important consequence of a decision made in 1959 by Franco, under pressure from his principal source of financial assistance, the United States, to open up the Spanish economy. Until that time, Spain had pursued the same protectionist, self-sufficiency economic policies that Prebisch was promoting in Latin America. It shifted to open economic policies at about the same time that South Korea and Taiwan did.

It used to be said that Europe ended at the Pyrenees, or, alternatively, that Africa began at the Pyrenees. There was some truth in those quips. Spain's condition in 1960 evidenced the continuing influence of the Counter-Reformation and the substantial rejection of both the Enlightenment and the industrialization that had helped to transform other European societies (and, far more than the rest of Spain, the Basque provinces and Catalunya). The *apertura* led to rapid growth of tourism, the value of which increased from $129 million in 1959 to $16.8 billion in 1988. Foreign investment rushed in. Spain developed not only a web of business relationships with the West but also scholarly, artistic, religious, military, and labor relationships.

From 1960 to 1970, Spain's GDP growth averaged 7.1 percent; from 1970 to 1980, 3.5 percent; and from 1980 to 1992, 3.2 percent, which translates into 2.8 percent per capita with the population growing at only 0.4 percent annually. Interestingly, Spain still reported adult illiteracy (5 percent) as late as 1990, the highest among the high-income economies. But income distribution, which was as badly skewed as the typical Latin American country forty years ago, is today among the most equitable, along with Sweden, Norway, Belgium, Finland, the Netherlands, and Japan.

Spain's culture has been transformed in the past half-century, at least with respect to those values and attitudes that influence how politics is conducted. Fifty years ago, Spain was run by a military dictator, Francisco Franco, the last in a centuries-old line of caudillos. The tradition of a Spanish military institution above the law persisted. Spain's intolerance, its propensity for polarization and confrontation on one hand and anarchy on the other, had been reconfirmed in the horrors of its Civil War. The Catholic Church was a major, conservative actor in Spanish politics (the Vatican had sent Franco a congratulatory cable following his defeat of the Republican forces). The Spanish left had demonstrated its radicalism and intransigence during its two years in power, 1931 to 1933, sometimes referred to as the Red Biennium.

Today, Spain has functioned within democratic norms for more than two decades, and most observers believe that the process is irreversible. The transition to democracy was facilitated by the Communist Party leader Santiago Carrillo and Cardinal Vicente Enrique y Tarancón. The left has shifted perceptibly toward the center under Felipe González, who served as Prime Minister from 1982 to 1996, when the center-right leader José María Asnar's Popular Party defeated González's Spanish Worker's Party, mostly because of endless corruption scandals in the González administration, but also because of high levels of unemployment.

The Church, having facilitated the transition to democracy, has remained substantially aloof from politics, and Spain today is clearly a secular nation. After a final, thwarted *pronunciamiento* in 1981 by a group of reactionary officers, the military has progressed to the point where it is fully under civilian control. The extent of change in Spain's military culture is suggested by the comment of Lieutenant General Manuel Gutiérrez Mellado, Deputy Prime Minister and Minister of Defense in the transition government of Adolfo Suárez that followed Franco's death, who was labeled a liberal by Franco's Old Guard: "I don't mind being called a liberal if that means that I admit to not being utterly right all the time, that I am ready to discuss things with whomever wishes to discuss things, that I prefer that there should be no more fratricidal wars, that I want Spain to belong to all Spaniards."[38]

The economic picture is less bright, Spain's earlier rapid growth notwithstanding. The Spanish economy is heavily dependent on foreign investment and tourism, while Spaniards depend heavily on the government. Foreign capital and know-how dominate industry. With Volkswagen's acquisition of the Spanish automotive company SEAT, there is now no Spanish-owned company manufacturing automobiles. Ninety-eight percent of Spain's enterprises are family-owned. There has been no growth in the number of jobs generated by the private sector during the past ten years, and the unemployment rate is extremely high, on the order of 20 percent of the workforce as of this writing, the consequence in part of weak entrepreneurial traditions (less weak, of course, in the Basque provinces and Catalunya). More Spaniards depend on the public sector—either for employment or pensions—than on the private sector.

Table 3.1 appears in *The New Values of the Spaniards*, a 1991 study by Francisco Andrés Orizo, a prominent political scientist in Madrid.[39] Orizo waggishly observed to me in a conversation in Madrid late in 1994 that Spain had evolved from a preindustrial to a postindustrial society without having passed through an industrial phase.

Table 3.1

	Spain (1988)	France (1985)	USA (1985)
Percentage of people who believe that the state is responsible for all citizens, including solution of their problems.	75%	44%	26%
Percentage of people who believe that citizens are responsible for their own welfare and solving their own problems.	23%	49%	74%

IMPLICATIONS FOR LATIN AMERICA

At one time or another in the 1970s, Argentina, Brazil, Chile, Paraguay, Bolivia, Uruguay, Ecuador, Peru, Panama, Nicaragua, Honduras, El Salvador, and Guatemala were all run by military dictatorships, and Mexico was still in thrall to the one-party dictatorship of the Partido Revolucionario Institucional (PRI). Today one finds elected civilian governments in all of them, and in the Mexican case, there is considerable evidence that the domination of the PRI for sixty-five years may be coming to an end. Is Latin America following Spain's irreversible process of democratization?

And what of the opening up of economic policy, which occurred in Spain more than thirty-five years ago but which is a phenomenon of the past decade in most Latin American countries? (Chile, which now has more than ten years of experience with an open, stable economy, is exceptional.) Is Latin America destined to repeat the relatively high growth rates Spain achieved between 1960 and 1970, to be followed by significantly slower growth, high unemployment, and heavy dependency on foreign investment and the government?

The probability of irreversibility of democracy is high in Costa Rica, Chile, and Uruguay, where democratic institutions—and civic culture—are most deeply rooted. At the other extreme are countries like Paraguay, Bolivia, Guatemala, and Honduras, where there is little evidence of real change, for example, with respect to abuse of power by

the military, the trappings of free elections notwithstanding. Elections
have taken place in the Dominican Republic and Venezuela for thirty
or more years, yet the fragility of these societies and the disappointing-
ly slow pace of change are apparent from the probable fraud in the
Dominican elections of 1994, two coup attempts and judicial proceedings against two presidents in Venezuela in this decade, and the continuing dominance of elderly, traditional politicians.

The irreversibility of democracy in Latin America, as well as the
capacity of capitalism and the market to produce significantly higher
and better-distributed levels of well-being, including employment
opportunities, will depend on the reinforcement of the universal
progress values. Latin America as a whole will be powerfully influenced
by what happens in Argentina, Brazil, Chile, and Mexico, and it is to
these countries, and particularly to recent trends in their political, economic, social, religious, and cultural evolution, that I shall turn after
considering the negative impact of intellectuals in the United States on
relationships between the United States and Latin America.

4

The Destructive Role of American Intellectuals (and the Savaging of the United Fruit Company)

The academic community in the United States bears a considerable responsibility for the prolonged estrangement of Latin America from the United States. The 1960s radicals, whose influence is disproportionately felt in academe to this day, propagated the message that the United States is a greedy, irresponsible, imperialistic power. Realizing Joseph Schumpeter's prophecy in 1942 that the success of democratic capitalism would nourish an intellectual class hostile to it, the sixties intellectuals also viewed capitalism as evil and U.S. corporations as avaricious exploiters.[1]

This message was welcomed by the left in Latin America, which had been saying essentially the same thing about the United States for much of this century, and which influenced the direction of policy in many countries. Strong bonds formed between U.S. and Latin American intellectuals, often supported financially by U.S. foundations, the Ford Foundation prominently among them. The Latin American Studies Association (LASA), which counts as members many of our social scientists who specialize in Latin America, evolved into a *dependencista*, an anti-American claque.[2]

Symptomatic of the radicalized mind-set of a good part of the LASA membership was the LASA annual meeting in Bloomington, Indiana, in October 1980, where Sandinista Junta member Sergio Ramírez and Foreign Minister Miguel d'Escoto were given a hero's ovation, while James Cheek, then Deputy Assistant Secretary of State for Latin America, was jeered and heckled. In a subsequent LASA newsletter, Harvard professor Jorge Domínguez, LASA president at the time, described the Bloomington meeting as "one of the darkest moments of my professional life . . . appalling . . . scandalous . . . damnable."[3]

The irony of the Bloomington meeting was exquisite. Cheek, a distinguished and enlightened career officer, had played a crucial role in the U.S.'s disengagement from the Nicaraguan regime of Anastasio Somoza Debayle in 1974. His reputation as a liberal led to his being ostracized during the Reagan administration. When Bill Clinton was inaugurated, Cheek was given his choice of ambassadorial assignments in Latin America. As of this writing, he is our ambassador in Argentina.

Andre Gunder Frank, an American born in Germany between the world wars, is one of the fathers of dependency theory. The first sentences of his enormously influential work, *Capitalism and Underdevelopment in Latin America*,[4] published in 1967, read,

> I believe . . . that it is capitalism, both world and national, which produced underdevelopment in the past and which still generates underdevelopment in the present. . . . [I]t is the structure and development of capitalism itself which, by long since penetrating and characterizing Latin America and other continents, generated, maintain, and still deepen underdevelopment.[5]

Central to Frank's thesis is the Marxist theory of the "loss and misappropriation of economic surplus in the process of capitalist underdevelopment."[6] The national bourgeoisie and foreign, principally U. S., investment are the instruments and beneficiaries of this "capitalist expropriation of surplus,"[7] leading to two transcendental conclusions: (1) "National capitalism and the national bourgeoisie do not and cannot offer any way out of underdevelopment in Latin America;"[8] and (2) (in the last sentence of the book) "evidently, the only way out of Latin American underdevelopment is armed revolution leading to socialist development."[9]

Frank's view of capitalism and imperialism in the Hemisphere captured the ideological essence of the far-left North American Congress on Latin America (NACLA). In a scholarly community in which guilt feelings, utopianism, socialism, anti-Americanism, and elitist arrogance combined to produce the kind of intoxication manifested at the Bloomington LASA meeting, NACLA's message—essentially a call to socialist revolution—was viewed as well within the framework of serious scholarly debate. NACLA's "scholarship" was largely focused on exposing "imperialism," and other evils, in the U.S. government and U.S. business in Latin America.

I got a taste of NACLA's pernicious mischief in the Dominican Republic, where I was the deputy director of the USAID mission after the 1965 revolution. One of the junior USAID officers was surreptitiously collecting notes and documents which, after leaving the organization, he fashioned into a scurrilous article that appeared in a NACLA journal. The article was wholly consistent with the NACLA view that the U.S. government foreign-policy establishment was peopled by reactionary exploiters and lackeys of Wall Street. He knew very well that many of his USAID and embassy colleagues (including the ambassador, John Hugh Crimmins, and myself) sympathized with the revolution and that we were doing everything we could to help improve the opportunities and living conditions of the Dominican masses.

In those same years in the Dominican Republic, I met Susanne Jonas Bodenheimer (she is known today as Susanne Jonas), who is one of the NACLA leaders. We had several talks about the revolution and the prospects for the Dominican Republic, but she gave me no sense of the extremeness of her views. A few years later, in 1969, she published a paper, "The Ideology of Developmentalism: The American Paradigm-Surrogate for Latin American Studies," which appeared in the *Berkeley Journal of Sociology*.[10] (She was then associated with the University of California at Berkeley. She now teaches Latin American and Latino studies at the University of California at Santa Cruz.) In that paper, Jonas echoes the views of Andre Gunder Frank, whom she frequently cites. She argues that the then mainstream "developmentalist" scholarly theories about Latin America were substantially wrong (with which, of course, I agree, although for entirely different reasons) but goes on to assert, with classic chutzpah, that those views "are more accurately characterized as expressions of an ideology than as solid foundations of scientific research."[11]

Jonas's criticism of the developmentalists contains some important truths:

> [They seem] to project a pious hope that development can be achieved without paying the high cost of removing the social and economic obstacles, that the impoverished masses can somehow be upgraded without infringing on the interests of the established elites. This myth has found its ultimate expression in the Alliance

for Progress, which projected the vision of powerful established interest groups (e.g., the landed, commercial, and industrial elites) becoming the agents of change in the name of enlightened self-interest. Attractive as this may seem to Americans motivated by a certain brand of reformism as well as by the concern for stability, it overlooks certain glaring conditions in Latin America: the fact that established interest groups have not voluntarily enlisted in the battle for thoroughgoing structural change . . . the fact that industrialization has not been accompanied by equalization of income or living standards . . . the fact that in most countries the lowest sectors of the population . . . are not organized or represented by any interest group.[12]

But as with Frank and Fernando Henrique Cardoso (the intellectual, not the politician), the solution for Jonas is a socialist revolution along the lines of Fidel Castro's: "the only possible example of *substantive* democracy and mass mobilization in Latin America [is] Cuba."[13] Interestingly, in reaching her revolutionary conclusions, she explores—and rejects—cultural explanations for Latin America's problems.

Richard Fagen, a professor of political science at Stanford, is a prominent Latin Americanist who has subscribed to dependency theory, sympathized with Fidel Castro's revolution, and consistently criticized both the motives and the conduct of U.S. policy toward Latin America. He co-edited a book with the Peruvian *dependencista* Cotler in 1974 in which he asserts that "coherence in the expression of anti-innovative activity and opposition to change . . . [form] the common core of U.S. policy in the hemisphere and the common denominator of Latin American opposition to that policy. . . . I would suggest that the national interest of the United States in Latin America has *in practice* been defined as *the preservation and extension of North American political, economic, and cultural influence and domination in the hemisphere at the lowest possible cost.*"[14]

Fagen himself leaves no doubt about the strength of his ideological commitment to socialism and his contempt for his own society, and with his own words clearly establishes his credentials as a polemicist rather than a scholar:

[G]iven the immense political, economic, and cultural power of the United States, and the historic misuse of that power, there is a clear responsibility to participate in what might be called "documented denunciation"—essentially muckraking and informational activity, often less than scholarly by conventional definitions, but absolutely vital if the worst excesses of the exercise of . . . American power, whether perpetrated by the Marines or by the multinationals, is to be held in check. . . . It implies prying into every corner and crevice of the policy-making process and the configurations of power.[15]

Among Fagen's policy prescriptions are "[l]iquidation of the Overseas Private Investment Corporation [OPIC], leaving capitalistic enterprises to run risks that supposedly entitle them to profits."[16] One wonders how Fagen reacts today when he reads of right-wing, budget-cutting Republicans who are calling for the liquidation/privatization of OPIC.

Like so many other American intellectuals, Fagen was entranced by the Sandinista revolution. In 1981, the Institute for Policy Studies, a left-wing think tank in Washington, published his photographic essay "The Nicaraguan Revolution—A Personal Report," in which Fagen labels the revolution "a bold experiment in social and economic reconstruction." The book is a paean to the Sandinistas; one senses that they fulfilled all of Fagen's most deeply felt aspirations, including a second socialist experiment in the Hemisphere and a bloody nose for Uncle Sam. Among the photographs appears *Comandante* (now *terrateniente*) Jaime Wheelock wearing his revolutionary fatigues.

The views of Frank, Jonas, and Fagen are representative of a generation of U.S. Latin Americanists, one that has skewed the opinions of vast numbers of young Americans toward an anti-American, anticapitalist, and even antidemocratic view of relationships within the Western Hemisphere. Dependency theory had for decades dominated the intellectual communities of the United States, Canada, Europe, Latin America, and the Third World in general. It has even developed a following among professors and students in as unlikely a country as South Korea.*

---

*I spoke to Korean professors and students in Kwangju and Pusan in 1990 about the dependency myth. The two lengthy sessions were strikingly similar in tone and content to discussions I have had with professors and students in Latin America and the United States. The irony, of course, is that South Korea has been one of the world's foremost examples of how a Third World country can benefit enormously from entrance into the same world market that the *dependencistas* blame for Third World poverty. Many of the Korean participants in the two sessions had studied in the United States.

Few of the dependency intellectuals have had the grace or courage, after the collapse of communism in Eastern Europe, the overwhelming defeat of the Sandinistas in the 1990 elections, the success of the "periphery" East Asian dragons in the world market, and the new wave of democratic capitalism in Latin America, to say, "I was wrong." In a recent book she co-edited, Jonas continues to attack capitalism—"neoliberalism," using the pejorative term popular in leftist bitter-end circles. But, like Marxists around the world, she is unable to advance an alternative to democratic capitalism. After all, those countries that have progressed the furthest toward "collective or redistributive norms [and] the quest for social justice that has inspired generations of leftists and progressives"[17] are all democratic capitalist societies. And the countries that have strayed furthest from the social justice goal, many of them in Latin America, have come around to democratic capitalism only in recent years.

Jonas does acknowledge one fundamental flaw in the traditional revolutionary program: "One of the most serious . . . weaknesses was the socialist Left's disdain for 'bourgeois democracy.' It has taken decades of painful experience with undemocratic, dictatorial governments to teach us to value democratic politics."[18] But the acceptance of "bourgeois democracy" means the acceptance of elections that produce conservative governments, and it remains to be seen how tolerant the bitter-enders will be of such governments, even though elected by a majority of voters.

Some members of the U.S. academic Latin Americanist mainstream are now claiming credit for the wave of democratization and market economic policies that has swept over Latin America. Joseph Tulchin, director of the Latin America program at Washington's Woodrow Wilson International Center, recently was quoted in the *Washington Post* as saying, "[Latin American students in the United States] came out of an atmosphere in which vitriolic diatribes against the United States were common, and they encountered a *tolerant* academy in the United States. They said, 'This is it? This is the enemy?' So they went home Jeffersonian democrats, and now they're in governments all around the hemisphere."[19]

What the Latin American students found, of course, was not a "tolerant" academy in the United States but a pandering academy that, with some exceptions, echoed the "vitriolic diatribes against the United

States," at least against the U.S. government and U.S. multinational corporations. We must ask ourselves what would have been the impact on Latin American students in the United States if they had encountered American academics who believed, as few did then but more do now, that dependency theory was essentially a myth and that Latin America was paying a dear price for blaming the United States for its problems.

In retrospect, a good part of the intellectual community in the United States, above all the Latin American specialists, looks like a bunch of bright, affluent, guilt-ridden, utopian elitists who never quite grew up—at a very heavy cost to those they were committed to help, and to their own society. Their excesses reverberate perniciously throughout the United States to this day: in their contribution to the political polarization of recent decades; in the increasing disrespect for others and the divisiveness in our society; in the mistrust of our institutions; in the drug epidemic that has claimed so many lives.

One casualty of those excesses is Lori Berenson, the young American who was sentenced to life imprisonment in Peru early in 1996 for her involvement with the pro-Cuban, terrorist Tupac Amaru Revolutionary Movement. An article in the *Boston Globe* noted that Berenson had studied briefly at MIT, where she apparently came under the influence of left-fringe professors Martin Diskin and Noam Chomsky, both proponents of the view that "Yankee imperialism" is chiefly responsible for Latin America's poverty and injustice, and both sympathizers with the Sandinista Revolution in Nicaragua.[20] Ms. Berenson's strong commitment to the cause of the revolutionary left in Latin America may thus combine youthful idealism with guilt feelings over our "culpability" for Latin America's condition.

The tragic irony is twofold: (1) few people today take dependency theory seriously, and that includes many Latin Americans of the left; and (2) the Sandinistas proved themselves to be as authoritarian, abusive of human rights, and greedy (witness their "*piñata*" looting after their overwhelming defeat in the 1990 elections) as the Somozas.

Lori Berenson thus joined a Peruvian terrorist group that has about as much credibility as its idol, Fidel Castro, who may yet go down in history as the last caudillo. And she joined it at a time when Latin America has put dependency theory behind it and seeks close economic and political ties with the United States.

Ms. Berenson is an adult, and she bears responsibility for her actions. But if, as the *Globe* article suggests, Professors Diskin and Chomsky were her mentors, they also bear some responsibility for this sad episode.

A CASE IN POINT: THE SAVAGING OF THE UNITED FRUIT COMPANY

The symbol par excellence of Yankee imperialism and the "ruthless"[21] activities of the multinationals was the Boston-based United Fruit Company—commonly referred to in Latin American intellectual circles as *el pulpo* ("the octopus") and the subject of a poem by the Chilean Marxist poet Pablo Neruda entitled "The United Fruit Co." (by the way, Neruda was the writer in the acclaimed Italian movie *The Postman*):

> The Fruit Company, Inc.
> reserved for itself the juiciest,
> the central seaboard of my land,
> America's sweet waist.
> It baptized its lands
> the "Banana Republics"
> and upon the slumbering corpses,
> upon the restless heroes
> who conquered renown,
> freedom and flags,
> it established the comic opera . . . [22]

The United Fruit Company was formed in 1899 of two large banana operations, the Boston Fruit Company, and several enterprises owned by Minor Keith. Keith had built a railway over the forbidding jungles, mountains, and rivers that separate Limón, Costa Rica's Caribbean port, from its capital, San José. The railway became Costa Rica's principal means of exporting bananas and coffee.[23]

During the early decades of this century, United's Central American operations faced increasing competition from the Standard Fruit Company and the Cuyamel Fruit Company in Honduras. United acquired Cuyamel, widely regarded as the best banana operation in the world, in 1930.* The man who had created Cuyamel from nothing was Samuel Zemurray, who became, with the sale of Cuyamel, for which he took 300,000 shares of United Fruit stock, the company's largest stockholder.

Samuel Zemurray had arrived in the United States in 1892 at the age of fifteen to live with relatives in Selma, Alabama. He was the son of a poor Jewish farmer in Bessarabia, and throughout his life he spoke English and Spanish with a heavy Yiddish accent. A Schumpeterian entrepreneurial archetype, Zemurray had accumulated considerable wealth before he was twenty by buying ripe bananas—too ripe to make it to the big markets in the north—on the Mobile docks and shipping them by train to nearby cities and towns. He became mesmerized by bananas, married the daughter of the New Orleans banana merchant Jacob Weinberger, and supported the ultimate winner of a Honduran civil war to get the concession for Cuyamel. Cuyamel's efficiency was chiefly attributable to the fact that Zemurray, a gifted manager who delegated authority and was regarded with admiration, respect, and affection by his subordinates, was on the ground in Honduras while the United Fruit management ran their operations from Boston.

By the end of 1932, United Fruit stock had plummeted—in Zemurray's view because of mismanagement—and Zemurray traveled from his home in New Orleans to Boston to talk to the company leadership. The meeting is described as follows by former United Fruit Vice President for Public Relations, Thomas McCann:

> He was greeted, frostily at best, by a board of directors which included Daniel Gould Wing, then chairman of the powerful First National Bank of Boston; former Massachusetts governor Channing H. Cox, direct descendant of two American presidential families, the Jeffersons and the Coolidges; the Lee half of Boston's most prestigious investment firm, Lee Higginson; and Bradley Webster Palmer, a leading Boston lawyer. Zemurray presented an incisive review of the company's mismanagement, backed by a bill of particulars which included the fact that the stock of United

*United Fruit was merged into United Brands in 1973 by the conglomerate wheeler-dealer Eli Black (who jumped to his death from the forty-fourth floor of a Manhattan skyscraper on 3 February 1975). United Brands was saved from bankruptcy by the Cincinnati businessman Carl H. Lindner in 1984 and is managed today by his son, Keith. The company name was changed to Chiquita Brands International in 1990.

Fruit Company had declined by almost 90 percent since he had become a shareholder. He demanded to know what the board intended to do.

Daniel Gould Wing responded for the other directors. He smiled thinly and in a reference to Zemurray's accent, said, "Unfortunately, Mr. Zemurray, I can't understand a word you say." Zemurray just looked at Wing for a few seconds then at the other Brahmin faces around the room. The story goes that he muttered something under his breath as he left. He returned shortly with his hands full of enough proxies to make translation unnecessary. Slapping them down on the long, oval table at 1 Federal Street, and speaking very clearly to avoid being misunderstood, Zemurray said, "You gentlemen have been fucking up this business long enough. I'm going to straighten it out." Wing and his clique were dumped from the board and Zemurray was back in bananas.[24]

Zemurray ran United Fruit until 1951, when he became chairman of the executive committee, in which capacity he served until 1956. He was directly involved in defending United Fruit's interests in Guatemala during the events that led to the overthrow of the Arbenz government, engineered by the United States. He served on the board of directors until 1957, by which time he was seriously incapacitated by Parkinson's disease, of which he died in 1961 at the age of eighty-four.

Zemurray was far from a ruthless tycoon. He was a liberal who fought Huey Long, supported and advised the New Deal, is warmly remembered by John Kenneth Galbraith,[25] played an important role in Israel's independence, and supported Adlai Stevenson in 1952 and 1956.[26] His philanthropic activities, many of them anonymous, were enlightened and far-reaching. Among them: the money to launch the New Orleans Child Guidance Clinic and a black women's clinic; support of two liberal publications, The Nation and The New Republic; two dormitories, a collection of Mayan arts, and $1 million for research on Central America for Tulane University (Tulane's presidents reside in Zemurray's town house); one of the most important tropical botanical gardens in the world, in Honduras; a chair in the arts at Harvard to be held only by a woman, which continues to this day (his daughter, Doris Stone, who once told me that he gave away more than he kept, attended Radcliffe).

A profile of Zemurray in the 19 February 1951 issue of Life Magazine noted, "He has always found it hard to turn down appeals for help from anyone who ever worked for him and is particularly generous to needy Central Americans. In New Orleans there is an old joke about this: 'If you want anything from Sam Zemurray, ask for it in Spanish.'"[27] The Pan American Agricultural School in Zamorano, Honduras, which started operations in 1941, was Zemurray's creation. (His daughter told me that he had transferred his United Fruit salary check in toto to the school starting in 1940.) Lest he be accused of self-interest, Zemurray insisted that no graduates be recruited by United Fruit. Today, the school is one of the best agricultural universities in Latin America and is particularly noted for the hands-on approach of its graduates, who number more than three thousand. Doris Stone served on the board of the school until her death in 1994. Her son, Samuel Zemurray Stone, a prominent Costa Rican political scientist, has also served on the board.

MYTH VERSUS REALITY

My first overseas assignment with USAID was in Costa Rica in 1964–65. I arrived in San José with a number of naive and arrogant ideas about Latin America, foremost among them the belief that Latin America was in trouble because we had neglected it. I didn't subscribe to the Yankee imperialism/dependency explanation, but I certainly had a profoundly negative view of the United Fruit Company. (At that time, I had no idea who Samuel Zemurray, who had died three years earlier, was.) I had been in Costa Rica some months when I received an invitation to visit the United Fruit operation in Golfito, on the Pacific coast.

What I saw in Golfito astonished me. A banana operation is visually impressive because of its transformation of vast stretches of jungle into orderly, productive lands served by efficient transportation, packing, and port facilities. The visual impact was magnified by the tidiness of the company town itself. But what impressed me most was the way United treated its Costa Rican workers. They lived in well-built houses; their children attended schools built and staffed by the company; and all had access to good health facilities. United's plantation workers were paid twice the going wage. And the company was increasingly bringing Costa Ricans into managerial positions. In sum, the United workers lived in conditions vastly superior to those of the average Costa Rican *campesino*, underscoring how much better United treated its employees than did most Costa Rican farmers and businessmen. It was precisely what one would have expected, knowing who Samuel Zemurray was and how much United Fruit came to reflect his persona.

United Fruit and Guatemala

To be sure, United Fruit involved itself in local politics, and that almost surely included favors for politicians and bureaucrats. But, as Hernando de Soto has argued, that is what Latin America's traditional "mercantilist" economics is all about—cozy relationships between businessmen and government.[28] United Fruit could not have survived if it didn't play the same game played by national businessmen. It is also true that Zemurray himself had hired mercenaries in 1910 to support an insurgency in Honduras that led to a new government favorable to him.

United Fruit had problems with organized labor. But in Central America, the few strong unions were principally those that were organized in the banana lands; their leadership was mostly communist;[29] and they were tolerated by Central American governments, which have traditionally discouraged strong labor unions to protect the interests of national businessmen. The United Fruit operations in Central America were a natural, easy target, their good treatment of their employees notwithstanding: they were foreigners, they were "rich," and it was easy to label them as "exploiters." The labor movement in Central America owes a profound debt of gratitude to United Fruit.

I have no doubt that United Fruit did everything it could to defend its interests in Guatemala in the early 1950s when the Arbenz government expropriated 400,000 unused acres of United Fruit's total of 550,000. Stephen Kinzer's and Stephen Schlesinger's *Bitter Fruit* [30] and Piero Gleijeses' *Shattered Hope: The Guatemalan Revolution and the United States 1944–54* both see the United States as a fundamentally selfish, hegemonic force in Latin America and United Fruit as the symbol of the allegedly rapacious activities of U.S. companies that operate there, although *Bitter Fruit* places substantial blame on United Fruit while *Shattered Hope* concludes that United Fruit was not central to the U.S. decision to intervene. Kinzer and Schlesinger, who were well aware of Zemurray's philanthropic activities and liberal leanings but did not mention them in their book,[31] chose to cast him as a robber baron.

An example: "Zemurray, though he detested the social reforms in Guatemala, had managed to accommodate himself to the new unions."[32] Kinzer, who subsequently wrote a book sympathetic to the Sandinistas following several years as the *New York Times* correspondent in Nicaragua in the 1980s,[33] and Schlesinger were also aware of United's major contribution to the economies of the countries in which it operated and its generally excellent treatment of its employees.[34] But they make no mention of the economic benefits and grudging mention of employee treatment:

> In some senses, the Fruit Company was benevolent and paternalistic. Its workers enjoyed better conditions than most farm laborers in Guatemala. The company provided adequate housing and medical facilities and even established a school for employees' children. (Critics liked to charge that the Guatemalan people indirectly paid for this largesse many times over through uncollected taxes on United Fruit property and exports.)[35]

Gleijeses, with whom I participated in a seminar on Guatemala some years ago and who comes across as a doctrinaire anti-American, acknowledges that "there is some truth" in the highly favorable findings of the Stacey May/Galo Plaza/National Planning Association study of United Fruit (discussed shortly) but subsequently makes it clear that "some truth" for him means "precious little."[36] With respect to United's treatment of its employees, he concludes: "For the company, this squalid record was a source of pride."[37] What is astonishing in Gleijeses's book, in which the United Fruit Company is one of the principal villains and in which its history is analyzed in some detail, is that he makes no mention whatsoever of Samuel Zemurray, although he was fully aware of the profound imprint of Zemurray on the Company.[38]

In the utopian, anticapitalist, anti-American world view of many Latin American and U.S. intellectuals of recent decades, there should have been some saint around who combined daring, courage, entrepreneurial creativity, dedication, and skillful management with the charitable, socialist, revolutionary concerns of the Maryknoll priests. In the real world, Samuel Zemurray probably came about as close to the utopian model as humans can. In the utopian world view of the intellectuals, U.S. multinational corporations should behave like charitable institutions, and U.S. government officials should behave as their adversaries. John Coatsworth, a professor of history and director of the

David Rockefeller Center for Latin American Studies at Harvard, critically notes,

> Throughout [Central America], U.S. diplomats routinely pressured the Central American governments to grant concessions and contracts to U.S. firms rather than to British (or other European, and now Japanese) companies. The identification of U.S. diplomacy with the interests of such U.S. businesses as the United Fruit Company . . . and the Chase Manhattan Bank between 1900 and the 1950s symbolized this policy.[39]

Does Professor Coatsworth believe that U.S. diplomats should have pressured Central American governments on behalf of British, other European, and Japanese companies? Does he believe that the British, other European, and Japanese embassies were in the habit of pressuring Central American governments on behalf of U.S. companies? Does he believe that the activities of U.S. business overseas are contrary to our national interest and the interests of receiving countries and consequently not to be promoted by our embassies? Apparently so, an inference that is reinforced by Coatsworth's recent advice that Central Americans look to Western Europe and East Asia for economic aid and political support.[40]

Coatsworth himself judges that United Fruit's role in the U.S. government's overthrow of Arbenz was not central: "[Guatemalan Communist Party leader José Manuel] Fortuny was probably right when he concluded that 'they would have overthrown us even if we had grown no bananas.' Defending [United Fruit] coincided with other U.S. policy objectives, chief of which was maintaining U.S. dominance over its Caribbean clients."[41] That is in my view a fundamental misreading of the history of U.S. involvement in the Caribbean Basin. Preclusion of influence by countries hostile to the United States—Germany at the time of World Wars I and II, the Soviet Union and Cuba during the cold war—has been the chief objective of U.S. policy in Central America and the Caribbean throughout this century and explains U.S. interventions not only in Guatemala in 1954 but also in Nicaragua in 1912 and 1982; the Dominican Republic in 1916 and 1965; and Haiti in 1915. The investments of United Fruit and other U.S. companies notwithstanding, Central America's economic significance to the United States is minuscule. Our investments in Canada alone exceed our investments in *all* of Latin America, as does our trade (see chapter

9). In the 1980s, I calculated that the entire Central American market—Guatemala, El Salvador, Honduras, Nicaragua, and Costa Rica—for U.S. products was about the same size as that for Springfield, Massachusetts.[42]

Imperialism? Exploitation?

The National Planning Association's 1958 assessment of United Fruit's impact on six countries in which it was operating at that time (Ecuador, Costa Rica, Panama, Honduras, Colombia, and Guatemala) was prepared by Galo Plaza, a highly respected former president of Ecuador and OAS secretary general, and Stacy May, a Dartmouth economics professor and adviser to Nelson Rockefeller. Their report arrives at "inescapable" conclusions[43] that will startle not only *dependencista* professors but the ostensibly informed citizen in Latin America, North America, and Europe as well:

> [T]he benefits accruing to the local economies in the producing areas are about four and one-half times larger than their proportionate contributions to capital investment. . . . Upon almost any criterion of reckoning, this constitutes a remarkably good bargain for capital-poor countries. . . .
>
> On every measurement that we have been able to devise, the return realized by producing countries from banana exports is extraordinarily high compared with any other agricultural endeavor in which they engage.
>
> On the measurement of yield per worker employed in agriculture, the returns from United Fruit operations were about five times the average. . . . In all cases, the wages paid by the United Fruit Company were substantially higher than the average for agricultural employees.
>
> By every economic measure that we have been able to apply, the contribution of the United Fruit Company to the economies of the six countries is enormously advantageous when regarded from the viewpoint of their national interest. . . . [I]t has been leaving within the production area more than $7.00 for every dollar in profits withdrawn. . . . The company's total tax payments . . . have been running in recent years to a sum that about equals its dividend withdrawals from profits. . . .

On the very important consideration of the effect on balance of payments . . . foreign exchange contributions to the local economies . . . amounted to almost $76 million, or to about 62 percent of their total exports.

Since it was organized in 1899, the profits after taxes of the United Fruit Company have averaged under 13 percent on net assets . . . compared with the 14.9 percent average return on net assets shown for 1,843 leading U.S. manufacturing corporations in 1955 in a tabulation made by the First National City Bank.

The . . . Company has made numerous additional contributions to . . . progress. . . . [It has] opened up vast areas of low, hot, humid, and heavily forested terrain. . . . It has supplied the basic facilities—roads, railways, port and communication facilities, electric power . . . hospitals and schools that have made this possible. It has introduced modern scientific agricultural methods and equipment, and has trained hundreds of thousands of the local inhabitants in their use. . . . It has pioneered in health and sanitation measures. . . .

[I]ts furnishing of hospital, dispensary, and sanitation services has been generally excellent. . . . With respect to the provision of educational facilities, United Fruit usually goes well beyond what is required by law . . . the company provides for its workers places of worship, clubs, recreational facilities, and athletic fields and equipment upon a scale and of a standard that are matched by few, if any, locally owned agricultural enterprises. . . . In the important field of housing, the company record again is good to excellent. . . . On balance, it is probably fair to appraise United Fruit performance in the field of labor relationships over the years as generally in advance of current practices.

And in historical summary:

[I]t is far from our intention to dismiss all criticism of United Fruit Company performance. . . . While we have not attempted the forbiddingly difficult, and probably impossible, task of appraising the rights and wrongs of the voluminous chronicle of charges and countercharges arising out of the days of banana pioneering, we are willing to believe that the early "banana hands" did not always fully exemplify the virtues and rectitude associated with the ideals of chivalry. But the same could be said of the political and commercial environments in which they had to work. On balance, it is doubtful that they seriously depreciated the prevailing ethical currency. Within a more recent time span . . . there can be no doubt that the company has made a very earnest effort to live up to the enlightened obligations of "good citizenship."[44]

The history of the banana industry since 1954 bears out the May-Plaza findings. United Fruit's assets are today owned by Chiquita Brands International, the world's largest producer of bananas. Chiquita operates in Panama, Costa Rica, Honduras, Colombia—and Guatemala, where its former lands are now owned by Guatemalan interests that produce for Chiquita. Chiquita grows about half its bananas on land it either owns or for which it has long-term leases (its assets in Latin America were valued at $864 million in 1994); the other half comes from contract arrangements with national producers, as in Guatemala. The pioneering of United Fruit, Zemurray's Cuyamel, and other American companies has made possible an industry that has produced tens of billions of dollars of benefits for Latin America—benefits that would either not have materialized or been vastly smaller were it not for the vision, creativity, and fortitude of the pioneers. They, and above all Zemurray, have also left a legacy of social responsibility that has prodded Latin American companies toward better treatment of their own employees and greater recognition of their obligations to their societies.

5

Argentina: First World to Third World?—And Back?

The state is impersonal: the Argentine only grasps personal
relationships. That is why, for the Argentine, to steal from the
government is not a crime. I state a fact. I don't justify or
excuse it.
—José Luis Borges, "Nuestro Pobre Individualismo"

There is a story about a conversation between two foreign diplomats in Buenos Aires. The first one says, "This country really puzzles me. I've been here five months, and I don't understand what's going on." The second responds, "Congratulations! You're brilliantly perceptive! I've been here five *years*, and I've just come to the same conclusion!"

The Argentine historian Carlos Waisman poses the puzzle, broadly, in this way:

> [T]he country's economic and political development has been curvilinear. The century 1880–1980 can be divided into two halves, whose characteristics are sharply different. Up to the Depression, Argentina was both a fast-growing economy and an expanding and relatively stable liberal democracy. The political crisis appeared in 1930, when the establishment of a military regime interrupted almost seventy years of constitutional legality, and the economic crisis became evident around 1950, when stagnating tendencies emerged. There was, then, a reversal of economic and political development, and the period between the Depression and the end of World War II was the watershed.[1]

Waisman's analysis of Argentina's economic trajectory is substantially confirmed by the research of the economic historian Angus Maddison: in 1900, Argentina's per capita gross domestic product, although half that of the United States, Great Britain, and Australia, was twice as great as Japan's, slightly greater than those of Finland and Norway, and slightly smaller than those of Italy and Sweden. In 1950, Argentina still led Japan, and its level of prosperity was about equal to that of Italy, Austria, and Germany (these four countries, of course, experienced extensive—vast in the case of Japan and Germany— destruction during World War II). But by 1950, per capita GDP in the United States was three times greater than in Argentina, while Switzerland, Canada, Australia, and Great Britain were twice as afflu- ent. By 1987, Argentina's per capita GDP was one-quarter that of the United States, one-third the average of the advanced democracies.[2]

But when Waisman says that Argentina was "a relatively stable liberal democracy" until 1930, he is off the mark. Until suffrage reforms in 1912, democracy did not really exist in Argentina. The traditional land-based oligarchy manipulated the political system, principally by its control of suffrage but also by rigging elections. Universal male suffrage was enacted in 1912 because of the establishment's fear of violence by the disenfranchised. The reform led to the victory in 1916 of Hipólito Yrigoyen of the opposition Radical Party. Of that transition, Carlos Rangel says, "[o]ligarchic democracy became chaotic democracy, full of inner contradictions, demagogical, ineffectual, incapable of holding in check the factions and the forces of disintegration that are characteris- tic of Hispanic societies."[3]

These "forces of disintegration" clashed in a week of violence— "the tragic week" in January 1919—when the military, police, firefight- ers, socialists, anarchists, and other activists engaged in a series of melees that brought death and injury to hundreds and almost resulted in the overthrow of Yrigoyen. His intransigent treatment of any oppo- sition is reminiscent of the intolerant "Red (leftist) Biennium" (1931–33) and equally intolerant "Black (rightist) Biennium" (1934–36) in Spain that preceded the Civil War—and with similar, if slower and less bloody, consequences.

In 1930, with economic hard times intensifying, the seventy- eight-year-old and probably senile Yrigoyen was overthrown by the mil- itary, supported by the oligarchy. Militarism and authoritarianism, which had dominated Argentina's early history and would soon produce the Perón dictatorship, were latent and ready, echoing Sarmiento's warning a hundred years earlier of the tendency of his countrymen toward "the dominance of brutal force, the preponderance of the strongest, authority without limits and without responsibility, justice administered without laws, without debate."[4] While it has its own unique features, Argentina's political development is clearly in the Latin American mainstream.

Until the Great Depression, Argentina competed in the same economic league with Australia and Canada. But by 1930, those offspring of Britain had sunk deep democratic roots into their soil, to a depth that Argentina has not approximated, even today. Should we conclude that culture operated in the political sphere but not in the economic, that, as Waisman and others argue, a combination after 1929 of a negative international climate and bad policies explains Argentina's subsequent economic stagnation?

I believe that Argentina's apparent economic success during the "golden age" from 1880 to 1930 was chiefly the result of three factors: (1) Argentina's supremely rich resource endowment, above all in the vast, deep, fecund soils of the pampas (with respect to natural resource endowment per capita, Argentina is among the richest countries in the world); (2) foreign investment, technology, and markets, above all British; and (3) economic policies that promoted exports. This judgment is consistent with the analysis of the late Carlos Díaz Alejandro, a highly respected Cuban-American economist who specialized in Argentina:

> The economic usefulness of pampean land was not discovered overnight, as in the case of an oil deposit, but arose as a result of a combination of growing European needs for primary goods, technological progress in transport, and an increasing interest by Argentine policy makers in promoting exports, foreign investment, and immigration.[5]

Foreign investment constituted half of fixed capital in Argentina in 1913, but dropped to a third in 1927. Interestingly, the Argentine economy decelerated between 1914 and 1929, in part because of the decline in foreign investment but also as a consequence of the relatively slow rate of growth of the European economies during World War I and the next several years. The post–1930 Argentine economic debacle was precipitated in important measure by adverse trends in the world economy and the understandably inward-looking reaction of Argentine policy makers. But the success of an import-substitution replacement for the traditional export-promotion policies depended on the existence of a dynamic entrepreneurial and managerial class, which did not exist in Argentina, like in most other Latin American countries (except Brazil and Chile, as we shall see in the next two chapters) and indeed in Spain, as I noted in chapter 3. In Argentina's case, the entrepreneurship and management—and technology—that drove its apparent economic success was furnished largely by foreigners, especially the British.

Various writers, Argentines and foreigners, have adduced geographical, historical, policy, and institutional factors to explain the Argentine puzzle. And all these factors are relevant. But geography is not destiny, as Australia has demonstrated. A country, even a remote country, has at least some control over its historical evolution. The evolution of institutions ultimately reflects the values and attitudes of a society. And one has to ponder why the political and intellectual leaders of Argentina persisted with erroneous policies for much of that country's history.

I am far from the only person to interpret the Argentine puzzle as essentially a cultural phenomenon. In chapter 1, I mentioned Mariano Grondona's typology of development-prone and development-resistant cultures. Grondona is a prominent Argentine intellectual and television talk-show host; his model of a development-resistant society is Argentina. Among others, Argentines and foreigners, who share the belief that culture chiefly explains Argentina's history are the American historian Thomas F. McGann,[6] the novelist V. S. Naipaul,[7] the Argentine writer Delfín Garosa,[8] and the Argentine political scientist Carlos Escudé, who concludes his insightful and provocative book *The Failure of the Argentine Project*[9] with the words,

> [T]he war of the Malvinas [Falkland Islands] should be a strong reminder of the potential for irrationality and madness present in a pathological and irredentist culture. And works like this book should serve to remind us of the importance of studying culture, again and again, not only to understand socio-economic and political processes, but also to understand the making of decisions of enormous historical significance.[10]

ARGENTINA'S IMMIGRANT POPULATION

In *Reversal of Development in Argentina*, Waisman argues against a cultural interpretation of the Argentine puzzle because of the country's "curvilinear" history—which I think ignores some compelling continuities, as well as similarities to other Latin American countries—but also because the cultural explanation "does not take into account the major difference between Argentina and the standard 'Hispanic' countries: the immigrant origin of the majority of the population, together with the fact that most immigrants were of non-Hispanic origin."[11] However, as Waisman acknowledges, many of them were of "traditional Catholic-Latin background."[12]

Tomás Roberto Fillol was a graduate student at Massachusetts Institute of Technology when he wrote *Social Factors in Economic Development* more than three decades ago.[13] Convinced that Argentina's failure principally reflected traditional values and attitudes, he stressed that Argentina is *not* European—not in the modern Western European democratic-capitalist mainstream—but predominantly Spanish and Italian; and there is not that much difference between the two southern European Catholic countries in a cultural sense. The majority of the Italian immigrants came from the southern part of Italy, the Mezzogiorno,[14] whose cultural pathology was illuminated forty years ago by Edward Banfield in his classic *The Moral Basis of a Backward Society*,[15] and more recently by Robert Putnam in *Making Democracy Work*.[16]

To be sure, a significant percentage of the immigrants were northern Italians, who have demonstrated their economic creativity not only in Italy but in Brazil and other countries. The northern Italians are also more disposed to association, to horizontal, democratic relationships, than the southerners, as Putnam documents. Moreover, about 20 percent of Argentina's inhabitants are of neither Spanish nor Italian extraction, including the largest Jewish population in Latin America.

There is evidence, noted by Waisman, of a disproportionate participation by immigrants in Argentine industry and commerce, a phenomenon of crucial significance to Brazil's dynamism, as we shall see. But Argentina's immigrants were subjected to a conscious program of Argentinization, above all in the schools, that was designed by the establishment to mold the immigrants in the image of what Carlos Escudé refers to in *The Failure of the Argentine Project* as the Argentine "homo patrioticus." In Escudé's view, whatever the antecedence of the immigrants, their children were likely to learn authoritarian, militaristic, nationalistic, and dogmatic values.[17] He believes that among the other consequences of the manipulation of the education system by the elites may have been the suppression of economic dynamism and creativity.[18]

ARGENTINA SHIFTS COURSE TOWARD THE FIRST WORLD

Argentina's history between 1930 and 1982 might aptly be described as going from bad to worse to disaster. We have already mentioned the failure of Yrigoyen and the Radicals to consolidate democracy after the suffrage reforms gave them fourteen years in power. The 1930 coup d'état was led by General José F. Uriburu, whose provisional presidency was followed by fraudulent elections in 1932 and 1938. During the early years of World War II, Argentina showed considerable sympathy for the Axis, and the military, who were committed to a nationalistic, corporatist vision of Argentina, again intervened in 1943 to preempt the accession to power of the pro-British aristocracy. But as the prospects of the Axis waned, the generals, including Juan Domingo Perón, who became vice president in 1944, shifted their ground and finally, in March 1945, declared war on Germany and Japan.

The early years of the import-substitution economic strategy inspired by the Depression were relatively prosperous. By 1943, industry had overtaken agriculture in economic importance, spawning a rapidly growing urban labor force that both precipitated a population explosion in Buenos Aires and created an important new political force, the *descamisados* (the "shirtless ones"), on which Perón rode to power in 1945. For a few years, he captured resources from agricultural exports and channeled them into wage increases for workers and the politically popular nationalization of foreign enterprises. But the longer-run effect was to discourage agricultural production, which fell by more than 50 percent. Against the backdrop of hard times provoked by his policies, and Perón's threat to arm the *descamisados*, he was overthrown by the military in 1955 and sent into exile.

Perón, and the generals who followed him, were the heirs of the "barbarian" current in Argentine history and culture that Sarmiento warned about in *Facundo*, the subtitle of which is "civilization and barbarism," and the real target of which was Juan Manuel de Rosas, the dictator who dominated Argentina between 1829 and 1852. Escudé notes, "before the fall of Rosas, the country and its culture presented a typical Latin American profile ... [that] ... bears a striking resemblance to the Argentina of Perón."[19] Naipaul describes Peronism as "protest, despair, faith, machismo, magic, *espiritismo* [mysticism], revenge"[20]—not characteristics one associates with the civic culture that nurtures democracy.

After three years of military government under General Pedro E. Aramburu, during which a Peronista uprising was crushed, Arturo Frondizi, a Radical, won clean elections and was inaugurated in 1958. Frondizi ran headlong into Argentine economic nationalism when he negotiated oil exploration contracts with U.S. companies. When he permitted the Peronistas to run in the 1962 provincial and congressional elections, anti-Perón factions of the military revolted, leading to the departure of Frondizi. Elections were held in 1963, and the winner, Arturo Illia, also a Radical, promptly canceled the foreign oil contracts. Unable to reconcile military factionalism and resurgent Peronism, Illia was deposed by the military in 1967.

The military held on to power until elections were held, in 1973, with the economy in disarray and the society polarized, and with increasing activity by left-wing terrorist groups. The victor was Hector J. Cámpora, a Peronist, who soon resigned, paving the way for the return of Perón, who won new elections with more than 60 percent of the vote—the electorate was still seeking a caudillo magician—and was inaugurated on Columbus Day, 1973. He died eight months later, with Argentina still in crisis. He had moved to the right in his eighteen years of exile, and many left-wing Peronists who were alienated by his policies joined the terrorist *Montoneros.**

Crisis then turned to farce. Perón's legacy to his country was his second wife, Isabel, a former cabaret dancer who, as vice president, succeeded him on his death. Her principal adviser was José López Rega, a mystic and soothsayer. Montonero violence accelerated, and the now anti-Peronista military returned to power in 1976 under General Jorge A. Videla.

---

*The *Montoneros* took their name from a group who fought for Argentina's independence from Spain early in the nineteenth century.

Impressed and worried by the Allende debacle in Chile and the *Tupamaro* violence in neighboring Uruguay, the Argentine military initiated the "Dirty War" against the left, which, to be sure, was also guilty of bloody abuses. Due process has never been one of Argentina's—or Latin America's—strengths, and it was totally ignored in an indiscriminate campaign of counterterror and torture, as also occurred in post-Allende Chile and, in a less brutal version, in "civilized" Uruguay. One of the Argentine military's horrifying practices did not come to light until 1995, when a former navy pilot admitted dropping live, drugged alleged leftists from airplanes into the sea, a practice apparently condoned by some Catholic chaplains.[21]

We are again reminded of Sarmiento's warning to Hispanic America 150 years ago:

> Terror is a sickness that infects people like cholera, smallpox, or scarlet fever. And after you have worked for ten years to inoculate against it, the vaccine fails to work. Don't laugh, people of Hispanic America, when you see such degradation! Remember that you are Spanish, and that is how the Inquisition educated Spain. Be careful, then![22]

Sarmiento's warning underscores the outrageous nonsense of the implication in Costa-Gavras's 1972 movie *State of Siege* that the U.S. government introduced torture to Latin American security forces. That movie, by the way, strongly influenced the U.S. Congress's decision to dismantle overseas police advisory programs. But, as Naipaul stresses, "[t]orture is not new in Argentina. And though Argentines abroad, when they are campaigning against a particular regime, talk as if torture has just been started by that regime, in Argentina itself torture is spoken of—and accepted—by all groups as an Argentine institution."[23]

THE FALKLANDS DEBACLE: THE TURNING POINT

Against a backdrop of the Dirty War, accelerating inflation aggravated by the oil shocks, and economic stagnation (during the 1970s, Argentina's industrial growth was among the world's slowest), the military presidency passed from General Videla to General Roberto E. Viola and then General Leopoldo Galtieri. In a desperate, adolescent adventure aimed at galvanizing popular support for his government,

Galtieri invaded the Falkland Islands in 1982. The Falklands had been a British possession since 1833, and the islanders considered themselves British. Prime Minister Margaret Thatcher responded promptly and powerfully. A British expeditionary force overwhelmed the Argentine occupying forces, restored British control, and humiliated not only Galtieri but the entire Argentine military establishment. Popular support for Thatcher in Britain reached record heights. Galtieri fell, and his successor, General Reynaldo Bignone, promised elections in 1983.

The Argentines refer to the Falklands as the Malvinas Islands and, the irresponsibility and opportunism of the Argentine military notwithstanding, it soon became fashionable in U.S. intellectual circles to substitute *Malvinas* for *Falklands*. This change of labels presumably demonstrated solidarity with a "victim of imperialism," particularly appropriate in academe after the Reagan administration made clear its support for the Thatcher policy. I have heard a former Assistant Secretary of State for Latin America mention "the Malvinas" and an American law professor refer deprecatingly to "Margaret Thatcher's *invasion* of the Malvinas."

The sympathies of some U.S. intellectuals notwithstanding, the Argentine military was disgraced before their own countrymen, and a chain of events was set in motion that, if history were just, would have led Argentina to erect a statue of Margaret Thatcher in Buenos Aires. Had the British accepted the Falklands invasion as a fait accompli, as the Argentine generals hoped, the Argentine military would doubtless have remained in power several additional years and might conceivably still be there today. And not only would Argentina's progress have been adversely affected. With the Argentine military still in power, General Pinochet might have had second thoughts about stepping down in Chile, as might the Brazilian generals. The wave of democratization that has washed over most of Latin America might have been little more than a ripple.

The Falklands disaster may prove to be an example of what I call the trauma theory of cultural change. This theory argues that disaster forces a society to reexamine its basic values and attitudes, as well as its goals and institutions. A few examples: the arrival of Commodore Perry in Tokyo Bay in 1853 with the power to bring Japan to its knees, leading to the Meiji Restoration; the collapse of the Ottoman Empire and the near-colonization of Turkey by Greece that led, in 1923, to

Atatürk's cultural revolution; the wholesale bloodshed and destruction of the Spanish Civil War, which attenuated traditional Spanish intransigence, intolerance, and violence; and the Allende/Pinochet episode in Chile that recreated a sense of unity and national purpose and suppressed ideological extremism.

In the event, a civilian president, Radical Raúl Alfonsín, was elected on 30 October 1983, defeating the Peronist candidate, Italo Luder, 52 percent to 40 percent. During his almost six years in office, Alfonsín succeeded both in creating an environment of political civility and in starting a process that would lead to the emasculation of the military. General Videla and Admiral Emilio Massera, chief architect of the Falklands adventure, were condemned to life in prison, Viola to sixteen years in prison, Galtieri to house arrest. (They were all pardoned by Alfonsín's successor, Carlos Saúl Menem, who had himself been imprisoned by the military.) During Alfonsín's term, elements of the military rebelled on three occasions but were defeated each time. We are reminded of the attempted *pronunciamiento* of General Jaime Miláns del Bosch against the government of Leopoldo Calvo Sotelo in Spain in 1981, in all probability the last whimper of a military institution conditioned to view itself as above the law.

Alfonsín's principal problem was the economy: stagnation, galloping inflation, and mountainous debt driven by the oil shocks and high interest rates. In mid-1985, he introduced Plan Austral, a stabilization program based on wage and price freezes, fiscal austerity, and a new currency. The plan succeeded for a few months in dramatically reducing inflation, and Alfonsín's Radicals won a big victory in the October 1985 congressional elections. But labor, particularly the Peronista unions under Saúl Ubaldini, agitated against the wage freeze as the stabilization program took hold. The Church, which fiercely opposed Alfonsín's proposal to legalize divorce, and diehard elements of the military and the extreme left imparted additional centrifugal forces to the volatile environment. In 1986, Alfonsín succumbed to the political pressures and started to relax the stabilization program. Inflation revived, and the Alfonsín administration effectively ended. With inflation in four digits, the Peronista candidate Carlos Saúl Menem won big over Radical Eduardo Angeloz in the May 1989 elections. Reviled by the people and in despair, Alfonsín resigned five months early, and Menem was inaugurated in July rather than December. A regime that had started as a *fiesta cívica* following a half-century of nightmare ended as another installment of the nightmare—but with democratic continuity intact.

I visited Argentina late in 1988 and again late in 1989, the latter a stop on a speaking tour. The country was in a state of deep psychological depression comparable to that of Peru under the increasingly ominous threat of the *Sendero Luminoso* in the late 1980s and early 1990s. Argentina appeared to be relentlessly governed by Murphy's Law, and few Argentines thought it would be otherwise in their lifetimes. Vast amounts of capital had fled to the safety of western and Uruguayan banks.

I'm afraid that the message of my 1989 lectures aggravated the gloom of some Argentines. By that time, a Spanish-language edition of my book *Underdevelopment Is a State of Mind* had been published in Buenos Aires, and my focus on the power of culture was interpreted—incorrectly—as arguing that Argentina was in permanent, irreversible decline. I remember the at once incredulous and credulous reaction of Argentine audiences when I pointed out that Brazil's per capita GNP then exceeded Argentina's, according to World Bank data. (Many Argentines look down their noses at the Brazilians.)

THE SURPRISING MENEM

Carlos Saúl Menem, three-time former governor of La Rioja province and the self-styled heir of Juan Perón, appeared to Argentina and the world as a flamboyant, nationalistic populist. The Catholic convert son of Syrian Moslem immigrants, Menem had been imprisoned for five years following the overthrow of Isabel Perón by the military. His easy 1989 victory over the Radical candidate Angeloz was chiefly the consequence of the economic chaos of the Alfonsín years. But, evoking Perón, Menem promised during the campaign both a 50 percent increase in wages and repudiation of the vast foreign debt Argentina had incurred, particularly following the oil shocks of 1973–74 and 1978–79. Had he implemented either promise, Argentina's economic disaster would have become a catastrophe.

Instead, he committed himself to a program of economic stabilization, privatization, encouragement of foreign investment, reduction of tariffs, and export promotion, with limited results at the outset—inflation exceeded 1,000 percent in 1990 and reached an annual rate *over 20,000* percent in March—but increasingly successful after he shifted the Harvard-educated economist Domingo Cavallo from Foreign Minister to Minister of Economy early in 1991. Annual inflation dropped below 100 percent in 1991, 20 percent in 1992, 10 percent in 1993, and 5 percent in 1994 as the Argentine peso was anchored to the dollar. GDP growth, which had been negative in the 1980s and flat in 1990, surged to 8.9 percent in 1991, 8.7 percent in 1992, 6 percent in 1993, and 7.1 percent in 1994—in part as a consequence of the 1991 initiation of MERCOSUR, a promising economic integration scheme initially involving Argentina, Brazil, Paraguay, and Uruguay, and now Chile. But the high growth of those years surely also reflects a partial recovery of what was lost during the many years of stagnation, and several more years of sustained high growth must be achieved before Argentina can reasonably be grouped with Chile with respect to stability and growth, particularly after the Mexican crisis ripple effects in South America. Preliminary estimates for 1995 show a 5 or more percent decline in GDP.[24]

The stabilization and development program has not been without costs. Unemployment has risen; many protected industries have failed; many pensioners face penury; and the provinces have suffered disproportionately. Menem and his team argue, sensibly, that time is needed to consolidate and distribute the benefits of a dynamic economy. But the question remains whether Argentina, with its incipient, fragile democratic institutions and lacking in both civic and entrepreneurial culture, will display the necessary patience and restraint.

Cavallo, as Foreign Minister, and the economist Guido di Tella, who succeeded him, have encouraged Menem to turn his back on the Peronist, and indeed Argentine, tradition of friction with the United States and pursue instead what Carlos Escudé labels a "citizenry-centric" foreign policy—that is, one in which the prime consideration is citizen welfare rather than national power, ideology, or consolidation of domestic power, the latter three of which have often driven foreign policy in Latin America, as I mentioned in chapter 3.[25] The result has been an unprecedented warm relationship between Washington and Buenos Aires, including symbolic Argentine military support of the Gulf War and visits by President Menem to Washington and by President Bush to Buenos Aires.

Menem infuriated many Argentines when he pardoned 210 military officers convicted during the 1980s of Dirty War crimes. But he also cut military spending in half and reduced the personnel strength of the armed forces from 100,000 to 20,000. The budgetary and personnel reductions, coupled with the discrediting of the military in the Falklands invasion, the Dirty War, and several failed military uprisings, have left firmly under civilian control a military institution that for much of Argentina's history had been the ultimate power.

The prudence and wisdom of the Menem economic, foreign, and military policies have played to a counterpoint of nepotism and corruption in Menem's inner circle and the widely publicized and scandalous breakup of his marriage. But as economic stability and growth took hold, his popularity surged to the point where a deal he worked out with Alfonsín to permit a second presidential term was translated into law in 1994. (The first term is for six years, the second for four. All subsequent presidential terms will be for four years, with one reelection.)* A few months later came the collapse of the Mexican economy and the "tequila effect" that reverberated throughout Latin America. The Argentine economy, which, like the Mexican, was heavily dependent on foreign capital flows and repatriated flight capital and has been running a large trade deficit, was shaken. Cavallo had declared his independence of the International Monetary Fund (IMF) just a few months before and had to reverse course, woo the IMF, and impose a rigorous austerity program, including a sharp contraction of credit, which aggravated Argentina's already serious unemployment problem and the shaky financial condition of many state-owned banks.

The biting austerity program and swelling unemployment notwithstanding, Menem won a handsome reelection victory on 14 May 1995, and Argentina appears to have weathered the tequila effect, although not without a significant drop in the growth rate and high levels of unemployment. Two crucial questions remain to be answered: Will Argentina's nascent democracy hold together under the stresses of economic transformation? And will the economic transformation be sufficiently dynamic to slash unemployment and produce growing pros-

*There is ambiguity about the number of legal reelections; by some interpretations, there is no limit.

perity for the masses? The answers to those questions depend in large part on the extent to which traditional Argentine values and attitudes are changing.

IS ARGENTINA'S CULTURE CHANGING?

Argentina's political history, at least until 1983, has been dominated by authoritarianism, militarism, and disrespect for the law. That history evokes the history of Spain until the death of Franco in 1975 and of the Italian south, the two principal wellsprings of the Argentine people. Several observers, the Argentines Grondona and Escudé among them, have linked Argentina's antidemocratic traditions to a personalistic, familist, fatalist, and mistrustful world view that evokes Ortega y Gasset's metaphor of "invertebrate" Spain—a society that lacks the cohesiveness to function as an organic whole.

Argentina's economic history suggests a shortfall in entrepreneurship, in part the consequence of an economic tradition in which the accumulation of wealth was often the consequence of governmental favors or the exploitation of public office for personal gain. The traditions of corruption are deeply rooted in Argentina. As we shall see in the next chapter, the fact that Brazil's per capita GDP has grown more than twice as fast as Argentina's in this century is in large measure the consequence of the greater creativity and dynamism of Brazilian businessmen, disproportionately the descendants of non-Iberian immigrants.

But, as we have seen in the case of Spain, at least with respect to the values and attitudes that influence political performance, culture changes, and both political systems and economic policies can promote cultural change. Argentina has now functioned for more than a decade within democratic political forms (although it still has a way to go with respect to democratic *norms*—for example, an independent, apolitical, and professional judiciary). As James L. Busey has observed of another Latin American context, "Previous stability lays the ground for understanding which makes possible future stability; previous chaos and resultant hatreds arouse deep bitterness which makes more difficult the task of establishing stable, constitutional government."[26]

The open economic policies that Franco had no choice but to adopt in the late 1950s contributed to a much broader opening of Spain to the West and, ultimately, to the adoption of western political norms. The open economic policies pursued in Chile during the Pinochet dictatorship led both to rising prosperity, in which Chile's entrepreneurial traditions were revived and reinforced, and to the return to democracy in 1989. We have already noted how the Allende-Pinochet trauma attenuated the confrontational, polarizing currents in Chilean society, in much the same way that the horror of the Spanish Civil War contributed to the moderation of Spanish politics.

Marita Carballo, an Argentine sociologist who heads the Gallup office in Buenos Aires, has compared value and attitude data samples for the years 1984 and 1991 and noted some interesting—and in some respects encouraging—trends. While popular support for democracy has intensified notably, "[t]he later data reveal an enormous decline in the confidence accorded . . . the parliament, the system of justice, and civil servants."[27] Carballo notes an intensifying interest in participation in politics, especially through several private public-interest organizations that have sprung up in recent years, including *Poder Ciudadano* (Citizen Power) and *Ciudadanos en Acción* (Citizens in Action). She concludes: "The public is less disposed to be told what to do and more adept at telling the government what *it* should do."[28]

Carballo's data show a positive change with respect to the work ethic. In 1984, 60 percent of respondents wished that work had less importance in life. In 1991, 73 percent of respondents felt that such a diminution of the importance of work would be undesirable. "People generally are satisfied in their work and take greater pride in it."[29] And Carballo notes that there is a far greater concern with motivation, challenge, personal development, and participation in decision making in the workplace, consistent with a worldwide trend influenced in part by Japanese management techniques.

The trends Carballo notes are encouraging with respect to the consolidation in Argentina of both a civic culture and a work culture, or ethic. Menem's victory in the 1995 elections in the wake of the collapse of the Mexican peso and the biting austerity measures imposed by his government both tends to confirm those trends and is a reason for some optimism about the political maturing of the Argentine electorate—and democratic continuity and capitalist creativity.

But it would be rash to conclude that Argentina's experiment with democratic capitalism is irreversible. In a seminar at Harvard just before the 1995 elections won by Menem, Mariano Grondona insisted that "Argentina hasn't yet reached the point where institutions are above people, as in Chile. And it still has a long way to go with respect to social justice, education, public health, saving, and the competitiveness of its economy."[30] Grondona also noted that the incipient Argentine economic "miracle" bears a stronger resemblance to the now-collapsed Mexican "miracle," with its heavy dependence on foreign capital, than to the more solid Chilean model, with its emphasis on exports and savings. Like Mexico in the years preceding the 1994 crisis, Argentina has run a substantial, persistent trade deficit, while Chile's balance has been neutral to positive.

THE NEW ARGENTINES—AND THE OLD

I visited Buenos Aires for several speaking engagements in March 1995, at which time I was invited to return in July to be a speaker at the annual meeting of the prestigious Association of Banks of the Argentine Republic. Both of my earlier books had been published in Buenos Aires, so the association was well aware of my views on the root causes of Latin America's—and Argentina's—underdevelopment, which was confirmed by the title of the lecture they assigned to me: "Underdevelopment Is a State of Mind—The Argentine Case." I was gratified that an organization of the Argentine establishment was interested in considering the cultural explanation for Argentina's peculiar history. But, with dependency theory now discredited and increasing numbers of Latin American professionals exploring the cultural explanation, I was not surprised.

Before my lecture, I met with representatives of two of the non-partisan public-interest organizations that have sprung up in recent years: Ciudadanos en Acción and Poder Ciudadano. Ciudadanos en Acción is akin to the League of Women Voters in the United States, although several of its activists are men. The two representatives I met with, Mercedes Muro de Nadal and Cristina Miguens, were convinced that many of Argentina's problems are rooted in culture, the weight of which they felt in their efforts to promote interest in electoral reform. Miguens and her psychiatrist husband Miguel Hoffman lead the Infancy and Human Development Foundation, which focuses on the relationship between infant and parents as a crucial determinant of personality formation.

Poder Ciudadano was formed in 1989 by a group of professionals, many of them lawyers, several of whom have studied in the United States. Its principal objective is to promote civic responsibility and participation. Among its members are Luis Moreno Ocampo, who has been the Federal District Attorney for Buenos Aires and was a prosecutor during the mid-1980s trials of the military and police; Mona Moncalvillo, a prominent journalist who is affiliated with the Peronist *Justicialista* Party; Teresa Anchorena, the Assistant Secretary of Culture during the early years of the Radical Alfonsín government; Manuel Mora y Araujo, a noted sociologist who is active in the Union of the Democratic Center party; and Marta Oyhanarte, a lawyer who became famous through her efforts to investigate the disappearance of her husband during the Dirty War.

Corruption—Poder Ciudadano refers to it as "hyper-corruption"—is one of their principal targets, and promotion of transparency in government is one of their principal goals. In this connection, Poder Ciudadano recently established a data bank on politicians seeking office in the 1995 elections, to include information on their personal finances and involvement in civil or criminal court cases. José Octavio Bordón of the *Alianza Frente del País Solidario* (FREPASO), who ran second to, but well behind, Menem, and Radical candidate Horacio Massaccesi, who ran a distant third, received Poder Ciudadano representatives cordially and provided them with the data they sought. Menem refused to meet with Poder Ciudadano or to provide the data.

The traditions of philanthropy and support of public-service organizations are scant in Argentina, as they are throughout Latin America, and much of the financing of Poder Ciudadano has come from institutions in the United States. Poder Ciudadano's efforts to promote interest in its activities have been successful with respect to media attention, but it continues to operate on a shoestring. The destiny of organizations like Poder Ciudadano and Ciudadanos en Acción is linked to the destiny of democracy in Argentina. If the organizations flourish and become self-sufficient, one can reasonably infer that civic culture is taking root.

The weight of the cultural problem will be apparent from an incident in which I was involved during the annual meeting of the Association of Banks of the Argentine Republic on 5 July 1995. The meeting had been inaugurated by President Menem, and President Cardoso of Brazil was to follow Economics Minister Cavallo as the closing speaker. The program included more than fifty speakers and panelists, the large majority of them prominent Argentine financiers and economists. The meeting was held at the posh Alvear Palace Hotel. I received a note asking me to visit one of the hotel rooms for reimbursement of my travel expenses and payment of an honorarium. When I entered the room, a representative of the association handed me a wad of hundred-dollar bills. I told him that I would much rather be paid by check, particularly given my absentmindedness and proclivity to lose things. He told me that the association had considered payment by check but that several of the speakers had asked to be paid in cash— "the tax question, you know."

ARGENTINA'S PROSPECTS

Democracy and the market are not enough to assure Argentina's landing in the First World. As Venezuela and the Dominican Republic have demonstrated over the past three decades, democratic forms do not assure democratic reality. And as Brazil has demonstrated during the same period, export-driven economic dynamism does not necessarily assure greater social justice.

Cultural change is a slow process, but in its aspirations for modernity, democracy, prosperity, and justice, Argentina can count on some important advantages: extremely rich natural resources; a highly educated citizenry by Third World standards (the World Bank reports adult illiteracy in Argentina at 5 percent);[31] good physical infrastructure; more than ten years of democratic continuity; enlightened and skillfully executed economic and foreign policies during the Menem administrations; and a chain of failures, abuses, and disasters that have been at the same time highly painful, costly, and instructive. Protestantism, particularly Pentecostal Protestantism, is making inroads on the Roman Catholic monopoly in Argentina,[32] although not as dramatically as in neighboring Brazil and Chile, where as much as 20 percent of the population is now Protestant.[33] Whether in its propagation of the Protestant ethic or in the competition it poses for the Catholic Church, the Protestant movement is likely to be a force for constructive cultural change, particularly with respect to the promotion of the values of work, frugality, education, merit, and community.

If Argentina's political, intellectual, media, religious, business, and labor leaders come to realize the influence of culture in Argentina's disappointing history and its crucial role in the country's modernization; if they work to change the traditional values and attitudes through, for example, educational reform, reform of the system of justice, decentralization, modern management techniques, and a focus on child-rearing practices; and if they are successful in preserving the democratic experiment and open economic policies in the face of the inevitable pressures, some of them rooted in traditional culture, to abandon them—then Argentina could be firmly anchored in the First World within a generation. Among the indicators of progress toward that destination would be:

- the growth of entrepreneurship, as evidenced by declining unemployment, expanding industrial production, expanding exports;
- higher savings rates, reflected in higher investment levels and slower growth of imports;
- substantially greater tax compliance;
- growth of philanthropy and philanthropic institutions;
- growth in the number and influence of private associations, particularly those focused on public-interest issues;
- a truly independent, professional judiciary;
- the disappearance of the name Perón from the contemporary political lexicon.

Argentina may well follow the Spanish model: deepening of democratic institutions to irreversibility, but with an economy heavily dependent on foreign capital, technology, and entrepreneurship for its dynamism. Given its vast natural wealth and its head start, this formula could lead Argentina to the First World faster than any other Latin American country, with the possible exception of Chile.

6

Brazil: Is the Future Now?

Brazil's history presents three salient—and contrasting—features: (1) rapid and sustained economic growth in this century; (2) extreme inequality in the distribution of income, wealth, land, and opportunity; and (3) difficulty in building democratic institutions. The latter two are typical of Ibero-Catholic culture and were equally true of Spain and Portugal until their Europeanization in recent decades. But sustained high economic growth is not typical. Each of the three features must be examined if we are to get some sense of where Brazil, sometimes referred to as "the country of the future—always," may be heading in the twenty-first century. Is the future now for Brazil?

THE ECONOMIC MIRACLE

Brazil is richly endowed with natural resources. It possesses large reserves of iron, manganese, nickel, tin, chromium, bauxite, beryllium, copper, lead, tungsten, and zinc. Gold, silver, and precious and semi-precious gemstones are extracted in commercial quantities. And its petroleum production is steadily increasing to the point where it accounts for half of national consumption. Brazil's hydroelectric resources are vast and now account for about 90 percent of electricity generation.

Brazil is also richly endowed with agricultural resources. From the mid-sixteenth to the mid-seventeenth centuries, the plantations of Northeast Brazil dominated world sugar production, and sugar continues as a major crop today, for export, domestic table consumption, and conversion to alcohol for vehicle fuel. Coffee was introduced in Brazil in the first half of the nineteenth century and soon became its principal export. Brazil is the world's largest exporter of coffee and orange juice concentrate; the second largest exporter of cocoa and soybeans/soymeal; and a

124

major exporter of meat and hides. But today, Brazil's manufactured exports are three times greater than its exports of primary products.

From 1900 to 1987, Brazil's average annual GDP growth—4.8 percent—was the second fastest in the world, after Taiwan (5.1 percent) and ahead of Japan (4.3 percent). In 1900, Brazil's GDP was the nineteenth largest in the world. In 1987, Brazil had climbed to tenth place, and World Bank statistics for 1993 show it in ninth place, ahead of China.[1] During those almost ninety years, Brazil's population growth averaged 2.4 percent, which left it tied for fourth with South Korea in terms of average annual growth of GDP per capita (2.4 percent). Japan's per capita GDP growth was highest at 3.1 percent; Taiwan was second at 2.8 percent; and Norway and Finland tied for third at 2.6 percent.[2]

But even eighty-seven years of rapid growth do not assure prosperity if the starting point is acute poverty. The World Bank lists Brazil's per capita GNP at $2,930 in 1993, barely edging into the category of upper-middle-income countries. Japan's per capita GNP was $31,490 in the same year; Finland's was $19,300; South Korea's was $7,660.[3] Brazil was a very poor country indeed at the turn of the twentieth century, and we need both to understand why that was true and what happened in the twentieth century to transform Brazil from economic stagnation and acute poverty into economic dynamism.

Unlike its neighbors who fought for independence from Spain, Brazil passed peacefully from colony to independence in 1822 and took the Portuguese Prince Regent Dom Pedro as its first emperor. Portugal's economic policies were similar to the mercantilist policies of Spain with respect to its colonies. That meant that Brazil exported what it produced—principally sugar, gold, and gemstones during the colonial period—to Portugal and increasingly to England, with which Portugal had a special trading arrangement from early in the eighteenth century that endured after Brazil's independence. Brazil imported from Portugal and England everything it needed but didn't produce, and that was a great deal in the undiversified Brazilian economy. Mercantilism also meant the Portuguese tried to control agricultural, commercial, and industrial activity in the colony, part of a general policy of suppression of Brazilian competition with the homeland, although not as suffocating as in the Spanish colonies.

A further brake on economic development was the Ibero-Catholic anti-entrepreneurial, anti-work tradition, which also explains to a large degree Portugal's economic backwardness. Raymundo Faoro observes of the typical upper-class Portuguese of the seventeenth century: "All productive activity was painful and dishonorable: agriculture, even the commerce that he tolerated, and industry. He was bored by the absence of a spiritual goal, of glory, in these occupations."[4] In 1987, the World Bank listed Portugal's per capita GNP at $2,830, the lowest in Western Europe and only $800 higher than Brazil's at the time. In Brazil's case, the anti-entrepreneurial, anti-work values were magnified by the persistence of slavery until 1888. *Trabalho e para cachorro e negro*, goes the old Brazilian saying—"Work is for dogs and blacks." And the elitist view of education also doubtlessly contributed to economic stagnation: in 1871, when Brazil's population totaled about ten million, only about 150,000—1.5 percent—were in primary schools, less than 10,000 in secondary schools.[5] (Portuguese mercantilism had led to the suppression of the printing press until 1808.)

The 150,000 Brazilian youngsters in primary schools probably represented no more than 5 percent of primary school–age children. In 1873, 28 percent of primary school–age Japanese children were in school, and that figure would rise to more than 95 percent by 1905.

Immigrant Entrepreneurs

Brazil's size and resource endowment, both vast, are not sufficient to explain its rapid growth in the twentieth century. If size and natural resources were sufficient, large, rich, and relatively underpopulated Argentina would be one of the most prosperous countries in the world. (Argentina is five-sixths as large as India but with less than 4 percent of India's population.) In fact, Argentina, its resource-based growth in the late nineteenth century notwithstanding, has grown less than half as fast as Brazil in this century in terms of GDP per capita.

Clearly, economic policies are relevant. Brazilian governments, civilian and military, have tended to concern themselves more with economic development than have Argentine governments. But Brazil's economic policy record, particularly with respect to currency stability and the role of the state in enterprise, is far from laudable.

The principal explanation of Brazil's economic growth resides, I believe, in the emergence of a large and dynamic Brazilian entrepreneurial class, agricultural *and* industrial, particularly in São Paulo and other southern states. It is entrepreneurship that chiefly explains the contrasts in Brazil's and Argentina's economic performance. But where did the entrepreneurs come from, if the Portuguese tradition is anti-work and anti-entrepreneurial?

Until 1818, Portugal prohibited the migration to Brazil of other than Portuguese nationals and slaves. Soon thereafter, colonies of German-speaking Swiss were established in Rio de Janeiro and Bahia. In the middle of the nineteenth century, increasing pressure against slavery led São Paulo coffee growers to look to Europe for laborers. The Germans who constituted the bulk of the immigrants until that time adapted poorly to plantation work, and Brazil sought new immigrants, particularly from southern Europe. From 1884 to 1939, more than four million people migrated to Brazil. Italians, most from the north, were the single largest group, accounting for one-third.[6] Wherever they came from, they encountered a laissez-faire environment in Brazil that contrasted sharply with the Argentine elite's efforts to force immigrants into the traditional Argentine mold.

Most of the immigrants settled in São Paulo, including 70 percent of the Italians and virtually all of the Japanese, who today number about one million. Most of the Germans and eastern Europeans settled in the southern states of Rio Grande do Sul, Santa Caterina, and Paraná, where they started in small-scale agriculture. But many were artisans, and the mercantilism-nurtured virginity of the Brazilian market encouraged them to move out of cottage industries into larger-scale manufacturing. Germans started the first textile mills, in 1874, and the first mechanical looms, in 1880. In 1920, 55 percent of Brazilian firms producing leather goods were owned by Germans. A 1950 census of industry in Rio Grande do Sul and Santa Caterina showed that almost 80 percent of the owners were of other than Portuguese extraction, more than half Germans.

By 1950, Italians accounted for almost 48 percent of all industrial activity in the São Paulo metropolitan area, while those of Portuguese extraction accounted for 15 percent. Germans accounted for 2 percent of São Paulo's population but 10 percent of industry.

The first Japanese immigrants arrived in 1908 and focused on small-farm agriculture. Japanese today are the dominant producers of fruits and vegetables consumed in São Paulo. The one million

Brazilians of Japanese antecedence are also disproportionately influential in industry, banking, and the universities.

Today, in part because of the laissez-faire environment immigrants encountered in Brazil, in part because of their success, and in part because of intermarriage with Luso-Brazilians, the entrepreneurial spirit is more developed in Brazil—at least the south of Brazil—than in most other Latin American countries.

Industry Displaces Agriculture

From colonial times through the first decades of the twentieth century, Brazil was a predominantly agricultural country. As late as 1919, agriculture accounted for 79 percent of total production, industry 21 percent. By 1939, industry's share had grown to 43 percent.[7] World Bank data show industry accounting for 69 percent and agriculture for 31 percent in 1960, industry 77 percent and agriculture 23 percent in 1993.

The industrialization of the Brazilian economy has its roots in the immigration of the late nineteenth and early twentieth centuries. But the policies of Getúlio Vargas (1930–45, 1951–54), Juscelino Kubitschek (1956–61), and the military chiefs of state starting with General Humberto Castelo Branco (1964–67) nourished those roots. During Vargas's fifteen-year dictatorship, he reoriented the Brazilian economy away from primary exports to import substitution industrialization, favoring urban over rural interests. Brazil's pattern of increasing state involvement in the economy can be traced back to Vargas. Kubitschek sustained Vargas's initiatives, introduced sectoral planning, and encouraged foreign investment.

The economic policies of Castelo Branco, crafted by his Planning Minister, Roberto Campos, were visionary, as we look back at Brazil's economic history from the vantage of the last years of the twentieth century. Campos pressed for expansion of exports, foreign investment, fiscal stability, a freer market, and decentralization, policies that are being pushed today by President Fernando Henrique Cardoso. The Castelo Branco/Campos policies were the launching platform for the Brazilian "miracle" between 1965 and 1980, when annual GDP growth averaged 9 percent, driven chiefly by export expansion, which averaged 9.4 percent annually. During those years, the sociologist Fernando

Henrique Cardoso, then with ECLAC, and other prominent Brazilian intellectuals such as Helio Jaguaribe were refining their socialist, anti-imperialist, anti-American dependency ideology and promoting import substitution as the only way to avoid the "exploitation" of the world market and foreign investment.

Brazil's rapid growth between 1965 and 1980 is mostly the consequence of good policies. One is reminded of the performance of the Chilean economy after somewhat similar policies were installed late in the 1970s during the Pinochet dictatorship, and the performance of the Argentine economy after President Menem established similar policies starting in 1990. And the high inflation/heavy foreign borrowing policies pursued by Brazil and Argentina in the wake of the oil shocks of the 1970s explain in large measure the slow growth (*negative* growth in Argentina's case) of the 1980s.

Policies *do* matter, particularly in explaining short-run economic phenomena. But when we view the evolution of the Brazilian economy over the span of this century, what is most striking is the sustained high level of growth driven first by industrialization and then by industrial product–led exports. (Interestingly, Brazil has for several years been experiencing an agricultural boom as increasing amounts of its vast interior lands are opened up.) Brazil's growth-promoting economic policies were generally better than Argentina's during this century, but not that much better and only rarely good. Entrepreneurship has driven the Brazilian economy, even during periods of policy miasma. And that entrepreneurial energy is largely the contribution of immigrants.

INEQUALITY, INJUSTICE

For many years, the World Bank has presented an income-distribution table in its annual reports. Data do not appear for about 40 percent of the 132 countries listed. But of the 60 percent that do appear, the most inequitable is Brazil: in 1989, the top 20 percent of Brazilians accounted for 67.5 percent of all income; the top 10 percent accounted for 51.3 percent; the bottom 40 percent accounted for just 7 percent. For comparison purposes, the top 20 percent in Japan, among the most equitable of the advanced countries, accounted for 37.5 percent; the top 10 percent for 22.4 percent; the bottom 40 percent for 21.9 percent of total income. Brazil's income distribution is more inequitable than substantially poorer, highly inequitable countries like Guatemala, Honduras, Kenya, and Tanzania. Moreover, in the 1980s, Brazil's income distribution worsened.

A recent ECLAC study shows Brazil with 38.5 percent of its population below the poverty line in 1990 and 16.4 percent living in indigence.[8] (These figures may be overstated because they may not adequately reflect Brazil's vast informal economy.[9]) Fifty-five percent of adult Brazilians living in urban areas and 89 percent of those living in rural areas had five years of education or less—worse than in Guatemala and Honduras.

Brazil also suffers from sharp regional inequalities that make it, like Italy and Turkey, look like two different countries: an extremely poor northeast, with social indicators (such as infant mortality, life expectancy, secondary school enrollment) roughly comparable to those of very poor Bolivia; and a more affluent and progressive south. Yet the social indicators for the South are not all that impressive, corresponding roughly to those of Mexico.[10]

Why should a country so rich in natural resources and with one of the most dynamic economies in the world evolve with such extreme social injustice? Obviously, insufficient resources have been channeled into public education and health, and opportunity has been severely restricted ever since colonial times, above all in the north. But what explains the chain of public policy decisions that has perpetuated this pattern of injustice and deprivation? Why have the elites who have run the country—the land-based aristocracy, often referred to as the "colonels," charismatic politicians like Getúlio Vargas, the military— accorded low priority to issues of social justice?

The substantial absence of democratic political institutions is a relevant factor. When the masses don't vote, or their votes are not counted, political leaders are less likely to be responsive to their needs and aspirations. The voting population actually decreased from 2.5 percent in 1894 to 2 percent in 1926. Women could not vote until 1934, the same year in which the secret ballot was introduced. Those same reforms opened voting to all literate people over eighteen, but adult literacy at the time was only about 20 percent.[11] The reforms were enacted during the Vargas dictatorship, and their implementation was spasmodic until Tancredo Neves was elected in 1985, ending two decades of military domination of politics.

Slavery is another factor that may help to explain Brazil's social injustice, particularly since it persisted until 1888, twenty-five years after the slaves were emancipated in the United States, fifty-four years after slavery was ended in the British Empire. Many writers, including Sir Arthur Lewis, David McClelland, Carlos Rangel, and the Nicaraguan politician and intellectual Salvador Mendieta, have stressed the negative values that slavery inculcates in both the slave and the master: distaste for work, focus on present needs, devaluation of education, undermining of the idea of community and social responsibility, callousness on the part of the master, sycophancy and rage on the part of the slave. I believe that the cultural legacy of slavery for many Brazilians whose ancestors were slaves is still palpable as a force that operates from within them to depreciate work and education and stifle upward mobility. I believe that a similar phenomenon is in play in the United States and that it is a greater obstacle to progress for blacks today than is white racism (which Gallup Poll data indicate has declined sharply in recent decades), above all for those blacks who have not escaped the cultural continuum of slavery, segregation, and the ghetto.[12]

But the principal explanation for Brazil's extreme social injustice resides, I believe, in the absence from Brazilian culture of a sense of community, of the identification of Brazilians with one another. The phenomenon is Ibero-Catholic in its roots: Brazil is an "invertebrate" society, to use Ortega y Gasset's description of Spain, suffering from a "particularism" he defines as

> that state of mind in which we believe that we need pay no attention to others. . . . Taking others into account implies at least an understanding of the state of mutual dependence and cooperation in which we live. . . . Among normal nations, a class that desires something for itself tries to get it by agreement with other classes. . . . But a class attacked by particularism feels humiliated when it realizes that in order to achieve its desires it must resort to these organs of the common will.[13]

To be sure, there are some important differences between Spain and Portugal that are reflected in differences between Hispanic America and Brazil. *Soberbia*—pride, with overtones of arrogance, haughtiness, intolerance, and vanity—is a dominant feature of traditional Hispanic culture.[14] Portuguese culture is softer, more resilient, less confrontational; in the Portuguese bullfight, the bull does not die. The Luso-Brazilian tradition is one of live and let live—precisely the words that former U.S. ambassador to Brazil John Hugh Crimmins used some years ago to describe to me the qualities that differentiate Brazil from Hispanic America.

"Live and let live" would explain the laissez-faire environment that European and Japanese immigrants found in Brazil, an environment in which they flourished and became Brazil's engine of economic development—in contrast to the experience of immigrants in Argentina. But "live and let live" in Brazil also implies self-absorption, familism at the expense of the broader society, and the absence of a sense of social responsibility and community. The behavior of the Brazilian at home, where with family and friends he is warm, respectful, and responsible, contrasts sharply with his dealings with strangers, which are commonly characterized by callousness, rudeness, and disrespect. One gets a strong sense of this driving a car in Brazil. The Brazilian José Oswaldo de Meira Penna observes: "The Brazilian, motorist or pedestrian, does not submit to the rational imperatives of community life but believes that it is necessary to . . . rebel against traffic signals, the police, and traffic regulations."[15]

Brazil is not generally a "civic" society, although there is clearly much more civic culture in the south than in the north, reversing the pattern of Italy. The contrast between the Brazilian's behavior within the family and outside the family is analyzed trenchantly in *A Casa e a Rua (At Home and on the Street)* by the Brazilian anthropologist Roberto DaMatta, who notes, "If I am buying from or selling to a relative, I neither seek profit or concern myself with money. The same can happen in a transaction with a friend. But if I am dealing with a stranger, then there are no rules, other than the one of exploiting him to the utmost."[16]

That kind of attitude has a lot to do not only with inequitable distribution of income, wealth, and opportunity but also with nepotism, corruption (including in the courts), tax evasion, and the absence of philanthropic activity. It also breeds mistrust.

During a speaking tour in several Brazilian cities in 1988, I accompanied my wife to a shoestore in Belo Horizonte where she bought a pair of sandals. One clerk helped her to find the sandals and gave her a receipt, which she then took to a cashier, who may well have been a member of the family that owned the store. After paying the cashier, she was given another receipt, which she took to another clerk, who wrapped the sandals and delivered them to her. In Canada, the United States, Western Europe, or Japan, one clerk would have handled the entire transaction. But in Brazil, as in Chile (see chapter 7) and elsewhere in Latin America, management's presumption is that employees will steal unless a system of checks and balances—highly inefficient, I might add—is in place.

To summarize, many factors contribute to Brazil's extreme inequality and injustice. But the principal factor is a family-centered, antisocial value system that evokes Edward Banfield's classic analysis of the Italian south in *The Moral Basis of a Backward Society*.

THE LONG ROAD TO DEMOCRACY

Brazil's postcolonial monarchy lasted until 1889, one year after slavery ended. What followed was forty years of limited experimentation with republican systems that is often referred to as the Old Republic. In fact, the landed aristocracy pretty much ran the country, with the military lurking in the background, much as the Argentine landed aristocracy ran Argentine politics between 1880 and 1916. The franchise in Brazil, as I have noted, was exercised by a tiny minority—2 percent of the population—who were denied the secret ballot.

Getúlio Vargas came to power in 1930 through a coup that ignored the results of an election ostensibly won by Júlio Prestes, a coup that succeeded when the military refused to defend the outgoing president, Washington Luis—"the first time the Brazilian military deposed a civilian president."[17] Vargas set to work building a *Novo Estado*—a New State—that had some of the characteristics of Argentina during the Perón dictatorship, including the courting of labor. But, like Perón, Vargas increasingly resorted to deficit financing, and Brazil's chronic and severe problems with inflation date from the early Vargas years, just as Argentina's date from the early Perón years.

Given Brazil's backwardness and social injustice, it is not surprising that a Communist movement developed during the Depression. Luis Carlos Prestes, a Robin Hood figure who became the Communist leader, exploited smoldering discontent in 1935 to provoke an uprising led by disgruntled military units. The uprising was put down by military members loyal to Vargas, leaving "an allergy for communism in the armed forces"[18] that would endure for many decades.

Vargas was ousted by the military in 1945 when it appeared that he was maneuvering to perpetuate his dictatorship in the face of a national consensus for democracy, a consensus born, in part, from the democratic fervor that followed World War II and from Brazil's active military support of the Allies. Eurico Dutra won the elections; Vargas was elected as a deputy in the Congress. Vargas, now espousing "anti-imperialism" and complaining about Brazil's "dependency," ran for president in 1950 and won. His policies were moderately leftist and prejudicial to foreign investment. Corruption was rampant in his government, and his left-leaning policies, which again stimulated inflation, and the courting of the extreme left by his Minister of Labor João Goulart provoked the military to act. On 24 August 1954, in circumstances reminiscent of Salvador Allende in Chile in 1973, Vargas shot himself when the military attempted to oust him, thereby becoming a martyr and hero of the left.

Juscelino Kubitschek, who had been the moderate governor of Minas Gerais, won the 1955 elections, leaving the military uneasy because of his links to Vargas. But his five years in power carried Brazilian democracy to its zenith. Creative, purposeful, and with a vision of Brazilian greatness, "he promised 50 years of progress in five, and he did not entirely fail."[19] He opened the door to foreign investment, and the economy boomed, driven chiefly by the industrial sector. He substantially expanded Brazil's electricity and highway infrastructure. And he built Brasilia, in the heart of Brazil, as a symbol of a new nation, although he went deeply into debt to do it. His ideas helped to shape John F. Kennedy's Alliance for Progress.

Brazil appeared to be moving toward political maturity when the 1961 elections were won by the reformist Jânio Quadros of the conservative opposition, and power passed peacefully from the ins to the outs. But Quadros was both eccentric and inept—his behavior in office invites comparison with that of Juan Bosch, who was elected president of the Dominican Republic late in 1962 and served for seven tumultuous months before he was ousted by the military. After seven comparably tumultuous months in office, in which he accomplished little but succeeded in antagonizing almost everyone, Quadros resigned, apparently in the belief that his resignation would be rejected by the people, the military, and the Congress, and that he would remain in power with a strengthened hand. But "Congress happily accepted the resignation, hardly anyone stirred, and the military kept the ex-president incommunicado to prevent his stirring up trouble."[20] Brazil's hopeful experiment with democracy was on the ropes.

Quadros was succeeded by his vice president, João Goulart, who had also served as vice president under Kubitschek. An affluent landholder, a populist, and an opportunist (he was an admirer of Perón), Goulart increasingly tied his political fortunes to the left. He wooed labor, now under Communist control, and attempted to drive a wedge between the military officers and the enlisted men, whose unionization he encouraged. In an economy marked by spiraling inflation, Goulart's "political ineptness and bombast"[21] led to confrontation with the military and, on 31 March 1964, his overthrow. The democratic experiment was over.

The circumstances of the demise of the Goulart government are also reminiscent of the overthrow of the Allende government and of Allende's suicide, in 1973. In both cases, presidents governed in the interests of their partisans, not of the entire citizenry. In both cases, partisan governance constituted a threat to the institutional viability of the military, who felt they had no alternative but to act. And in both cases, the United States has been blamed for "ending democracy."

I digress to a speaking tour of South America I made early in 1995. In two countries, Bolivia and Brazil, I was told the same funny yet sad joke: "Do you know why they don't have coups d'état (*golpes de estado* in Spanish) in the United States? Because there is no American embassy in the United States!" The joke is sad because it perpetuates the myth of U.S. responsibility for Latin American *golpes* in a region where the typical manner of changing governments has been the *golpe* since long before the United States established embassies. Unquestionably, the United States was directly involved in the 1954 overthrow of the Arbenz government in Guatemala (a country, by the way, that had known little else than dictatorships and *golpes* throughout its history as an independent country). And the Reagan and Bush administrations obviously supported the contras' efforts to overthrow the Sandinista government in the 1980s. But it is a leap, often ideologically driven, from those two cases to the presumption that the United States is responsible for every attempted *golpe* in Latin America in recent history.

In the case of Chile, no scholar or politician has uncovered any shred of evidence of U.S. involvement in the coup d'état, although many in the U.S. Congress and the media went to extremes to do so. I saw Roberto Campos, the economic czar of the government of General Humberto Castelo Branco that succeeded Goulart, during my 1995 trip and asked him whether there was anything to the oft-heard (above all in U.S. academic circles) allegation that the United States engineered Goulart's overthrow. Campos's response (in English): "Rubbish!"

The Military in Power (1964–85)

Brazil's history has been powerfully influenced by what Raymundo Faoro, using a term of Max Weber's, has labeled the "patrimonial state":

> Faoro stresses the role of the central government bureaucracy in managing the interventionist policies of the patrimonial regime. Unlimited by popular influence [because democratic institutions have rarely functioned in Brazil], the *patronato político* (patronal political authority of the public sector) established the parameters within which the social and economic structures of Brazilian society evolved. State capitalism provided the major impetus for economic growth; the limited franchise and the elitist domination of public policy-making by the public functionaries, the clergy, the military, and the landowners assured a hierarchical social system that over time stratified society into two groups: upper and lower.[22]

Faoro's "patrimonial state" is very similar to Hernando de Soto's "mercantilism," a corrupting system of favors and rents through which government and favored elements of the private sector mutually prosper at the expense of nonfavored business people and the consumer.[23] But to blame these institutions for the social injustice and corruption found in Brazil, Peru, and indeed most of Latin America misses the point. What has permitted these societies to evolve such unfair and inefficient institutions? And why have the democratic institutions that would inevitably have precipitated the demise of patrimonialism/mercantilism not been in place? We are again reminded of Tocqueville's wisdom: patrimonialism/mercantilism reflected the values and attitudes of their architects and managers, elitist values and attitudes that stressed the individual and the family over the community; that discouraged the free flow of ideas—and even of broad-based education; that shunned basic concepts of fair play; that saw government as an instrument to advance the narrow interests of a few at the expense of the many.

Roberto Campos, Castello Branco's planning minister, and Finance Minister Octávio Bulhões designed an economic strategy that emphasized fiscal stabilization through increased tax revenues and restraints on government spending; emphasis on education and infrastructure in public investment; export promotion, including exchange-rate adjustments to avoid overvaluing of the cruzeiro; modernization of capital markets; increased savings and investment; and incentives for investment in the poorer areas of Brazil, above all the northeast. The strategy was principally responsible for the high growth rates Brazil experienced between 1968 and 1980, averaging 9 percent annually (between 1968 and 1974, growth averaged 11 percent annually). Exports increased from $1.9 billion in 1969 to $20.1 billion in 1980, driven by manufactured products.[24] A fiscal deficit that amounted to 4.3 percent of GDP in 1963 had declined to 0.3 percent by 1971. Inflation, which had exceeded 100 percent in 1964, declined to about 20 percent during the period 1968–74.[25]

From the vantage of the mid-1990s, Campos looks like a courageous prophet—"an ardent defender of economic liberalism and the market economy, he advocated privatization and Brazil's insertion into the world economy at a time when socialism and pseudo-nationalism thrived."[26] Campos's positive attitudes about the United States alienated him from the Latin American intellectual and political mainstream, and Brazilian leftist-nationalists referred to him as "Bob Fields"—the English translation of "Roberto Campos." Among those who opposed his views then were the leftist nationalist Fernando Henrique Cardoso and the political scientist Helio Jaguaribe.

When I visited Brazil in 1995, I talked not only with Campos, whom I had first met in 1988, but also with Jaguaribe. The extent to which Cardoso and Jaguaribe have shifted their views to the Campos position was apparent from my conversations. They had nothing but the highest praise for Cardoso and his program of stabilization, privatization, and openness to the world market and foreign investment. I pointed out to Jaguaribe the similarity of our conversation to that of my conversation with Campos. He smiled and noted that the gap between the two had narrowed considerably.

Castelo Branco had hoped to transform the traditionally chaotic, personalistic Brazilian political system into a more stable democracy. In 1963, there were thirteen parties, all organized from the top down around leaders, often charismatic. Castelo Branco forced the thirteen to merge into two: the pro-government National Renovating Alliance (Aliança Renovadora Nacional—ARENA) and the Brazilian Democratic Movement (Movimento Democrático Brasileiro—MDB). But he manipulated the electoral system to assure the dominance of ARENA. He chose to step down in 1967, at a moment of considerable unpopularity because of his economic austerity policies, and was succeeded by Marshal Artur da Costa e Silva, one of whose announced goals was "to establish true democracy in Brazil."[27]

Costa e Silva installed a totally new cabinet with Antônio Delfim Netto as his economic czar. Delfim Netto, whose political intuition Campos admired,[28] sustained the stabilization/export/investment policies crafted by Campos. But the austerity program, and particularly the loss of real worker income, provided a rallying point for students, leftist priests (many of them Western European), and labor leaders and led to an urban guerrilla movement, violence, press criticism, and a forceful clampdown by the military on political activity—including the shutting down of Congress—and freedom of expression. Costa e Silva suffered a stroke in August 1969 and was succeeded by General Emílio Garrastazu Médici who, like his predecessors Castelo Branco and Costa e Silva, called for a return to democracy and "free universities, free parties, free trade unions, and a free church."[29]

Unlike his predecessors, Médici had the advantage of the economic boom born of the Campos policies. But leftist violence and terrorism continued, including the kidnapping of U.S. Ambassador C. Burke Elbrick, who was released when fifteen political prisoners were released by the government. Médici responded with repression: torture was employed by the security forces and some activists "disappeared," although only a tiny fraction of the numbers of "disappeared" persons in Argentina and Chile, underscoring the contrast between intransigent, intolerant Hispanic-American culture and "live and let live" Luso-American culture. But the revolutionaries failed to attract mass support, and as the economy, now guided by Mario Simonsen, roared ahead, Médici became increasingly popular, with the support of 90 percent of the population by one estimate.[30]

Médici handpicked his successor, General Ernesto Geisel, of German Lutheran antecedence, who took office in March 1974. He had the bad luck to be on the receiving end of the first OPEC oil "shock," which doubled Brazil's bill for imported oil from $6.2 billion in 1973 to $12.6 billion in 1974. Geisel faced two options: to impose austerity or to borrow, chiefly from abroad. The heir of the Castelo Branco, Costa e Silva, and Médici "miracle," Geisel was not disposed to retrench, and he opted for the borrowing strategy, as did Argentina and subsequently oil-exporter Mexico, sowing the seeds of the debt crisis of the following decade. This was the moment when the East Asian "dragons," who imported virtually all their oil, chose to tighten their belts, with reduced (but still substantial) growth for a few years, followed by a return to the astonishingly high (8–10 percent annually) growth rates they have enjoyed since the mid-1960s—with no significant additional indebtedness. Brazil's gross debt was $12.5 billion in 1973, $98 billion in 1986.[31]

Recall from chapter 3 my 1995 conversation with Uruguayan Senator Alberto Couriel about the causes of Latin America's "lost" economic decade, the 1980s. Couriel initially blamed the foreign banks for the debt crisis. When I reminded him how the East Asians had managed the oil shocks, he extended the blame to Latin American policy makers. But the principal culprit, not often so-identified in Latin America, perhaps out of Third World loyalty, was OPEC and the skyrocketing price of oil.

Geisel's administration veered away from the authoritarianism of his predecessors toward what was then called "decompression" and subsequently "opening" (abertura). He attempted a reconciliation with the Church, several of whose leaders were Liberation Theology activists, and whose "base communities" had become a major political force. He substantially ended torture and press censorship, and he oversaw clean congressional elections, which the opposition MDB won. The press, the bar association, the Church, labor, and intellectuals pressed their demands for greater social justice and political participation.

Geisel also handpicked his successor, General João Baptista Figueiredo, former chief of intelligence, who was inaugurated early in

1979—the year of the second oil shock and dramatic increases in world market interest rates—with signs that the economy was in trouble. Simonsen resigned as planning minister when his austerity plan was rejected. He was replaced by Delfim Netto, who had no choice but to devalue the *cruzeiro* substantially, adding further inflationary pressures. Inflation exceeded 100 percent in 1980, 200 percent in 1983 and 1984.

The New Republic and the New Fernando Henrique Cardoso

In the face of economic hard times, Figueiredo continued and expanded on the Geisel *abertura* policies. ARENA, the party supporting the military, and the opposition MDB were disbanded, and Brazilian politics again fragmented into numerous smaller parties built around one leader. Despite strong pressures for direct election of the next president, including mass demonstrations in several cities, left-of-center Tancredo Neves was selected by the electoral college in 1984. The military was unhappy with the results but let them stand, and the New Republic was born. Of the constitution that was subsequently passed by the Congress sitting as a Constituent Assembly, Riordan Roett says, "The process was a tortured one, with many elements of the populist-nationalist position written into the document. The final product . . . not only is cumbersome but also severely constrains rational decision making."[32]

Neves became ill just before his inauguration and died soon thereafter. His vice president, José Sarney, thus became the first civilian to lead the country since 1964.

Sarney made one attempt to stem inflation—the Cruzado Plan, a stabilization program that looked promising in its early months and then collapsed. In 1987, the Sarney government declared a moratorium on debt payments, the effect of which was to isolate Brazil from other Latin American debtors like Argentina and Mexico. Inflation became hyperinflation.

Fernando Collor de Mello defeated the candidate of the left, the labor leader Luis Inácio da Silva ("Lula"), in the 1989 elections. Collor, who had campaigned on a platform of economic stabilization and liberal market reforms, assumed the presidency in March 1990 with inflation exceeding 1,000 percent annually. His efforts to control inflation were unsuccessful and stifling of growth, and the intense odor of corruption in his administration led to impeachment proceedings and his removal from office. Vice President Itamar Franco took over as interim president in October 1992. After firing three other finance ministers, Franco shifted Foreign Minister Fernando Henrique Cardoso to finance in May 1993 to develop a stabilization program. The program called for major cuts in government spending, aggressive tax collection, and reduction of the indebtedness of state governments to the federal government, at the same time pushing economic *abertura*, the free market, and privatization. In part because of the MERCOSUL* integration scheme that had brought Brazil and Argentina (and Paraguay and Uruguay) into a dynamic new trade relationship in 1991, the Brazilian economy was again growing, but it was not until 1994 that the stabilization program took hold. Inflation dropped precipitously, and Cardoso rode the wave of price stability to defeat Lula easily in the October 1994 elections.

The "new" Fernando Henrique Cardoso has jettisoned his earlier socialist, "dependency" ideology and is now fully committed to the liberal model: a free economy open to the world market and foreign investment, reduced tariff protection, and privatization of state enterprises. Cardoso has sought good relations with the United States, despite the traditional anti-American nationalism of *Itamaraty*, Brazil's powerful foreign ministry.[†] Cardoso has also singled out inequitable distribution of income and opportunity as a high-priority target, giving special attention to education. Driven by new incentives and foreign investment, the economy was booming—at an annual rate of 10 percent—in the first quarter of 1995. Cardoso's problems have been complicated by the collapse of the Mexican peso, which the Brazilian left blames on the "neoliberal" policies that Cardoso is pursuing. The "Tequila effect" has contributed to balance-of-payments pressures that have resulted in selective tariff increases and quantitative limits on imports (for example, automobiles from Argentina). But progress has been made on privatization (the state enterprises are a major contributor to fiscal deficits), and *The Economist*'s mid-1995 assessment of the Brazilian economy is bullish.[33]

---

*The Spanish equivalent is "MERCOSUR."

†The extent of *Itamaraty*'s influence is apparent from its traditional veto power over the naming of the foreign minister.

WHITHER BRAZIL?

What can we conclude about the prospects of a country whose rich resource endowment and impressive sustained economic growth—often in the face of poor economic policies—contrast with extreme social injustice and sluggish development of democratic institutions? Do recent favorable economic and political developments suggest that Brazil is finally within reach of its promising future?

President Cardoso does not lead a mature democracy. Brazil is still a familistic society without any real tradition of civic culture. The fragmented political parties are rarely more than an extension of charismatic personalities and, in the absence of an ideological or philosophical binder, are intrinsically unstable. The Brazilian sociologist Maria Lucia Victor Barbosa notes a phenomenon common to almost all of Latin America: "In Brazil, democracy is confused with elections."[34] Other elements normally associated with modern pluralistic systems, for example, due process in the judicial system, intermediating associations between government and the individual, civilian control of the military, equality of opportunity, are at best incipient in Brazil. Victor Barbosa goes on to observe, "democracy presupposes . . . equality of opportunity that begins with the satisfaction of basic human needs, a condition clearly not achieved by Brazil, an extremely unequal society where economic underdevelopment coincides, as inevitably it must, with political underdevelopment."[35] A foreign observer described the Brazilian legislature to me as "typically Third World." It recently voted itself a thirteenth, fourteenth, and fifteenth month of annual salary.

Victor Barbosa concludes that Brazilian underdevelopment is rooted in Luso-Brazilian culture, a view shared by Roberto Campos.[36] He agrees with Faoro's thesis that patrimonialism is deeply ingrained in the Brazilian psyche and that it is an obstacle to progress in part because it enshrines status rather than achievement and merit: "This society doesn't believe in competition because of the Iberian patrimonial, mercantilist tradition, strengthened by the Church's prejudice against profit. The market psychology has not yet caught on." There is still a strong current of statism in Brazil, and that includes members of Cardoso's government, Planning Minister and presidential aspirant José Serra among them in the view of some. On the other hand, the trauma with hyperinflation is deeply etched in the minds of most Brazilians, as was apparent from Cardoso's surge in popularity when his stabilization program worked.

Campos is also concerned about population growth, currently about 2 percent per year, and pervasive corruption, much of which has to do with the patrimonial public-sector traditions: "Sixty percent of the scandals are related to government contracting; 20 percent are due to over-regulation; and 20 percent can be attributed to the 'hero without morals' that Brazilians so admire."

But Campos is encouraged by the existence of a large pool of entrepreneurs in Brazil, in contrast to Argentina, where, he believes, Perón killed off the entrepreneurial spirit, an opinion shared by Jaguaribe.[37] If MERCOSUL defies the tradition of failed integration schemes in Latin America (see chapter 9), it could add an important impetus to Brazil's economic performance. And Campos is generally hopeful about Brazil's future, in part because of Brazilian entrepreneurship, in part because he is convinced that Cardoso is moving purposefully in the right direction. Campos and Jaguaribe, and the influential Brazilian economist Dionisio Dias Carneiro,[38] also agree on the crucial role of privatization of state enterprises as a means of achieving fiscal stability and lower interest rates.

Campos views the burgeoning Protestant movement in Brazil as a positive factor, among other reasons because it is promoting family planning and contraception, in contrast to the Catholic Church. The growth of Protestantism in Brazil has been, to use David Martin's word, "dramatic."[39] The initial impetus came from European, particularly German Lutheran, immigrants, of which General Geisel's family is an example, and Presbyterian and Baptist immigrants from the U.S. South after the Civil War. But by the mid-twentieth century, Pentecostal sects had become dominant in a wave of conversions from Catholicism that has brought the number of Protestants to about one-fifth of Brazil's total population today. "Protestants [are] marked out by their dislike of alcohol, promiscuity, and dancing, and by their attachment to work and social mobility," notes Martin.[40]

While some of the converts had already achieved middle-class status, many more were poor, and many were black. "To the black, joining any Protestant denomination is in itself an advance: A cultural advance because Protestantism is the religion of the book and therefore of literate people; it is the religion of the United States, of a world power. A social advance because on every level the Protestant tends to rise and enter the middle class."[41] I have yet to see data that confirm this upward mobility. But I would be surprised if, in due course, such data do not appear.

ON BALANCE

What is the net of this mix of liabilities and assets, of centrifugal and centripetal forces? Much depends on the success of the Cardoso program. If the stabilization program holds, which depends much on the success of the privatization initiatives and continued rationalization of the federal government's financial relationships with the states, and if inflation is curbed during the balance of his term, then the odds of long-term stability and growth will improve measurably. But this will not be easy, particularly with an immature, fractious legislature and the persistence of influential statist and nationalist forces in the society, to say nothing of the extreme social inequities that are likely, at least in his first years in power, to defy President Cardoso's reform programs.

To some extent, Cardoso's—and Brazil's—success depends on favorable conditions in the world economy. Another disaster of the proportions of the 1994–95 collapse of the Mexican peso could be lethal for Brazil's aspirations, since foreign capital and markets have an increasingly important role in its economic growth.

One cannot discard the nightmare scenario in which political pressures or external economic factors force the scrapping of the stabilization program, inflation reappears, the *real* steadily loses its value, the lower classes are hurt disproportionately, demonstrations and violence multiply, and the military return to power.

But it seems to me that the net of the positive and negative factors should leave one hopeful, if not optimistic, that Fernando Henrique Cardoso's administration will prove to be the turning point in Brazil's history. Brazil's intrinsic economic dynamism, magnified by good policies, should create a larger pie during Cardoso's four years, and widespread awareness of extreme social injustice in Brazil is likely to translate into some progress toward its correction. Even if MERCOSUL follows other, earlier Latin American integration schemes into oblivion, the opening up of the Brazilian economy is likely to lead to increased competitiveness for a country that has emphasized exports longer than any other in Latin America. And in the long run, Brazil, not Mexico, may prove to be the key to the success of NAFTA and full integration of the economies of the Western Hemisphere.

I, like Francis Fukuyama, have argued that economic pluralism will inevitably tow political pluralism in its wake.[42] Some may argue that the Brazilian case demonstrates the wrongness of that view, since Brazil has experienced rapid sustained growth without achieving either social justice or sustained political pluralism. But we must be mindful that Brazil's economic dynamism has occurred until recent years within a cozy government-business patrimonial system that substantially denied access to outsiders—far from open and pluralistic—and, more broadly, within an individualistic, familistic culture. Prosperity, the free market, the decline of statism, conscious efforts by the political and intellectual leadership to transform Brazilian culture, increased priority for education (including civic education), and the rise of Protestantism may in time create a civic culture and permanently transform the political landscape. But, in the case of Brazil, at least another decade must pass before one can be confident about the irreversibility of democracy.

7

The Chilean Miracle: Policies, Culture, or Both?

Since the mid-1980s, in the wake of the introduction of the free-market, export-promotion policies of a group of neoclassical economists often referred to as the "Chicago boys,"* the Chilean economy has grown steadily at an average of 6 percent annually, reaching an East Asian pace of 10 percent in 1992. The "Tequila effect" of the collapse of the Mexican peso at the end of 1994 gave pause to the Argentine and Brazilian economies, but the Chilean economy scarcely missed a beat; ECLAC's early estimates are for 8 percent growth in 1995. Most observers see nothing short of a major political crisis that could stem Chile's growth for the foreseeable future.

In 1989, Chile returned to democracy after the sixteen-year Pinochet military dictatorship. Prior to the victory of Salvador Allende in 1970, Chile was generally considered, along with Costa Rica and Uruguay, an atypically democratic Latin American country. Democracy appears to have been substantially reconsolidated during the administration of Christian Democrat Patricio Aylwin (1990–94) and Eduardo Frei Ruiz-Tagle (1994–). But civilian control of the military is not complete, as the world was reminded when the generals resisted the 1995 Supreme Court upholding of the conviction of General Manuel Contreras and Colonel Pedro Espinoza in the 1976 assassination in Washington of Orlando Letelier, a supporter of Salvador Allende. (Both were subsequently incarcerated in a jail built especially for them.) The military problem notwithstanding, it is clear that Chile has substantially put behind it the intolerance, polarization, and hostility of

*Several of the Pinochet economic advisers (for example, Sergio de Castro, Sergio de la Cuadra, Alvaro Donoso, Miguel Kast, Juan Carlos Méndez, Cristian Larroulet, and Rolf Luders) did graduate work at the University of Chicago.

the Allende years (1970–73) and the Pinochet dictatorship (1973–89) and returned to the civility, at least by Latin American standards, that has historically characterized it.

It is only with respect to income distribution that Chile today looks like a typical Latin American country: in 1992, Chile's most affluent 20 percent of the population accounted for 60 percent of national income, its top 10 percent for almost 46 percent, just slightly more equitable than Guatemala and Honduras.[1]

The Chilean case provokes four key questions:

1. What explains Chile's atypically democratic and relatively peaceful (by Latin American standards) history?
2. What explains Chile's extremely inequitable income distribution?
3. What does the Chile case tell us about the relationship between economic and political development?
4. Does the Chilean miracle demonstrate that, at least with respect to economic development, culture is irrelevant, and that good economic policies can assure success without reference to the culture within which they operate?

But before we turn to those questions, we need to take a look at Chile's geography and history.

AN ISOLATED, RICH COUNTRY

In the geographical sense, Chile may be the most peculiar-looking country in the world. It is more than 2,600 miles from north to south, almost as wide as the United States is from east to west. That is roughly the same, both in distance and terrain, as the span from Baja California, to Alaska. But as long as it is, Chile is comparably skinny: its widest east-west dimension is about 200 miles; at Santiago, slightly north of the middle of the country, the distance between the Andean border with Argentina and the Pacific is about 100 miles. Its vast north-south span notwithstanding, Chile is only slightly larger than Texas in area.

About 80 percent of Chile is in the temperate zone. The country stretches from the Atacama Desert and the Peruvian border in the north to Tierra del Fuego and Cape Horn in the south, substantially closer to Antarctica than the southern reaches of Africa and Australia/New Zealand. Its southern coast is similar to the coast of Alaska, glaciers and all. The Andes form most of its eastern border, which is shared briefly with Bolivia and then, for about 2,000 miles, with Argentina. The Andes present the most rugged terrain in the Western Hemisphere (Mount Aconcagua, in Argentina near the Chilean border, rises to 22,831 feet and is the loftiest in the Hemisphere), and their visibility through much of the narrow strip of land that is Chile contributes to a strong feeling of isolation.

Chile is rich in mineral resources, and its agricultural resources should be sufficient to satisfy national consumption and permit substantial export of high-value fruits and vegetables. Chile is among the world's largest exporters of copper, and it dominated the world nitrate market during the last decades of the nineteenth century and the first decades of the twentieth. Its climate is mostly temperate. Virtually any agricultural product or livestock can be grown in the many microclimates found in Chile's 38 degrees of latitude. And it is blessed by the coincidence of its growing season with winter in the vast European, North American, and East Asian markets for fresh fruits and vegetables. Only about 7 percent of its land is available for crop production and 20 percent for pasture, although its forestry resources (about 17.5 million acres) are extensive—and extensively exploited.[2] The rest is largely the rugged Andean region and the northern desert. For comparison, more than half of Argentina, which is almost four times larger than Chile, is available for crop production.[3]

Chile's early colonial history is not notably different from that of most other Latin American countries. The Spanish colony was founded by some of the same conquistadors who played a key role in the subjugation of Peru, Diego de Almagro and Pedro de Valdivia most notably among them. The first colonists were not peaceful permanent settlers like the atypical colonists of Costa Rica. They were, like their counterparts in Mexico and Peru, soldiers of fortune seeking wealth in gold and Indians—and ultimately a life of prosperous leisure in Spain. They were predominantly from Extremadura, Castille, and Andalucía, forged in the reconquest of Spain from the Moors, disdainful of agriculture and commerce.

The conquistadors did not find much in the way of precious metals. What they did find were the warlike, resolute, and resourceful

Araucanian Indians. Chile's history through the seventeenth century was dominated by continuing conflict with the Araucanians, a southern tribe of which, the Mapuches, never surrendered and maintained physical control of a good part of the southern half of the country until it was essentially ceded to them as a reservation in 1866. A combination of Chile's poor precious metal endowment and the problem of subduing the Araucanians led to neglect by the motherland, although the array of Spanish colonial institutions in Chile was similar to that elsewhere in the empire. The *encomienda*, the award of large tracts of land and the Indians thereon (essentially in slavery) to prominent Spaniards, established land tenure and social patterns—a landed aristocracy and a lot of poor agricultural workers—that endured well into the twentieth century.

Chile's reputation for stability and civility began to develop after independence in 1818, although the eighteenth century had witnessed a transition from the instability and bloodshed of the wars against the Araucanians to the consolidation of large-scale ranching and farming. Bernardo O'Higgins led the battle for independence and acted as an enlightened dictator from 1817 to 1823.* But civilian government followed. After several years of rule, the Liberal Party was ousted by force in 1830 by Diego Portales and the Conservatives, who in 1833 promulgated a durable constitution, "based on a strong presidency, strictly centralized administration, and the wholesale fixing of elections, a practice which lasted until 1891."[4] (We are reminded of politics at the same time in neighboring Argentina.) In the last decades of this period of Conservative domination, the Liberals were permitted access by the Conservatives, the former ultimately displacing the latter as the dominant party. By this time, urban middle sectors were emerging, a process nurtured in part by the University of Chile, which was established in 1842. (Its first rector was the renowned Venezuelan jurist Andrés Bello.) Chileans took pride in these signs of political and social progress and came to regard their country as the "model republic" of the region—a view widely shared abroad.[5]

---

*O'Higgins's father, Ambrosio, was an Irishman who rose through the ranks of the Spanish colonial bureaucracy to become captain general of Chile and viceroy of Peru. The younger O'Higgins completed his studies in England, where he was befriended by Francisco de Miranda, whose notes on the contrast between the post-independence United States and pre-independence Latin America were cited in chapter 3.

Chile was successful in the nineteenth century in two other respects: in warfare against its neighbors and in economic development. It defeated the Peruvian-Bolivian Confederation in 1839 and was victorious against the same two foes in the War of the Pacific, which lasted from 1879 to 1883 and in which "a sequence of brilliant campaigns gave the country total victory, a definite superiority complex, and possession of the Peruvian and Bolivian deserts, rich in nitrate, for which there was growing demand abroad as fertilizer."[6]

Chile had established itself as an important exporter of agricultural products earlier in the nineteenth century. It had shipped substantial quantities of wheat to California and Australia during their gold rushes. The use of nitrates in fertilizer until the advent of synthetic nitrates about 1930 meant vast export income for Chile, as did its rich endowment in copper. Although the mining and export of nitrate and copper were principally in the hands of foreigners, particularly the British and Americans, Chileans were noted for their entrepreneurship in the Southern Cone, and they provided a considerable impetus to the growth of the Argentine economy as well as their own.[7]

Chile thus experienced a remarkable transformation in the nineteenth century. Its evolution toward political pluralism was more rapid than that of any other South American country, including Argentina and Uruguay. It displayed an uncommon economic dynamism. Yet its social structure continued to be dominated by a landed aristocracy, on the one hand, and a rural proletariat, on the other.

THE BASQUES—AND OTHER IMMIGRANTS

How can one explain this transformation? Clearly, several factors are relevant, including rich resource endowment, a favorable climate, and a geographic position at once remote and advantageous. But a principal explanation for Chile's progress, I believe, is immigration from Europe, above all of the Basques:

> Between 1701 and 1810, some 24,000 immigrants arrived in Chile from Spain [about doubling the number of Spaniards] and forty-five percent of these came from Navarre [a province just east of the Basque Country, whose people share many Basque traditions] and the Basque provinces. Everyone agrees on the extraordinary

impact these . . . groups had, including [the renowned Basque writer] Miguel de Unamuno who called Chile along with the Jesuit order the two great creations of the Basque people. Their road to economic success and social prominence ran from commerce to the countryside to office. . . . Luis Thayer Ojeda, one of the most accomplished of many Chilean genealogists, thought that "three-fourths of the distinguished personages of nineteenth-century Chile were of Basque descent."[8]

Today, the Basque impact is diluted by intermarriage, immigration from other parts of Europe, and modernization more generally. But Basque-surname families are still disproportionately prosperous and influential, and in the nineteenth century they played a premier role in Chile's economic and political development.

The Basque provinces, on the Bay of Biscay near the French border, have long been considered, along with Catalunya, the most progressive, prosperous, and democratic regions of Spain. Their entrepreneurial tradition contributed to a degree of industrialization in the nineteenth century that far exceeded that of the rest of Spain. Before industrialization, their land-tenure patterns were dominated by small farms, in contrast to the plantation—*latifundio*—patterns in most of Spain. The earliest successful experiments in Spain with the cooperative form of organizing private enterprises occurred in Mondragón, near Bilbao, the capital of the Basque province of Vizcaya. The Basques took advantage of their head start in industrialization to move quickly and influentially into finance, a sector where they are highly influential today.

It is true that Basque industrialization was stimulated by the British, who found near Bilbao rich deposits of the red hematite ore they needed for Bessemer steel production in the middle of the nineteenth century. But long before that, the Basques had earned a reputation for industriousness and creativity.

François Depons, a Frenchman who lived in Caracas for some two decades at the turn of the nineteenth century, described economic life in Spain's Venezuelan colony in a book published in 1806.[9] Depons noted that

plantation owners . . . ordinarily live in the cities . . . where expenditures . . . reflect the plantation's production, but are calculated in accordance with the most fertile and abundant year. Consequently, it is only exceptionally that income exceeds spending, and rather than economizing to improve the crops, they load themselves up with debts and attribute those debts to bad weather and defective laws, when they are due only to the lack of order among the owners. . . . The plantation owner who visits his estates once a year is satisfied that he has taken care of his interests. He has often not even informed himself on the work being done on his plantation. . . . A country which holds agriculture in such contempt does not deserve the favors of nature.[10]

Depons then notes some exceptions to this pattern of extravagance and waste:

As proof of the advantages agriculture would reap if the owners lived on the estates, suffice it to observe the farms which prosper, those which sustain themselves . . . it will be noted that [they] are managed by their owners, who channel all their ambition into increasing their income and take pride in being farmers; in general those who act in this way are Basques.[11]

He also notes a parallel pattern in the city, including the success of a large company "due to their effective administrators, who always came from the Basque provinces, which seems to be the refuge for good customs."[12] In breaking down the population of Caracas, he notes:

[A] second class of Europeans resident in Caracas is comprised of those who came here to engage in industry or make their fortune. Almost all are from the Basque provinces or Catalonia. Both are equally industrious, but the Basques, without exhausting themselves as much, manage their businesses better. Willing to take economic risks and perseverant in agriculture, they tend to be more successful than the Catalonians. . . . The Basque is never intimidated by the size or the risk of a business proposition. He trusts even in chance.[13]

Other European immigrants also played a vastly disproportionate role in Chile's economic development. Tiny by comparison with the immigrant flow into Argentina (Markos Mamalakis notes that immigrants accounted for but 2 percent of Chile's 1950 population),[14] European immigrants were instrumental in the creation of the textile, glass, ceramics, printing, chemical, paper, metallurgy, pharmaceutical, and beer industries, as well as in mining, navigation, and railroading.* Immigrants from the Middle East, particularly the Lebanese, were also highly successful. The pattern of immigrant entrepreneurship evokes Brazil's experience, as does Mamalakis's conclusion that, "in the economic development of Chile, immigration has played a role vastly superior to that suggested by its modest proportions."[15]

FROM PRESIDENTIALISM TO PARLIAMENTARIANISM TO PRESIDENTIALISM

Toward the end of the nineteenth century, Chilean society was strained by resentment of Santiago in the provinces, disputes over the role of the Church, and the emergence of new wealth in the north. Growing political tolerance during the second half of the nineteenth century evolved into conflict between those committed to a strong presidency and those who believed in a dominant legislature. José Manuel Balmaceda's strong presidency ended in 1891 in civil war and his suicide, and power shifted to the congress for more than three decades, until 1924. Arturo Alessandri, a prominent "parliamentary" politician, who was elected to the presidency in 1920 on an ambitious reform platform and who pushed through a new constitution in 1925 that endured until 1973, was first ousted, then restored to power by the military, then replaced by Colonel Carlos Ibañez, who presided as a mildly repressive dictator from 1927 to 1931. After a brief chaotic period, aggravated by the Depression, during which a socialist republic was proclaimed, Alessandri was reelected, inaugurating a new period of presidentialism that lasted forty years.

It was during these years that significant numbers of conversions from Catholicism to Protestantism began. "In Chile, much of this growth has been associated with a Pentecostal breakaway . . . from the Methodist Church. From 1930 to 1960 this church alone grew from 54,000 to 425,000. From 1930 onwards Chilean Protestantism rapidly expanded as a whole. . . . The current [1990] Protestant population of Chile is certainly well over a million and variously estimated at between 15 and 20 percent of the total."[16] As elsewhere in Latin

---

*The American Henry Meiggs was one of the railroad pioneers. His nephew, Minor Keith, built the railroad from Costa Rica's Atlantic Coast to San José, used it to promote banana production, and was one of the founders of the United Fruit Company (see p. 95).

America, Chilean Protestants have a reputation for sobriety, hard work, family stability, and upward mobility.

Alessandri was succeeded in 1938 by Popular Front candidate Pedro Aguirre Cerda, whose Radical Party stood to the right of its two allies, the Communists and the Socialists, the most dynamic Marxist parties in Latin America. The Radicals remained in power until 1952, when the electorate, disenchanted with party politics and chronic inflation, turned to now-General Ibañez. His disappointing term was followed by the election of Alessandri's son Jorge, the candidate of the right, in 1958.

The Chilean left, the two principal parties being the Socialists and their usually more moderate partners, the Communists, continued as a major factor in Chilean politics and benefited from both the skewed pattern of distribution of income, land, wealth, and opportunity, and the expansion of the franchise: women were enfranchised in 1949, and the number of voters increased from about half a million in 1938 to 3.6 million in 1973. Nonetheless, when the right threw its support to the centrist Christian Democrat candidate, Eduardo Frei, in 1964, Frei won easily.

The two goals of Frei's ambitious "Revolution in Liberty" were accelerated economic development and greater social justice, which aligned it with John F. Kennedy's Alliance for Progress, of which Chile became a showcase. Frei initiated an ambitious land-reform program and invested heavily in education and housing. He "Chileanized" the American-owned copper companies by taking majority control of them, an initiative that was reluctantly accepted by the copper companies but applauded by many in Washington. While they alienated the right, these reforms did not satisfy the left, setting the stage for the 1970 elections that were to prove so costly to Chile.

ECONOMIC PERFORMANCE

In 1900, according to Angus Maddison, Chile, with a GDP per capita of $956 in 1980 dollars, was quite prosperous by Latin American standards as a result of fairly rapid growth during the nineteenth century. Chile's per capita GDP was more than twice that of Brazil, half again greater than Colombia, Mexico, and Peru, and three-quarters that of Argentina. The picture in 1987 had changed dramatically: Brazil's $3,417 per capita was the highest, yet Chile had overtaken Argentina.[17]

Between 1900 and 1987, the Chilean economy grew at an average 3.2 percent annually, the lowest of the six Latin American countries tracked by Angus Maddison (also including Argentina, Brazil, Colombia, Mexico, and Peru). Chile's population growth rate, at 1.7 percent, was the slowest of the six, but GDP per capita grew only 1.5 percent annually, compared with Brazil's 2.4 percent (and Argentina's 1.1 percent). Interestingly, during the period 1900–1950, with Chile's growth mainly export-driven, its per capita GDP growth (1.8 percent) was the same as Brazil's. During the period 1950–87, with Chile's economic policies stressing import substitution and state involvement in the economy during much of the period, its per capita GDP grew at 1 percent, while Brazil's grew at 3.2 percent, mostly the result of export expansion.[18]

Chile's growth in the nineteenth century was fueled first by agriculture and then by nitrate and copper mining. The latter two industries were largely in the hands of the British and the Americans, but Chile received a very substantial income from them on which the government and private sector came to depend. Some blamed the bonanza for "our economic inferiority," to use the title of Francisco Encina's popular 1913 jeremiad. Only a small part of the income was channeled to investment: the Chilean economist Patricio Meller notes that "for several years during the nitrate boom, imports of consumption goods such as wine, jewels, cloth, and perfumes were almost twice as large as imports of industrial and agricultural machinery."[19] (Imports were facilitated by an overvalued exchange rate.) Agriculture was increasingly neglected, and Chile began to import food. Mamalakis observes, "Massive riches generated by nitrate, copper, and even agriculture were used to support consumption-facilitating rather than investment- or production-promoting services. . . . What Chile has always needed most—a revolution in capital formation—did not occur and was not attempted between 1930 and 1973."[20] And that notwithstanding the creation in 1939 of the Chilean Development Corporation (CORFO), which "was given the Promethean task of bringing to Chile the secret fire that the industrial demigods of the developed nations had so successfully guarded in achieving self-propelled growth."[21] By 1974, CORFO was bankrupt.

During the 1960s, economic growth, facilitated by a crawling peg exchange rate system, averaged 5 percent, which, combined with a population growth rate of 2.4 percent, meant a per capita growth of 2.6 percent, slightly above the Alliance for Progress target of 2.5 percent. By the end of that decade, Brazil—not to mention the East Asian dragons—was growing at about 10 percent. But Brazil, and the dragons, was promoting exports to the world market, while Chile, the seat of the Economic Commission for Latin America (ECLA-CEPAL), was pursuing Prebisch's recipe of import substitution and heavy state involvement in the economy. While respectable, a 5 percent growth rate was insufficient to transform Chile the way 10 percent rates were transforming Korea, Taiwan, Hong Kong, and Singapore. And Chilean society resisted the social justice programs of the Christian Democrats, while the East Asian societies became increasingly equitable.

THE ALLENDE DEBACLE

There are several parallels between Spain in the 1930s and Chile in the 1970s. Both societies were highly inequitable, a condition that nurtured a strong and militant left. Chile had developed and benefited from a civic culture, but its institutions were unable to withstand a revolutionary program promoted by a government that saw itself responsible only to its own partisans, not to the broader society—much as did Spain's leftist government during the Red Biennium (1931–33) and again in 1936. The Chilean military, strongly influenced by Prussian traditions, were supposed to be among the most professional in Latin America. But when they saw their institution threatened, they behaved like the Spanish military, who had traditionally viewed themselves as above the law, as the ultimate arbiter of politics. In Spain, the consequence was a raging civil war, culminating in the Franco dictatorship that lasted almost forty years. In Chile, the consequence was what Mamalakis describes as "the disguised but relentless 1970–73 civil war,"[22] culminating in the Pinochet dictatorship, which lasted sixteen years.

The civil wars (if the reader will accept Mamalakis's characterization) and the ensuing dictatorships, as I argued in chapter 3, traumatized both societies and ultimately facilitated a healing process that attenuated the tendencies toward polarization, confrontation, and intolerance common to most Hispanic countries, a healing that in turn facilitated Spain's rapid transition to democracy after Franco's death in 1975 and Chile's return to democracy after the 1988 plebiscite.

The alienation of the right and the failure of the Frei program to coopt significant elements of the left led to Allende's victory with 36.6 percent of the vote. Conservative ex-president Jorge Alessandri ran second, with 35.2 percent, the left-wing Christian Democrat Radomiro Tomic third, with 28.1 percent. Of Allende's three years in power, Mark Falcoff observes: "Most of the issues which arose during the Allende years had long been debated in Chile, and were the object of comprehensive and far-reaching reforms. What was new after 1970 was the notion that the mere act of electing a Marxist president suddenly and magically released the country from the political and economic [and I would add cultural] constraints which had shaped policy outcomes in the past."[23]

The Allende government quickly became the darling of the academic/foundation community in the United States, much as Nicaragua's Sandinistas would nine years later. Here was a government committed to a revolutionary program of social justice, a redistributing of wealth and opportunity from the rich to the poor, in a patently unjust society. Here was a government that thumbed its nose at the United States (Allende's people, as well as many more moderate Chileans, were totally committed to dependency theory), among other measures by completing the expropriation of the American copper companies. And here was a government that was on the receiving end of some nasty policies contrived by the cold war paranoids, Richard Nixon and Henry Kissinger, and U.S. business interests in Chile (a criticism not without foundation).*

The Allende socialist revolution combined a sweeping agrarian reform and nationalization of private enterprises (150 formerly private industries were nationalized in 1971) with a broad array of social programs: day-care centers, school lunch programs, health and welfare services, subsidized housing, expanded educational opportunities for the poor. Except for the nationalizations, these are measures that centrists could easily support, assuming that the economy could also support them.

---

*My view at the time was, and to this day is, that U.S. policy toward Chile during the first six months of the Allende government was ill-advised and counterproductive. But those policies became more moderate thereafter, mainly as a consequence of the increasing influence of career people in the State Department, the liberal Deputy Assistant Secretary of State John Hugh Crimmins (see chapter 6) prominently among them.

But Allende's expansionary economic policies, consistent with the blindness of Marxist theory to practical questions of incentives, investment, markets, competitiveness, and management, focused on consumption and short-term political gain, above all through large wage increases, particularly for the lowest-paid workers. Drawing down on the substantial foreign exchange reserves inherited from Frei helped Allende achieve a growth rate above 7 percent in 1971, and while consumption was the principal engine of the growth, there was also a production response. But the government was forced to resort increasingly to the printing press as the economy began to falter in 1972. Investment plunged in the antibusiness climate, and foreign exchange reserves ran out. Inflation exceeded 150 percent in a stagnant economy in 1972, 500 percent in a declining economy in 1973.

Allende's economic difficulties were in small part the consequence of the drying up of U.S. aid as well as sharp reductions in lending by the World Bank and the Inter-American Development Bank, influenced by the United States. But his expansionary policies effectively destroyed Chile's creditworthiness, and it is unlikely, in the wake, for example, of the expropriation of the U.S. copper companies, the warmth of Allende's relationship with Fidel Castro, and his anti-American rhetoric, that the U.S. Congress would have endorsed continued lending to Chile even if the executive branch were so disposed. Moreover, as Falcoff observes, "[i]n rapid order New York and Washington were replaced by [probably to their subsequent regret] Moscow, Peking, Bucharest, East Berlin, and Pyongyang, as well as Paris, Tokyo, Sydney, Ottawa, Buenos Aires, Mexico City, Madrid, Brussels, Stockholm, Amsterdam and Helsinki."[24]

I digress briefly to the relationship of the United States with Sandinista Nicaragua, particularly during the first two years of the Sandinista revolution, 1979–81. Allende's three years coincided with the Nixon administration. The Sandinistas came to power toward the end of the Carter administration, which believed—correctly, in my view—that the hostility with which Allende had been treated at the outset by Nixon was both wrong and unwise. One consequence was a Carter policy of doing everything possible to help the Sandinistas, in the hope that a constructive relationship could be built with a left-wing Latin American government. We were the single largest source of financial, food, and technical aid (for which, by the way, I as

USAID director was responsible) during the first eighteen months. The Sandinistas then made it impossible for us to continue by providing arms and other assistance to the Salvadoran guerrillas, consistent with the announced Sandinista doctrine that sooner or later they would have to confront the ultimate "enemy of humanity . . . el Yanqui."*

We learned something from the Allende episode that influenced our policy. But the Sandinistas didn't, at least with respect to economics. They followed Allende's path to monetary expansion, inflation, contraction of investment, and, inevitably, economic decline. In the middle of 1980, with an economic disaster looming, we offered to provide the Sandinistas with the best American economic expertise available. They declined and chose instead a team of Bulgarians. (The World Bank today lists Bulgaria as a lower-middle-income country, at about the same level of per capita GDP as Guatemala.)[25]

Allende's policies polarized and ultimately shattered the imperfect structure of Chilean pluralism without offering a viable substitute. As Falcoff concludes,

> there *was* no Chilean road to socialism, in the sense that there never was a socialist political majority. . . . There *was* a Chilean road to soak-the-rich populism . . . unfortunately, it did not and could not work in economic terms. At best it could make life extremely difficult for Chilean capitalism, but a capitalism rendered inoperable does not ineluctably yield to a functioning alternative.[26]

Allende probably died by his own hand,[27] an ironically appropriate metaphor for that tragic moment in Chilean history. Many Chilean and American intellectuals have tried to blame the United States for his overthrow, a hypothesis that Senator Frank Church tried unsuccessfully to prove in subsequent Senate hearings. While a number of individuals and institutions played a role in the demise of Salvador Allende—and democracy—in Chile, the principal architect of that tragedy was Allende himself.

---

*The Sandinista anthem contains the words, "*Lucharemos contra el Yanqui, enemigo de la humanidad*" ("We shall fight against the Yankee, enemy of humanity"). We repeatedly tried to persuade the Sandinista leaders to change that line, to no avail.

THE PINOCHET DICTATORSHIP

The military government that followed Allende ruled Chile in a manner similar to military governments of that time in Argentina, Brazil, and Uruguay. As with his counterparts in those countries, the first priority of General Augusto Pinochet, who had been named army commander just a few weeks before the *golpe de estado*, was the extirpation of the left, a campaign that proceeded brutally and relentlessly for a decade or more at the cost of thousands of lives and untold suffering. The abuse of human rights was all the more shocking by contrast with Chile's civic traditions and its image as one of Latin America's few stable democracies. And it surprised many anti-Allende Chileans, who expected the *golpe* to be followed by early elections.

I must pause here and inquire into the roots of this disruption of Chile's (and Uruguay's) political traditions. To be sure, the Allende policies had torn Chile asunder. Yet some elements of the military establishment, led by Pinochet's predecessor, General Carlos Prats, respected the principle of civilian control of the military and opposed the *golpe*—and Prats was murdered in Buenos Aires a year later.[28] But when most of the military leaders concluded that a revolution was inevitable and that it would ultimately swallow both the democratic tradition and their own institution, they acted quickly and forcefully, following a historic militarist pattern well known in almost all Latin American countries—and Spain and Portugal.

Pinochet's sixteen years in power must be viewed as a cultural atavism reflecting the deep roots of traditional Ibero-Catholic authoritarianism; the Hispanic arrogance and proneness to confrontation—the *soberbia* to which Díaz-Plaja attaches so much significance; the fragmenting consequences of Ortega y Gasset's "particularism"; the dark eddy of human nature—magnified in Hispanic culture at least since the Inquisition—that tolerates and even derives pleasure from the suffering of others; and the Hispanic tradition of the military *pronunciamiento*—the ultimate expression of a military institution that functions above the law.

The Pinochet dictatorship evokes the Franco dictatorship in Spain in another sense: both introduced market economic policies that opened their countries to the world economy, breaking with decades of import substitution strategies that had perpetuated the corporatist

("mercantilist," to use Hernando de Soto's term) tradition of cozy relationships between a business oligarchy and government. In both cases,
one can infer that the subsequent movement toward (return to, in
Chile's case) political pluralism was positively influenced by economic
policies that opened opportunity to those formerly not among the few
favored by the corporatist system, policies that nurtured economic
dynamism in sharp contrast to the inevitable stagnation of self-sufficiency policies.

Pinochet's economic program veered 180 degrees away from
Allende's:

> The Chilean economic adjustment program of the 1970s stands
> out as an example of a drastic and rapid reform process. The bud-
> get deficit was cut sharply from 25 percent of GDP in 1973 to 1
> percent by 1975. A restrictive monetary policy pushed real inter-
> est rates above 50 percent a year. Price controls were lifted and
> subsidies eliminated in the domestic market. Quantitative restric-
> tions on trade were eliminated, and tariffs were cut to a uniform
> 10 percent by 1979. The multiple exchange rate system was con-
> solidated and combined with a large devaluation as an offset to
> the tariff reduction. The result was a post-liberalization surge of
> price inflation, which averaged 350 percent a year in 1974–75
> before declining to 85 percent in 1977. The government also
> began a rapid privatization program in which more than 300 firms
> with a total book value of about $1 billion were returned to pri-
> vate ownership.[29]

The harshness of the program and some errors in its management
were aggravated by the two oil shocks, with their attendant surge in
world interest rates, and a drop in world copper prices. In the 1974–75
recession, unemployment rose to 15 percent. In the 1981–82 crisis,
domestic demand fell by almost 25 percent, and unemployment exceeded 20 percent. "At this stage many evaluations concluded that the
Chilean economic adjustment program had been a failure."[30] Leftists in
Chile and around the world rejoiced in the "collapse" of this "neo-
liberal" capitalist experiment that had inflicted so much pain on the
Chilean people. But their rejoicing was short-lived:

> After some false starts, the government adopted a pragmatic and
> orthodox macroeconomic policy beginning in 1985. The key fea-

ture was a large depreciation of the real exchange rate that initiated an export-led expansion, financed by a tight fiscal policy to raise domestic saving, which had fallen to a remarkable low of 1.6 percent of GDP in 1982. Chile's [negative] trade balance was reversed from a deficit equal to 13 percent of GDP in 1981 to a surplus that peaked at 6.6 percent in 1986 and averaged 4 percent a year in the 1987–92 period. The growth of GDP averaged 6.2 percent a year in the 1983–92 period, and unemployment had declined to below 5 percent of the labor force by 1992.[31]

Chile was for much of this century a country with a very low rate of savings. Today, principally as a consequence of a policy that requires that 10 percent of one's salary be channeled to a personal retirement account, Chile's savings rate—above 25 percent of GDP—is the highest in Latin America. When I visited Santiago in 1995, I met two representatives of the Hong Kong government who had come to Chile to study the mandatory savings/retirement program. (The Hong Kong miracle reflects, in part, one of the highest savings rates in the world—above 30 percent.)

Today, the Chilean economy continues its impressive growth, impervious to the "Tequila effect," and most observers expect that growth to continue for the foreseeable future. Chile has become the probable next member of NAFTA. From my point of view (see chapter 8), Chile would have been a far better candidate than Mexico, above all because of its vastly stronger democratic traditions. But there are other good reasons:

> [Chile's] 11 percent tariff on imports, down from about 200 percent at one time, already makes its economy one of the most welcoming in the world. . . . Its laws are compatible with NAFTA, meaning few reforms are required. Its labor and environmental records meet required standards and are exemplary when compared with Mexico, where those two areas proved so controversial that they forced last-minute side agreements on NAFTA.[32]

With the economy in good shape, Pinochet believed that a majority of Chileans supported him. But in the 5 October 1988 plebiscite on his continuation in office, about 55 percent of Chileans voted against him.[*] That, of course, means that about 45 percent

---

[*]The government claimed that those opposed to Pinochet accounted for 54 percent; the opposition claimed 56 percent.

wanted him to remain in office, a substantial if minority show of approval (and better than that of the Sandinistas, who received 41 percent of the votes in the 1990 Nicaraguan elections). A process was set in motion that brought the return of constitutional government and the landslide election of the Christian Democrat Patricio Aylwin in December 1989. Aylwin was inaugurated in March 1990. His successor, the Christian Democrat Eduardo Frei Ruiz-Tagle, won easily four years later.

The military retained a degree of autonomy, and Pinochet was assured of his position as commander-in-chief of the army for eight years. And the military continues to receive a flat 10 percent of the dollars the state-owned copper enterprise CODELCO exports. But Chile is now a very different country from 1973. The Marxist left has been discredited by Allende's "disguised but relentless 1970–73 civil war,"[33] the collapse of socialism in Eastern Europe, and widespread acceptance of the "Chilean model" of free-market, export-based, pro-foreign investment economic policies—even by "Communist" China. Like their European counterparts, many of Chile's Socialists (who were earlier to the left of the Communists) moderated their ideology, severed their links to the Communist Party, became electoral allies of the Christian Democrats, and endorsed democratic capitalism. The political debate in Chile has narrowed appreciably to that found in mature democracies throughout the world: How much emphasis on economic growth? How much emphasis on social justice?

Let's return to the four key questions posed at the outset of this chapter:

1. What explains Chile's atypically democratic and relatively peaceful (by Latin American standards) history?
2. What explains Chile's extremely inequitable income distribution?
3. What does the Chile case tell us about the relationship between economic and political development?
4. Does the Chilean miracle demonstrate that, at least with respect to economic development, culture is irrelevant, and that good economic policies can assure success without reference to the culture within which they operate?

WHY IS CHILE DIFFERENT? HOW DIFFERENT IS IT?

This brief review of Chilean history has pointed to several factors that have influenced Chile's evolution: its unique geography and temperate climate; remoteness; favorable natural resource endowment; and the absence of precious metals and easily enslaved Indians, with a resultant loss of interest on the part of Spain that meant greater freedom of action by the Spanish colonists.

A key element of the explanation for Chile's atypical entrepreneurial tradition and economic dynamism, particularly in the nineteenth century, and the civility that has characterized much (but far from all) of Chile's political evolution is Chile's large Basque-descended population. I have also noted the disproportionate impact of non-Hispanic European and other immigrants on Chile's industrialization and export surge, similar to the Brazilian experience.

But Chile's history, while more progressive than that of many other Latin American countries, is unmistakably the history of an Ibero-American country. Like Argentina, its politics during the nineteenth century, including the outcome of elections, were manipulated by the elite. The early conservative governments resorted to repression. Two armed rebellions were mounted against Manuel Montt, president from 1851 to 1861. President José Manuel Balmaceda's suicide in 1891 was precipitated by a civil war. The military removed Arturo Alessandri from power in 1924, and Colonel Carlos Ibáñez ran a dictatorship from 1927 to 1931. A short-lived Socialist Republic was proclaimed prior to the reelection of Alessandri in 1932. Forty years later came Allende's "disguised but relentless civil war" and the sixteen years of Pinochet's military dictatorship.

It is against this backdrop that Chile's persistent social problem should be viewed. While its income distribution is highly inequitable by First World standards, by Latin American standards it is typical. In several respects, Chile is well ahead of most other Latin American countries: its 1990 adult illiteracy rate (7 percent) places it among the educational elite group of Uruguay, Argentina, Costa Rica, and Cuba. In 1992, 72 percent of high school–age Chileans were in school, also very high by Latin American standards (the figure was 43 percent for Costa Rica).

Chile's life expectancy (seventy-four years) and infant mortality (16 per 1,000 live births) place it close to the advanced democracies in these categories.[34] But its income distribution approximates that of Guatemala.

Three cultural factors help to explain the anomaly of Chile's inequitable income distribution—which, by the way, has not significantly improved since the economy got into high gear in the mid-1980s, although the real income of the lower classes has steadily increased. Chile's evolution toward political pluralism is largely the consequence of the relatively early appreciation by the elites that elections are a better way than guns of transferring power. Indispensable to that accommodation is trust that the opposition, once in power, will play the game by the rules, which means that the "ins" will not take undue advantage of their power and that they will accept the results of the next election. This is essentially the formula on which Costa Rica's democracy evolved.

But the formula, fundamentally a truce between competing factions, does not necessarily embrace the idea of fair play, a concept central to Anglo-Protestant polities. Nor does the formula depend on a sense of community, a value that can both nurture democracy and promote social justice, as in Japan. By Latin American standards, these values may be more developed in Chile and Costa Rica (and Uruguay) than elsewhere. But even in the case of Costa Rica, income distribution is quite inequitable by First World standards; it is comparable to that of Peru. And Costa Rica's efforts to promote social equality have been marked by a notable paternalism on the part of the elites: until recent decades, labor unions were discouraged, and the aspirations of the poor were met through policies, including large-scale feeding programs, that smacked more of charity than of development.

I might add that the degree of trust in Chile is comparable to that found elsewhere in Latin America, at least to the extent that the handling of money in commercial establishments is indicative. During my visit to Santiago in 1995, I purchased some articles in a pharmacy and ran into precisely the same cumbersome, multiclerk, cross-check procedures that my wife had encountered in Brazil (see pages 132–33).

In sum, Chile is different. But it is also clearly an Ibero-Catholic society.

The Interplay Between Political and Economic Development

Cause and effect run in both directions between politics and economics, and Chile is a case in point. Chile's somewhat hyperbolic nineteenth-century reputation as a "model republic" attracted the interest of foreign investors and immigrants. Its impressive economic growth in the nineteenth century produced the resources that enabled government to function more effectively and to make at least some of the social investments that assured a degree of progress for the masses—further reinforcing, thereby, the acceptability of political pluralism.

But in Ibero-Catholic societies, prosperity does not guarantee democracy. Brazil's economic miracle in the mid-1960s and 70s did not lead to a return to the democratic experiment until the military, frustrated by its inability to keep inflation under control, threw in the towel in the 1980s. Venezuela's oil-based prosperity has been accompanied by a fragile, unsteady, corruption-filled experiment with democratic institutions. Mexico's oil-based prosperity served more to reinforce the control of the Partido Revolucionario Institucional (PRI) than to promote pluralism. And in Chile's case, the relative prosperity of the Eduardo Frei Montalva years (1964–70) was insufficient to rein in the centrifugal forces that led to Salvador Allende, forces that are deeply rooted in Ibero-Catholic culture.

The Chilean case tends to confirm a phenomenon suggested by the East Asian and Spanish experiences: sweeping economic reform is easier to implement in an authoritarian environment than in a democratic one. If Pinochet had had to face the scheduled elections in 1976, with the economy still very wobbly, he might have been defeated, even assuming that most Chileans still supported the ouster of Allende and the heavy-handed, dictatorial measures of the military. The next election would have taken place in 1982, with the economy apparently on the verge of collapse. An opposition politician running on a platform that opposed the "neoliberal" economics of the Chicago boys would almost surely have won. In this respect, Pinochet's contribution to Chile's prosperity today is comparably significant to that of Chiang Kai-shek and his son, Chiang Ching-kuo, in Taiwan; Park Chung Hee in South Korea; and Franco (who reluctantly supported the opening up of the economy) in Spain.

The Interplay Between Culture and Policy

Late in 1993, I met with Arch Ritter, a Canadian economist at Carlton University in Ottawa who has focused on Chile in his work. As I explained my views on Latin America's underdevelopment, he grew obviously impatient, even angry. Like many of his colleagues, Ritter is an economist who is convinced that all you have to do is get the economic signals right in *any* culture to assure economic development. He rejects the idea that some cultures encourage economic creativity and produce proportionately more entrepreneurs than others, that some cultures encourage saving and investment more than others. I inferred that he considered my views racist.

I regret that it did not occur to me at the moment to ask him how he would explain the extraordinary performance of the Chinese in Thailand, Indonesia, Malaysia, the Philippines, the United States, and so on. After all, the Chinese (among the highest-level achievers in the United States) and the Puerto Ricans (among the lowest) all function with the same economic signals. A similar argument can be made about the Japanese in Brazil and Peru, the Jews wherever they have migrated.

About a year later, I met with David Hojman, a Chilean economist who teaches at the University of Liverpool. Hojman is convinced that the Chilean economic miracle is mainly the consequence of the market, export-oriented policies of the Pinochet government. And he believes that the new economic policies are changing Chilean culture, for example, with respect to the role of women. But he also believes that the foundation of the miracle far antedates Pinochet; that the miracle underscores the continuity between the Pinochet policies and those of predecessor governments (for example, the Pinochet creeping peg continual adjustment exchange-rate strategy was similar to that of Eduardo Frei's government in the 1960s); and that the cultural factors that have made Chile different are also relevant:

> [T]he Pinochet educational policies, and their results, were in fact
> a continuation and deepening of trends previously observed. Firstly
> . . . formal education in Chile has been more widely spread among
> the population than in other Latin American countries . . . [and]
> . . . public education has been less concentrated at the top (at the
> university level) than elsewhere in the region. . . . [A]s a result of

this, Chile has middle sectors which have been traditionally strong economically, socially, and politically. This means reasonably competent small- and medium-scale entrepreneurs; skilled manual workers, white collar employees in the public and private sectors, middle management and so on. . . . The third continuity has to do with certain aspects of the national culture . . . traditionally in Chile there has been more respect for institutions and the rule of law, less corruption and less of some forms of violent and other crime.[35]

I should note, in passing, that a recent study of business-related corruption in forty-one countries around the world placed Chile at the less-corrupt end of the spectrum (slightly less corrupt than the United States, by the way), while other Latin American countries and Spain were at the more-corrupt end.[36] We might also note that, by Latin American standards, Chile's military and police had long been considered among the most professional—until 1973—and the least corrupt.

I think that even Ritter would agree that the Chilean miracle has at least some roots that antedate the Chicago boys that are relevant to its recent success. Chile's entrepreneurial tradition and its impressive growth in the nineteenth century; its prosperity relative to the rest of Latin America at the turn of the twentieth; its early reputation as the "model republic" and the evolution of its democratic institutions—before 1970 and since 1989; its achievements in education and health; and the profound trauma of the Allende-Pinochet years all contributed to an indispensable foundation for the economic miracle of the past decade.

While the comparison is imperfect, Chile's political and economic evolution with respect to the rest of Latin America is similar to the Basque provinces' (and Catalunya's) evolution with respect to the rest of Spain.

One additional question remains: Why did the Chilean economy slow down through much of the twentieth century? Chilean historian Francisco Encina argues that the nitrate and copper bonanzas produced an easy prosperity that shifted the Chilean elite's attention away from saving, investment, and economic creativity toward consumption (which was facilitated by an attractive exchange rate).[37] And he was particularly troubled by the increasing emphasis on the professions and classics and away from practical learning in the education system. This view is reminiscent of the Buddenbrooks phenomenon. "In Thomas Mann's novel of three generations [*Buddenbrooks*], the first sought money; the second, born to money, sought social and civic position; the third, born to comfort and family prestige, looked to the life of music. The phrase is designed to suggest, then, the changing aspirations of generations, as they place a low value on what they take for granted and seek new forms of satisfaction."[38] A Chinese adage addresses "the three-generation cycle, from rags to riches to ruin."[39]

And there are other obviously relevant factors, including the end of the nitrate bonanza about 1930, as synthetic substitutes were developed; Chile's turning inward, along with much of Latin America, during the Great Depression; and the sustaining of that inward-lookingness during the decades of influence of Prebisch, CEPAL, and dependency theory.

Chilean culture is changing by the judgment of several analysts. President Clinton's first National Security Advisor for Latin America, Richard Feinberg, who was a Peace Corps volunteer in, and has written about, Chile (and who sympathized with Allende and was highly critical of the U.S. role in Chile in the early 1970s), expressed the view in a conversation in early 1995 that "Chile's culture has been totally transformed. It's more materialistic, more individualistic." Paul Sigmund also believes that Chile has undergone significant cultural changes in recent decades:

> Chile has indeed become more modern in its educational system, economy, social attitudes, and politics. . . . The old hierarchical, ascriptive, and semi-feudal structures and relationships still have left their traces, but Chile is evolving into a more democratic, equalitarian, and participatory society. . . . [Chile is in the process of eliminating] the rigidities of the corporatist organization of the economy which gave special privileges to specific groups and impeded the operation of the competitive market in economics and politics. Chile is still, fortunately, a society in which family and group attachments are strong, but they are increasingly combined with individualist and competitive entrepreneurial values.[40]

But the transformation is incomplete, in the judgment of several others. One informed foreigner in Chile observed during my 1995 visit that "Chile is halfway between Latin America and the First World. Isolation is still a serious problem. There is some danger in continuing [vertical] patron-client relationships without horizontal relationships to displace them. The Basques are disproportionately influential and prosperous, as are non-Spanish Europeans. But in most of their traits, Chileans are still Spanish. Ibero-Catholic culture is still here, and a struggle is going on. It won't be won for a generation."

Nor is Chile fully secular. The Roman Catholic church still retains substantial political power. Martín Hopenhayn, a prominent intellectual with whom I met in 1995, assured me that the best-qualified Chilean for the job of Minister of Education is José Joaquín Brunner. But, as I mentioned in chapter 1, the Church vetoed him because of his highly secular views. Mark Falcoff adds, "The Chilean Catholic church is now one of the most conservative in Latin America, and in social mores and matters of personal morality Chile is the most conservative country in Latin America. The Christian Democratic party is in thrall to the church, which still has a veto power on educational and other matters, including birth control."[41]

What conclusions can we draw about the interplay of culture and policy? Chile's divergent—but far from wholly divergent—spur from the Latin American main track is largely explained by a culture that has been shaped by Chile's unusual geography and climatic variations; by a resource endowment that did not interest the conquistadors but subsequently produced important mineral riches; by a disproportionate number of Basque immigrants; and, like Brazil and other Latin American countries, by a small but creative and influential group of non-Hispanic European and other immigrants.

The Chilean economic miracle of the 1980s and 1990s is chiefly the consequence of policies that have opened opportunities for Chilean producers in both the domestic and world market, at the same time limiting government involvement in production and distribution, and encouraging and facilitating foreign investment and technology transfer. As elsewhere in Latin America, the new policies hold the promise of breaking up the traditional, cozy, inefficient, and corrupting "mercantilist" relationship between government and the oligarchy, thereby providing new incentives for broad-based entrepreneurship. As has happened in South Korea and Taiwan—and as will happen in China in the next few decades, I believe—economic pluralism is likely to reinforce political pluralism.

We are again reminded of Daniel Patrick Moynihan's sage observation that "[t]he central conservative truth is that it is culture, not politics, that [in the long run] determines the success of a society. The central liberal truth is that politics can [in the short run] change a culture and save it from itself."[42]

AN ENDURING MIRACLE?

It is hard not to be bullish about Chile. Among Latin American countries, Chile is the one most likely to follow the Spanish model into the First World. Indeed, there are several striking parallels between Chile and Spain, including the sobering, tolerance-inducing effects of civil war and prolonged military dictatorship; residual postdictatorship problems with civilian control of the military; introduction of open, market economic policies during the dictatorship. But Chile has some advantages over Spain: its democratic roots are far deeper than Spain's; it has privatized its economy far more than has Spain; and it enjoys an entrepreneurial tradition that one cannot find in Spain outside of the Basque provinces and Catalunya. In this connection, Rudiger Dornbusch recently made an observation about contemporary Chile that has strong echoes from the nineteenth century: "Chileans have learned how to do business and Argentines have not—Chileans are all over Argentina making deals, merging, buying, and brokering."[43] Moreover, Protestantism is growing rapidly in Chile, bringing with it a more progressive value system that is likely to enhance the evolution of Chile's democratic political system at the same time that it promotes the work ethic and a stronger national sense of social responsibility.

If Chile sustains its growth rate at about 6 percent annually, the result will be an increase in per capita GNP of 4.5 to 5 percent annually. At that rate, it will take about three decades for Chile to reach the prosperity threshold of the First World (about $12,000 today).

Chilean business groups are far from unanimous about the desirability of Chile's entry into NAFTA.[44] Farmers and industrialists understandably fear the competition of efficient American and Canadian producers. But that competition, as well as the competition of efficient retailers like Wal-mart, will help the Chilean economy to sustain its momentum and to assure jobs and reasonably priced goods to the Chilean populace.

Spain's membership in the European Union has clearly strengthened both its commitment to democracy and its economic prospects. Chile's entry into NAFTA would help assure the irreversibility of democracy, sustained economic growth, and, in due course, Chile's landing in the First World.

In 1950, Spain was the most inequitable country in Europe with respect to distribution of income, land, wealth, and opportunity. Today, its income distribution is among the most equitable in the First World. Many of the forces that produced that transformation, including sound economic policy, democratic politics, a lively and influential media, migration from rural to urban areas, and redoubled efforts to expand and improve education, are clearly in play in Chile.

These same forces, as well as the Protestant surge and the work of some Catholic groups (for example, work-ethic Opus Dei is active in Chile as it has been in Spain), are transforming Chilean culture, and that transformation is probably irreversible, too. Unlike Argentina, Brazil, Mexico, Colombia, Venezuela, Peru, and other countries where the experiments with democracy and capitalism rest on a fragile cultural base that must be reinforced if they are to consolidate democracy and prosper, Chile's cultural base has experienced a steady if slow process of modernization since the eighteenth century, a process that has accelerated in recent years, a process that is probably now self-sustaining.

8

Mexico: The Failure of a Revolution, the End of a Dynasty

Seeing San Diego, one becomes aware of what Mexico could be if it hadn't experienced a demographic explosion and an explosion of corruption, graft, and nepotism, and political, moral, social, and economic degradation.
—MAURICIO GONZÁLEZ DE LA GARZA, El Occidental

Wherever you put your finger, pus comes out.
—A MEXICAN ATTORNEY GENERAL, QUOTED BY ALAN RIDING IN Distant Neighbors

Corruption is not a characteristic of the system. It is the system.
—A POPULAR SAYING IN MEXICO

It is early in November 1993, and President Bill Clinton is addressing a joint session of Congress prior to a crucial vote on the North American Free Trade Agreement (NAFTA). NAFTA is one of the Clinton administration's legislative priorities, as it was in the Bush administration. After stressing the recent growth of American exports to Mexico in response to the enlightened economic policies of Mexican presidents Miguel de la Madrid (1982–88) and Carlos Salinas de Gortari (1988–94), President Clinton has a flash of clairvoyance and candor and adds, "Oh, by the way, one year from now, the Mexican peso is going to drop from 3.5 to 8 against the dollar; we're going to have to put up $20 billion to bail Mexico out; our favorable trade balance of $5 billion with Mexico in 1994 will turn into a deficit of $15 billion in 1995, costing us 300,000 jobs;[1] President Carlos Salinas de Gortari will become a pariah in his own country and leave it; and it will be revealed that his brother, Raúl, holds upwards of $100 million in secret accounts in Switzerland and elsewhere."

In the light of President Clinton's candid comments, the House of Representatives and the Senate vote unanimously against NAFTA.[2] The vote accelerates Mexico's economic and political crisis so that its immediate architect, President Salinas de Gortari, takes the heat instead of his successor, Ernesto Zedillo. The Institutional Revolutionary Party (usually referred to by its Spanish acronym, PRI), which has run Mexico since 1929 as a one-party monopoly, is totally discredited and splits. The old-guard dinosaurs try to maintain the tradition of rigged elections, but the PRI reformists, backed by the opposition parties, invite the United Nations to send in hundreds of observers. The right-of-center Partido de Acción Nacional (PAN) candidate Vicente Fox wins handsomely with a mandate to clean house. The PRI dynasty ends in its sixty-sixth year. Mexico may be on the road to democracy.

One part of this tale is true: the content of President Clinton's vision of what would soon happen in Mexico. But neither he nor his advisers enjoyed clairvoyance, nor did he ever say anything publicly that suggested that the administration had any sense whatever of where Mexico was really heading. The AFL-CIO, Ross Perot, and Pat Buchanan opposed NAFTA, as did a number of liberal Democrats. But after much inflated rhetoric and arm-twisting by the administration, both houses of Congress approved it, only to be shocked a year later when the Mexican economy collapsed. Zedillo ended up holding the bag. Salinas, who at one point stood a good chance of heading the new World Trade Organization, left Mexico in disgrace. There has been much speculation since about his own involvement both in corruption and in the assassination of two prominent PRI politicians.

Thus, in the last years of the twentieth century, Mexico is living a deep crisis that is far from confined to economic issues. Its authoritarian political system is an unraveling cocoon, revealing, as each thread is peeled away, how profoundly the society has been infected by corruption and abuse of power. The presence of perhaps ten million legal and illegal Mexican immigrants in the United States who have left their country since 1965 (the figure includes their children born in the United States)[3] is a symbol of the failure of the Mexican Revolution of 1911 and the Partido Revolucionario Institucional that it spawned. It was intended to create the promised democratic society where citizens, particularly poor citizens, could influence their own destinies, improve their living conditions, and leave behind their centuries-old traditions of poverty, impotence, and hopelessness.

Mexicans often look back to the grandeur of the pre-Columbian Olmec, Toltec, Maya, and Aztec civilizations to establish their country as different from the rest of Latin America. They also see themselves as different because their northern neighbor is the United States. But, as we shall see, Mexico's history through the colonial period and independence displays many of the same patterns of authoritarianism and social injustice that have characterized most Latin American countries.

THE COLONIAL ROOTS OF UNDERDEVELOPMENT—AND CORRUPTION

The Aztec Empire that Hernán Cortés encountered in 1519 was surely one of the wonders of its time, the principal city of Tenochtitlán comparable in many of its amenities to sixteenth-century European cities. Although none of the pre-Columbian civilizations had discovered the arch, Aztec and Mayan architecture was both complex and striking, as today's visitors to the several restored Mayan sites in the Yucatán, Guatemala, and Honduras will attest. The Mayans had evolved an accurate solar calendar, and their agriculture and that of the Aztecs were sufficiently advanced to support large cities—Tenochtitlán is estimated to have had about 250,000 inhabitants when Cortés arrived.[4] (He soon thereafter destroyed Tenochtitlán and started building Mexico City on the same site.)

But for all the physical grandeur of the Aztec and Mayan empires, their societies looked more like pharaonic Egypt than sixteenth-century Europe, China, or the Ottoman Empire. For the Aztecs, the state existed for war, and war was a continuous condition of life. War was also an important source of candidates for the widespread practice of human sacrifice that the priests insisted was necessary to satisfy the gods, a ritual that often culminated in cannibalistic acts. The nobles, warriors, and priests exploited the masses, whom they considered inferior. Slavery was widely practiced.

The reaching back by Mexicans to the grandeur of the Aztec and Mayan empires reflects an understandable pride in their architectural and scientific achievements, as well, probably, as some dissatisfaction with the achievements of Mexico as an independent country, particularly by contrast with its neighbor to the north, whose pre-Columbian Indians knew no such grandeur. But the reaching back also romanticizes the condition of humans in those civilizations. And, above all, it exaggerates the influence of Aztec and Mayan culture on contemporary Mexicans (except perhaps for those Mexicans, particularly in the south, who continue the old languages and some of the customs). In Mexico, as elsewhere in Latin America, pre-Columbian Indian culture has been overwhelmed by traditional Spanish culture and institutions.

Cortés and his followers came to the New World principally to find precious metals and get rich. The chronicler of the Cortés expedition, Bernal Díaz del Castillo, wrote that their mission was "to serve God and His Majesty the King, to give light to those who were in darkness, and also to get rich—which all of us came looking for."[5] Most were from the lower classes and were uneducated. Many had fought in the Reconquest of Spain from the Moors and believed they were thereby entitled to wealth and leisure. Since this ultimately depended on mining silver and gold, which in most cases involved intensive manual labor, Indians were effectively enslaved for the purpose. When the Spaniards on Hispaniola and elsewhere ran out of Indians, who died off because of disease, particularly smallpox, and abuse, they began to import slaves from Africa.

A few priests, the Dominican Bartolomé de las Casas above all, tried to defend the interests of the Indians, but with limited effect. Las Casas was atypical. The Nicaraguan historian José Dolores Gámez observes, "The Catholic clergy, which . . . could have served to moderate the colonial yoke, was with very few exceptions another terrible scourge for the colonies. Intent on breaking the chains of their priestly vows, especially that of poverty, many priests came to the colonies hoping to enjoy a new existence, carefree and comfortable, and especially to satisfy their earthly ambitions."[6]

Mexico City became the viceregal capital of New Spain, which extended north through California and south to Panama. Lima became the viceregal capital of a Peru that extended from Panama to Buenos Aires. In the seventeenth century, Spain began to exercise tight, centralized control over the colonies through extremely detailed laws and decrees, and auditing arrangements. Given the enrichment motivation of most of the colonists, the laws and decrees often became gates controlled by officials who would open them only for a price. The sale of office was commonplace, the price predicated on the gatekeeper's yield. Bribery and influence also extended to those agents sent by the Crown to check on colonial officials. "The consequence was that inertia, corruption, bribery, and easy social relationships became commoner features of the administrative system than did enterprise, integrity, and honesty."[7]

Work was devalued. The prominent Mexican social critic Samuel Ramos observes,

> The conquerors were not workmen, but soldiers, who had to utilize the vanquished race in order to take advantage of their new possessions. Work in [New Spain] did not, therefore, signify a benefit that could alleviate need but an opprobrium suffered for the benefit of the masters. Mexican will and initiative lacked opportunity for development. Wealth was not acquired by work but by the unjust privilege that permitted exploitation of the poor. Trade was the monopoly of the classic Spanish storekeeper, who came to America only to carry back a fortune to his native land.[8]

In the broadest sense, New Spain was an extension of Old Spain and of its static, rigid, Catholic world view. The Mexican writer Edmundo O'Gorman describes this world view as flowing from

> the Catholic truth . . . that had resolved forever the question of the life of the individual and of the society; opposed to reforms and innovations, and to programs to transform nature, which were considered acts of arrogance since they implied modifications to the creation of the supreme divine wisdom. The world had no reason to be a paradise where abundance and prosperity would reign; it was a vale of tears, the place of banishment of the fallen Adam.[9]

New Spain and New England

What a contrast was New England with New Spain! The Massachusetts Bay Colony was settled in the 1630s by Puritans whose overriding goal in emigrating was to practice their Calvinist religion free of Anglican orthodoxy, "to . . . serve God's will and be free of temptation [in] a place where [one] would touch no unclean thing.'"[10] A candidate for membership in a Congregational church "had to stand before a highly skeptical group of elders, and satisfy them in three respects:

adherence to Calvinist doctrines, achievement of a godly life, and demonstrable experience of spiritual conversion."[11]

The Calvinist antecedents of Puritanism echoed in five fundamental ideas: *depravity*, the consequence of Adam's original sin, which was everywhere but which could be, indeed *must* be, defeated ("It is impossible to conceive of a disillusioned Puritan.");[12] *covenant*, by which the Puritans believed they had a contract with God that placed on them a heavy burden of responsible, righteous behavior; *election*, which meant that only a select, prosperous few were actually admitted to the covenant; *grace*, which was both an idea and an emotion that could be experienced only by the elect; and *love*, both God's for the Puritans and the Puritans' for one another. ("One leader told them that they should 'look upon themselves as being bound up in one *Bundle of Love*; and count themselves obliged, in very close and Strong Bonds, to be serviceable to one another.'"[13])

It should not then come as a surprise that the vast majority of Puritans migrated in families. Historian David Hackett Fischer, whose *Albion's Seed* brilliantly analyzes the power and persistence of America's British cultural roots, points out that in New Spain the ratio between men and women was 10 to 1, in Massachusetts, 1.5 to 1.[14] Most of the Puritans were middle class—yeomen, artisans, craftsmen, merchants. In 1660, two-thirds of the men and one-third of the women were literate.

In such a cultural context, the Calvinist elements of which would more than two centuries later serve as the grist for Max Weber's analysis of Protestantism and capitalism, it is not difficult to understand how the Massachusetts Bay Colony prospered, despite poor natural resource endowment. Nor is it difficult to trace the cultural roots of New England's strong tradition of self-government, including the direct democracy of the town meeting. And many other features of early New England that have so profoundly influenced the shape of our nation are also easy to understand: the tradition of excellence; the founding of Harvard University in 1636; the philanthropic obligation of the prosperous; the strong currents of austerity, simplicity, and community.

The Mexican writer Octavio Paz, who won the Nobel Prize for Literature in 1990, generalizes the contrast between the two Americas: "One, English speaking, is the daughter of the tradition that has founded the modern world: the Reformation, with its social and political consequences, democracy and capitalism. The other, Spanish and

Portuguese speaking, is the daughter of the universal Catholic monarchy and the Counter-Reformation."[15] In 1776 there were three thousand newspapers in the former British colonies. When Mexico gained its independence forty-five years later, three newspapers were in print.[16]

Independence: Mexico Tries to Deny Its Past

Mexico gained its independence from Spain in 1821 after ten years of sporadic fighting that started as an uprising of the masses against the colonial government, the great landholders, and the Church led, first, by a priest, Miguel Hidalgo y Costilla; then, after his execution by forces loyal to the crown, by another priest, José María Morelos y Pavón; and finally by Agustín de Iturbide, who had fought on the royalist side against Hidalgo and Morelos. Growing support for constitutionalism in Spain prompted Iturbide and key elements of the New Spain establishment that had opposed Hidalgo and Morelos to support independence as a means of perpetuating a monarchy. Iturbide was proclaimed emperor in May 1822. He was overthrown by the military less than a year later. In subsequent decades during which the army monopolized power, governments came and went at the rate of one a year, usually in the wake of *pronunciamientos*—the announced will of the army.

Whatever the rhetoric of the wars of independence in Latin America and the constitutions of the new countries, the practical outcome was substantial continuity with the backward social structures—and injustices—of the colony. Octavio Paz observes, "The Independence of Mexico was the denial of what we had been since the sixteenth century; it was not guided by a national vision derivative of our past, rather by a totally alien universal ideology. . . . It was, in essence, a manifestation of the Spanish and Arab traditions of patrimonialism . . . and it inevitably led to the *caudillismo* that has dominated our countries since Independence."[17] As in many other Latin American countries, Mexican Conservatives—generally more centralist, protectionist, and pro-Church—vied against Liberals, who were imbued with the humanist visions of progress that flowed from the American and French revolutions. But, as Edmundo O'Gorman stresses, the Conservatives were mired in an Ibero-Catholic culture that was antithetical to progress, and the Liberals could not bring about change because they, too, were hostage to that culture.[18] Inevitably, the conflict between the Conservatives and the Liberals lost focus and often seemed more concerned with power than with ideology. General Antonio López de Santa Anna, the dominant political and military figure during this period, served as chief of state in both Liberal and Conservative administrations.

By the 1830s, it was apparent that independence was no guarantee either of prosperity or stability. When Texas sought independence in 1835 (the Mexicans had encouraged migration of Anglo-Americans to Texas),[19] the Mexicans were able to defeat the insurgents at the Alamo but lost the war—and Texas—at San Jacinto a year later. When the Texans sought admission to the United States in 1845, Mexico decided to go to war[20]—a decision welcomed by many in the United States, including President Polk. The Americans overwhelmed the disorganized and bankrupt Mexicans, led by Santa Anna, and the Treaty of Guadalupe Hidalgo (1848), which rankles in the Mexican psyche to this day, awarded what is today Texas, California, New Mexico, Nevada, and Utah, and parts of Colorado and Wyoming, to the United States in return for $15 million in cash. Mexico lost more than half its territory.

The disaster of the Mexican-American war strengthened the hand of the more radical liberals, Benito Juárez, a Zapotec Indian from Oaxaca, most prominent among them, who sought to curtail the power of the army and the Church, the latter by wholesale confiscation of Church property. This led to a civil war from 1857 to 1860 that culminated in the installation of Juárez as president. But the liberal constitution of 1857, which established religious freedom, was of little practical relevance: Juárez presided over a bankrupt country, and his popularity declined as it became apparent that the beneficiaries of the confiscation of Church lands were not the campesinos, as the liberals had intended, but the large landholders—"accentuat[ing] the feudal character of our country," in Paz's words.[21] Mexico's bankruptcy and debts to France led to a French expeditionary force that, with the help of the Conservatives, set up Maximilian of Habsburg, the younger brother of the emperor of Austria, as emperor of Mexico in 1864. Maximilian's liberal intentions notwithstanding, he was executed in 1867 following the defeat at Querétaro of the French forces that had installed him.

But the Mexican government was still deep in debt—a condition that has reappeared throughout its history—and Juárez was unable to move his program for progress and prosperity forward. He died in 1872.

Four years later, the ambitious liberal general, Porfirio Díaz, seized power. Save for 1880–84, when one of his aides served as chief of state, Díaz was in power until 1911. The *Porfiriato* lasted thirty-five years.

PORFIRIAN POSITIVISM

Porfirio Díaz was a classical Latin American caudillo. The ideas of pluralism, decentralization, due process, and social responsibility were beyond his ken; his gesture toward democratic politics was to hold elections—and rig them.

Like politicians and intellectuals in Brazil, Chile, and elsewhere in Latin America, Díaz and his allies were influenced by Auguste Comte's "positivism"—a dialectic that was driving humankind from superstition through abstract theory to practical progress. Under his tutelage, a new generation of technocrats, the *científicos*, or scientists, rose to power (and wealth) promoting economic development and strong government. The positivist slogan "order and progress," which to this day adorns Brazil's national flag, was modified by Díaz to "plenty of administration and no politics."[22] The Mexican economy grew, stimulated by foreign investment, particularly from the United States; railroad construction; the discovery of new minerals; plantation agriculture; and some industry. The Mexican government's fiscal accounts became solvent, and Díaz could count on the financial resources to lubricate his system of centralized control. A middle class began to emerge, particularly in Mexico City. But the masses were still denied education and opportunity, and wages at the lower levels failed to keep pace with price rises. The trend continued toward consolidation of agricultural lands, accompanied by a growing rural proletariat. And the *Porfiriato* was corrupt to the core.[23]

The progress wrought by the *Porfiriato* failed to transform Mexico. Paz observes:

> The ideas of Spencer and John Stuart Mill demanded ... the development of heavy industry, a democratic bourgeoisie and the free exercise of intellectual activity. The Díaz dictatorship, based on great rural holdings, bossism and the absence of democratic freedoms, could not make these ideas its own without either denying itself or disfiguring them beyond recognition. Thus positivism became a historical superimposition much more dangerous than those that preceded it, because it was based on a misconception.

Between the landholders and their political and philosophical ideas an invisible wall of deception arose, and the expulsion of the Díaz regime followed almost inevitably.[24]

REVOLUTION WITHOUT TRANSFORMATION

By 1910, leaders opposed to *Porfirianismo* were springing up all over Mexico—in both a geographical and an ideological sense: Francisco Madero, an idealistic liberal from the north; General Bernardo Reyes, a Nuevo León caudillo; the Agrarian reformer Emiliano Zapata from Morelos; Pancho Villa, bandit and opportunist, also from the north. Díaz's rigging of the 1910 election led to his overthrow in 1911, and Madero was elected. But he lasted only fifteen months, at which point General Victoriano Huerta seized power and executed Madero. Less than two years later, in 1914, Huerta was forced into exile by a group of "Constitutionalists" whose only real bond was opposition to Huerta. The Constitutionalist leader was Venustiano Carranza, a liberal supporter of the martyred Madero, who promulgated a new, more liberal, but essentially rhetorical constitution in 1917. Zapata and Villa refused to support Carranza and fought on until Carranza's military, ably led by the Sonoran Alvaro Obregón, put an end to the fighting.

Mexicans in 1920 were exhausted, suffering from disease and malnutrition, and hostage to a corrupted military institution. But they benefited from an important new resource: oil production, which commenced in the first years of the new century and increased to the point where Mexico pumped one-quarter of what the world consumed.

Carranza was assassinated in 1920, and Obregón served as president from 1920 to 1924. He was followed by another Sonoran, Plutarco Elías Calles, who was president from 1924 to 1928 and effectively ran the government until 1934. It was Calles who, in 1929, formed the National Revolutionary Party (PRN), grandfather of the Institutional Revolutionary Party (PRI) that has run Mexico since 1946. The Sonorans can take credit for downsizing the army to the point where, in contrast to almost all other Iberian-culture countries, it has not since played a significant role in politics.*

---

*Rumors, apparently unfounded and astonishing to most observers, that the Mexican military was conspiring against the government of President Ernesto Zedillo caused the peso to plummet in November 1995.

It was during the 1920s that José Vasconcelos, a Oaxacan revolutionary, became the leader of educational reform in Mexico with a vision of a Cosmic Race—"the prodigal sons of a homeland which we cannot even define but which we are beginning at last to observe. She is Castilian and Moorish, with Aztec markings."[25] Paz identifies Vasconcelos as "the founder of modern education in Mexico," and goes on to say,

> The character of the educational movement was not the work of [this] one extraordinary man . . . but rather an accomplishment of the Revolution, and its realization expressed the finest and most secret element of the revolutionary movement. . . . Vasconcelos conceived of instruction as active participation. Schools were established, readers and the classics were published, institutes were created, and cultural missions were sent to the remotest parts of the country. At the same time, the intelligensia turned toward the people, discovering their true nature and eventually making them the center of its activities.[26]

But, like so many other aspects of the revolution, the educational reform faltered as subsequent governments lowered its priority and focused their attention increasingly on maintaining their power and perquisites. In 1995, 35 million Mexicans over the age of fifteen—more than a third of the total population—had not finished primary school, and only 18 percent had completed secondary school.[27]

Lázaro Cárdenas was elected in 1934 as a protégé of Calles, but he soon broke with his sponsor, and after an extended struggle Calles was exiled. Cárdenas committed himself to land reform and sponsored the *ejido* program, under which more than 40 million acres of land were transferred to small farmer communities to be tilled either individually or collectively, according to the wishes of the community. Cárdenas worked with leftist labor leader Vicente Lombardo Toledano to incorporate a powerful labor confederation into the ruling party, relabeled the Mexican Revolution Party (PRM) in 1937. The lack of union independence contributed to the extreme corruption of the labor movement. Jonathan Kandell notes that "labor leaders were secretly on the government payroll. They received kickbacks from management to forgo strikes or cut them short and to accept lower wage settlements for their rank and file. They also extracted bribes from workers in exchange for union membership."[28]

Cárdenas became the symbol of Mexican nationalism when he

expropriated the foreign oil companies in 1938, ardently supported by Mexicans across the political spectrum. He was succeeded in 1940 by Manuel Avila Camacho, who, like his successor, Miguel Alemán (1946–52), promoted industrialization and worked cooperatively with the United States. Starting in 1940, the Mexican economy experienced twenty-five years of rapid growth—averaging about 6.6 percent per year—within an import substitution strategy that would become the dominant economic policy of virtually all Latin American countries. But Mexico's population was growing at more than 3 percent per year, and the Mexican economy was unable to generate the employment necessary to absorb new entrants into the labor force. *Bracero* programs brought temporary Mexican workers into the United States to meet the labor shortages of World War II, and a substantial flow of illegal Mexican workers probably began at about the same time.

The PRM was relabeled the Institutional Revolutionary Party (PRI) by Alemán in 1946, by which time it had established a firm monopoly grip on Mexican politics. It was held together not only by its nationalist, socialist, populist, and "revolutionary" ideology, much of which was in any event rhetorical, but also by its ability to convert financial resources into political power, for example, by buying influence in the media. With its full control of the electoral machinery, the PRI could, if necessary, rig elections with impunity.* That same unchallenged control also encouraged corruption, a concomitant of government in Mexico since the early days of New Spain. Alan Riding says that Alemán, who had become a rich man as governor of Veracruz and Interior Minister, bought up a good part of Acapulco before a new airport and other infrastructure caused property values to soar.[29] It was common for public officials to "extract . . . huge bribes from private contractors."[30]

Alemán chose Adolfo Ruiz Cortines as his successor (1952–58). Ruiz Cortines gave women the vote, for what it might be worth, during his otherwise unnoteworthy administration. He and his successor, Adolfo López Mateos (1958–64), were beneficiaries of the continuing economic boom. López Mateos pushed domestic policies to the left and distanced himself from the United States on foreign policy, for example, by maintaining relations with Castro's Cuba. He was succeeded by

---

*One continues to hear that Carlos Salinas de Gortari was in fact defeated in 1988 by the PRI dissident, Cuauhtémoc Cardenas, son of Lázaro Cardenas.

the more moderate Gustavo Díaz Ordaz (1964–70) who confronted, along with his Interior Minister Luis Echeverría, intensifying student demonstrations that led to the massacre of large numbers (Riding estimates as many as 300)[31] at the Plaza of Tlatelolco in October 1968, shortly before Mexico hosted the Olympic Games.

Echeverría was tapped by Díaz Ordaz to succeed him and was inaugurated in 1970. Both Echeverría and his successor, José López Portillo (1976–82), tried to accommodate the left, in part through foreign policies that were usually hostile to the United States, in part through statist economic policies. (The state, which had accounted for little more than 10 percent of the economy before Echeverría, had in its hands 70 percent of the economy when López Portillo departed, according to Kandell.)[32] Echeverría had to face the consequences of the slowdown in the Mexican economy that resulted from the market limitations of the import substitution strategy and Mexico's failure to become competitive behind the high tariff barriers that protected it from imports. He resorted to a large devaluation and heavy foreign borrowing. López Portillo at first benefited from major new oil finds but then was also forced to devalue and borrow following the plunge of oil prices in 1981.

National economic adversity apparently did not adversely affect the personal fortunes of Echeverría and López Portillo. Keith Rosenn of the University of Miami Law School notes that CIA documents acquired by Jack Anderson "revealed that Echeverría made off with between $300 million and $1 billion during his tenure as President of Mexico. . . . López Portillo increased the take to somewhere between $1 billion and $3 billion. . . . [A] secret study commissioned by López Portillo himself estimated the total rake-off during his administration at $44 billion."[33] Rosenn goes on to cite the observation of Alan Riding that "[c]orruption is essential to the operation and survival of the political system. . . . [T]he system has in fact never lived without corruption and it would disintegrate or change beyond recognition if it tried to do so."[34]

DE LA MADRID AND SALINAS DE GORTARI: TECHNOCRATS "CORRUPTED BY THE IVY LEAGUE"

Official election results show that Miguel de la Madrid won the 1982 election with more than 70 percent of the vote, probably an exaggerated figure.[35] De la Madrid, who had done graduate work at Harvard, inherited an economic shambles that forced a massive (600 percent) devaluation and subsequently led to a moratorium on Mexico's debt payments that staggered world financial markets. Argentina, Brazil, and Chile had also overextended their credit-carrying capacity, and their debt problems coupled with Mexico's contributed to a crisis that undermined stability and growth in Latin America throughout the 1980s—widely referred to by economists as "the lost decade."

De la Madrid and his technocratic team, many members of which had also studied at prestigious U.S. universities, started a process of economic restructuring that reversed the inward-looking, nationalistic policies that Mexico had pursued for decades. Central to the reforms were budgetary austerity, trade liberalization, encouragement of foreign investment, and privatization of state enterprises, the large majority of which were losing money as a consequence of political influence in decision making and hiring, and corruption. The reforms were applauded by the International Monetary Fund, the World Bank, and the U.S. government.

The Mexican technocrats were proud of their achievements, and, with the help of the School of Political and Social Sciences at the Autonomous University of Mexico and the Center for International Affairs at Harvard University, they mounted a seminar on Mexican-U.S. relations that brought some thirty U.S. experts to Querétaro in May 1987. Among the Mexicans who spoke, several of whom had done graduate work in prestigious U.S. universities, were Secretary of the Interior Manuel Bartlett; Pedro Aspe, Undersecretary for Planning and Budget; Jaime Serra, Undersecretary for Revenues in the Finance Ministry; René Villarreal, Advisor to the Secretary of Energy and Mines; and Fernando Pérez Correa, Undersecretary of the Interior. All but Pérez Correa, who discussed electoral reforms, focused on the economic reforms.

It soon became apparent that the real purpose of the seminar was to offer the Mexicans an opportunity to tout the de la Madrid economic program to a group of influential American intellectuals. No serious address was made to the question of political liberalization, although the papers I brought back from Querétaro include a sheet of official letterhead with the monogram and name *de la Madrid*, the PRI logo, and "1982–1988" at the top. At the bottom is the slogan, "*Renovación moral, es exigencia del pueblo.*" ("The people insist on moral renewal.") I said little until the end of the seminar, when, discomfited by the obvious evasion of the political and social issues by the Mexicans, I chose to make a statement that I knew would be extremely unpopular with them and indeed with some of my American colleagues. I cite it here because of its relevance to Mexico's condition, and its relationship with the United States, a decade later:

> I would like to underscore an unspoken fact of life that touches on much that has been said here, a reality that makes it impossible to achieve the balanced, dignified relationship—a relationship of equals—between Mexico and the United States that we all seek. So long as the Mexican political system continues to appear to be a controlled system designed to assure the continuity in power of the dominant party; so long as the words "electoral fraud" float so prominently in the air; so long as Mexico has the image of institutionalized corruption at all levels of the society, but especially in the public sector; so long as Mexico continues as a country with some of the world's most inequitable indicators of distribution of wealth, income, land, and opportunity; so long as these conditions exist, a balanced relationship—a relationship similar to that enjoyed by Canada and the United States—cannot exist between Mexico and the United States.[36]

The economic policy of the de la Madrid administration pointed Mexico in a new direction, one that was reinforced and capitalized upon by his successor, Carlos Salinas de Gortari, who had done his graduate work at Harvard. But little progress was made toward "moral renewal," particularly as vast amounts of drug money circulated through the Mexican economy. Jack Anderson referred in 1984 to CIA reports that showed that de la Madrid had deposited $162 million in foreign bank accounts.[37]

Under Salinas, who was inaugurated in 1988, the Mexican economy rose from the doldrums of the debt crisis to international stardom. After years of stagnation, economic growth resumed modestly. The fiscal deficit, chronic after Echeverría, was sharply reduced, and inflation declined from 160 percent in 1987 to 8 percent in 1994. Debt restructuring reestablished Mexico's creditworthiness, and capital inflows soared. The Mexican stock market, enriched by privatized former public enterprises, became one of the "emerging market" magnets. Largely because of Mexico's success as well as the sustained excellent performance of the Chilean economy, Latin America started to attract new interest on the part of foreign investors. The "miracle" was capped by

Salinas's NAFTA initiative in 1991 and its approval by the United States and Canada late in 1993. The Latin American country that for four decades was probably most obsessed, after Fidelista Cuba, with dependency theory and Yankee imperialism, Mexico leaped into bed with the malevolent elephant it had once blamed for most of its woes. U.S. Republicans and Democrats (with some notable exceptions) alike applauded the new intimacy, as did the Canadians.

And then, shortly after Salinas's successor, Zedillo, was inaugurated at the end of 1994 and to the surprise of almost everyone, the Mexican economy collapsed, threatening the resurgent economies of Argentina and Brazil in what came to be called the Tequila effect. The value of the peso dropped from 3.5 to 8 to the dollar. Inflation surged as the price of imports more than doubled. To qualify for a $50 billion rescue package, including $20 billion in swaps and guarantees from the U.S. Exchange Stabilization Fund, Mexico was forced to make deep cuts in public spending and to raise interest rates above 50 percent. Unemployment soared. And, with Mexico's imports contracting sharply and the devaluation's incentives for exports, Mexico's earlier substantial trade deficit with the United States turned into a three-times-larger trade surplus.

What triggered the crisis? Michel Camdessus, Managing Director of the International Monetary Fund, explained it as follows:

> I would point to a number of factors. First, there were still weaknesses in Mexico's position at the start of 1994 that contained the seeds of the crisis that eventually occurred. In particular, the external current account deficit, running at 6½ percent of GDP in 1993, was very large by most standards, and was being financed by short-term capital flows. A steep real appreciation of the peso and a major deterioration in the private sector's savings performance had contributed to the emergence of this deficit. . . . Mexico's weak external position was exacerbated in 1994 both by a series of unfavorable developments at home and abroad and by shortcomings in Mexico's policy response, partly owing to the political hiatus following the elections in August. The uprising in Chiapas was the first in a series of dramatic adverse domestic developments that are well known; and also from early 1994 Mexico was confronted with a substantial rise in world interest rates, which prompted international investors to reassess the share of their portfolios invested in emerging markets. . . . And the policy response was not

adequate, the outgoing administration leaving to the new administration the responsibility of defining the adjustment strategy that was called for.[38]

I have no doubt that this is an accurate explanation of the immediate economic factors behind the crisis. But one must ask several questions that touch on deeper causes: Why didn't the Mexican authorities take action earlier? What lies behind the spending/importing binge that was an important factor in producing the imbalance between exports and imports? What lies behind the "dramatic adverse domestic developments," which include not only the Chiapas uprising but two political assassinations and increasing evidence of grand-scale corruption reaching to the highest levels of government? And how is it possible in this age of instant communications that the most sophisticated governments and private and public financial institutions in the world were so ill-informed about Mexico's situation?

The answers to these questions reach to the heart of Mexico's failed revolution, of its corrupt political system. The checks and balances of truly democratic societies—for example, independent judiciaries, legislatures, and media—have never been operative in Mexico, and that has been particularly true after sixty-five years of one-party monopoly. Government decision making occurs in opaque settings that make it much easier to conceal unpleasant facts, to dissemble, and to divert resources to personal ends. In the absence of a rigorous ethical code, a compelling vision of a more decent society, and a strong sense of public service and responsibility, the lack of transparency creates a corrupting environment in which public officials vie with one another for personal advantage and raw power. It is an environment that evokes the Kremlin, particularly in the last years of that failed revolution.

As we approach the end of the twentieth century, it is difficult to avoid the conclusion that, whatever its appearance of modernization, Mexico is a failure. It has denied most of its people adequate education facilities, the opportunity to influence their political destiny, economic opportunity, and fair treatment in a court system where political influence and money almost always win. Most of its intellectuals have spent the last four decades contriving specious theories that blamed Mexico's ills on the United States. Many of its politicians have engaged in populist excesses, anti-American posturing, and demagoguery while vastly enriching themselves.

How can one explain the failure of a society rich in natural resources and next door to the most lucrative market in the world, particularly when the other country that borders on the United States, Canada, has done so well? One novel explanation suggested to me by several Mexicans during a speaking trip I made to Mexico in late 1995 was that many of the Mexican politicians and technocrats who were believed to be guilty of corruption and abuse of power, including ex-presidents de la Madrid and Salinas de Gortari, had learned how to abuse power at Harvard, Yale, and other prestigious U.S. universities. (If we no longer exploit Mexico through our multilateral corporations and manipulation of the world market, we corrupt its leaders in our universities!)

But the roots of Mexico's failure are not to be found in the United States. They are deep in traditional Mexican values and attitudes, unmistakably derivative of the mainstream Ibero-Catholic values that lie behind the failure of Latin America more generally.

CULTURAL OBSTACLES TO PROGRESS IN MEXICO

Alan Riding is an experienced *New York Times* correspondent who served as bureau chief in Mexico City for six years, following which he wrote the book *Distant Neighbors*, published in 1984. It is one of the most comprehensive and probing examinations of contemporary Mexico, written by a person clearly sympathetic to the country but also very well informed about the Mexican reality and the forces that drive it. In the first pages of the book, Riding makes several observations about Mexican culture that evoke the ten values I have referred to in this book:

> [T]he Western sense of time has been resisted by Mexicans. Cultures that view birth as a beginning and death as an end can have no sense of a living past. For Mexicans, neither birth nor death is considered overly important . . . the future is viewed with fatalism, and as a result, the idea of planning seems unnatural. If the course of events is predestined, Mexicans see little reason to discipline themselves to a routine.
>
> [Mexicans] are forced to work hard but dream of a life of leisure. . . . The Mexican may work as hard as his Indian forefathers, but he dreams of emulating his Spanish ancestors, who

arrived to conquer and not to labor: the image of success is more important than any concrete achievement. . . . What counts to the Mexican is what he is rather than what he does, the man rather than the job: he works to live and not the inverse. . . . Status and appearances are crucial throughout society. The poor spend ostentatiously to hide the "shame" of their poverty. . . . The use of titles reinforces the sense of hierarchy that pervades society.

Businessmen gamble on large, fast profits rather than long-term expansion of a market; individuals prefer spending to saving . . . and even corruption reflects the concept of seizing an opportunity now and facing the consequences later.

. . . the country's own historical record of defeats and betrayals has prepared Mexicans to expect—and accept—the worst. The official heroes . . . have invariably been murdered, while the ideals enshrined in laws and constitutions have been universally betrayed. . . . Empty promises and outright lies come easily. . . .

The extended family is the principal safe haven where emotions can be shown without risk, where unquestioning loyalty is guaranteed, where customs are maintained. . . . When the Mexican male steps outside [the high walls that surround his home], he acts as if confronting a hostile society with which he feels minimal solidarity. The concept of commonweal barely exists and community approaches to shared problems are rare. . . . Efforts to organize voluntary work to build a school or a health clinic invariably fail. . . . Even among the wealthy, the idea of supporting charities is alien, with the result that many orphanages depend entirely on contributions from the foreign community.

The Mexican male's insecurity is best illustrated by his constant fear of betrayal by women. . . . Combining the Spaniard's obsession with honor and the Indian's humiliation at seeing his woman taken by force, Mexico's peculiarly perverse form of *machismo* thus emerges: the Spaniard's defense of honor becomes the Mexican's defense of his fragile masculinity.

Society as a whole functions through relationships of power, while individual rights are determined by levels of influence.[39]

Two prominent Mexican writers, Samuel Ramos and Octavio Paz, have peered deeply into the Mexican psyche and drawn conclusions that are consistent with Riding's perceptions.

Ramos's *Profile of Man and Culture in Mexico* was first published, in Spanish, in 1934. His argument pivots on the psychological doctrine of

Alfred Adler, a former disciple of Freud who focused his later studies on the inferiority complex. Ramos believes that Mexican males suffer from a gap in their self-image (inflated) and the reality of their personalities and circumstances—a gap that may be magnified by the contrast between Mexico and the United States. The resultant tension motivates the aggressive, *macho* behavior associated with the Mexican male, a behavior that may be an arc in a vicious circle: "Since the Mexican's sense of inferiority affects his spirit and since, furthermore, his social life in the nineteenth century was at the mercy of repeated anarchy and civil war, neither composure nor continuity of effort has been possible. Whatever has to be done has to be done quickly, before some new disorder interrupts the work."[40] Ramos goes on to note another Mexican cycle: "The same political comedy is performed periodically: a revolution, a dictator, a program of national restoration."[41]

Starting from his Adlerian foundation, Ramos soon arrives at conclusions similar to those of other critics of Ibero-Catholic culture. He notes the rigid, reactionary posture of the church and its profound influence on the education systems and social structures. He cites Salvador de Madariaga's emphasis on the extreme, antisocial individualism of Hispanic culture, which is also at the root of Ortega y Gasset's concept of the "invertebrate" Ibero-Catholic society, and which links to disrespect for the law and distrust of others. ("The Mexican does not distrust any man or woman in particular; he distrusts all men and women.")[42] He emphasizes the traditional hostility toward work and innovation, the focus on the present and the past at the expense of the future.

In *The Labyrinth of Solitude*, Octavio Paz repeatedly returns to cultural and psychological factors to explain Mexico's condition. He notes that the traditions of abuse of power, social indifference, violence, and cynicism apply to all classes. He sees all Mexicans caught up in a world view in which there are only two possibilities: either *chingar* (close to the vulgar English "to screw") others or be *chingado* by others. And he goes on to say, "It is impossible not to notice the resemblance between the figure of the *macho* and that of the Spanish conquistador. This is the model . . . that determines the images the Mexican people form of men in power: caciques, feudal lords, hacienda owners, politicians, generals, captains of industry. They are all *machos, chingones* ('screwers')."[43]

Paz also makes a searing statement about the centrality of the lie in Mexican life: "We tell lies for the mere pleasure of it, like all imagi-

native peoples, but we also tell lies to hide ourselves and to protect ourselves from intruders. Lying plays a decisive role in our daily lives, our
politics, our love-affairs and our friendships, and since we attempt to
deceive ourselves as well as others, our lies are brilliant and fertile."[44]
How can the idea of trust be inculcated in such a culture? Only if people learn that the lie as a way of life is ultimately destructive of the individual, his or her self-esteem, and the interests of the society and its
progress.

While sympathetic to many aspects of the Mexican Revolution
in this century, Paz concludes that it has failed to transform Mexican
society:

> [D]espite its extraordinary fecundity, it was incapable of creating a
> vital order that would be at once a world view and the basis of a
> really just and free society. The Revolution has not succeeded in
> changing our country into a community, or even in offering any
> hope of doing so. By community, I mean a world in which men rec-
> ognize themselves in each other, and in which the "principle of
> authority"—that is, force, whatever its origin and justification—
> concedes its place to a responsible form of liberty.[45]

THE DESTRUCTIVE ROLE OF MEXICAN INTELLECTUALS

It was not until early in the 1990s that Mexico, led by President Carlos
Salinas de Gortari, concluded that its best interests would be served by
an intimate economic relationship with its northern neighbor, one that
would both promote trade with the most dynamic national market in
the world and welcome the presence of U.S. multinational corporations. The Salinas initiative turned its back on decades of Mexican
anti-Americanism (of varying intensities, to be sure) and had to have
been extraordinarily unsettling to those Mexican intellectuals and
politicians whose stock in trade was scapegoating the United States, all
the more unsettling in the wake of the collapse of communism in
Eastern Europe and the landslide defeat of the Sandinistas in the 1990
Nicaraguan elections. Many of those Mexican leaders were "socialists,"
and they were comparably upset by Salinas's moves to reduce the role
of the state in the economy and his introduction of the free-market
policies that they pejoratively referred to as *neo-liberalismo*.

The criticism by the Mexican left of the Salinas economic initiatives has intensified with the economic crisis that began at the end of 1994. By that time, NAFTA was a fait accompli, and the United States had no choice but to bail Mexico out massively, in cooperation with the International Monetary Fund and other First World countries. By that time, also, the projections that had convinced the U.S. Congress to vote for NAFTA were worthless, as the tale at the outset of this chapter stresses. One can only speculate about what would have happened to the Mexican economy if the U.S. had not decided to support it. An economic catastrophe that led to a revolution would have been one reasonable scenario.

Their disparaging references to *neo-liberalismo* notwithstanding, few Mexican intellectuals are today promoting a return to socialism and import substitution, and many have concluded, reluctantly, that the intimate economic relationship with the United States is, on balance, a good thing.

What would have happened if Mexico had promoted close economic ties with the United States in the early 1950s rather than waiting until the early 1990s? Most observers would, I think, agree that Mexico would today be substantially better off economically, more technologically advanced, and more democratic.

Why did Mexico instead choose an arm's-length, sometimes confrontational posture toward the United States? The answer lies in the Mexican psyche, shaped by the trauma of the Mexican-American War and the intimidating success of the United States, which may well have contributed to the inferiority feelings emphasized by Samuel Ramos. The 1950s were also years in which the import substitution, *dependencia*-based strategy of Raúl Prebisch and CEPAL first reverberated throughout Latin America. Most Latin American countries, Mexico included, pursued foreign policies vis-à-vis the United States that were predicated on considerations of national power and prestige, the consolidation of internal power, and ideology, as Carlos Escudé has pointed out. Few Latin American countries (Costa Rica being an exception) pursued what Escudé labels a "citizen-centric" foreign policy, "one whose overriding objective was the well-being of the citizen."[46]

These political, ideological, and emotional forces were reflected in, and reinforced by, the voices of influential Mexican intellectuals, who generally viewed the United States as greedy, insensitive, and reactionary, if not evil. That the United States was the bellwether of international capitalism discredited the free market for those intellectuals and reinforced the socialist tendencies that were of biblical loftiness in the Latin American universities where many of them had studied. They were the children of José Enrique Rodó, the Uruguayan writer, and his *Ariel*.

Jorge Castañeda today writes columns for *Newsweek* and articles for *The Atlantic Monthly*, although until recent years, he was among the most strident anti-American intellectuals in Mexico. (He did his undergraduate work at Princeton.) With Enrique Hett, he wrote *The Economics of Dependency*, published in 1978, an explicitly Marxist tract that draws extensively on the theories of Andre Gunder Frank and the old Fernando Henrique Cardoso as well as the "imperialism" writings of Lenin.[47] The book is filled with Marxist cant, including the cause-and-effect relationship between, on the one hand, "capitalism" and "imperialism," chiefly in the United States, and Third World "underdevelopment" on the other. One of the authors' conclusions: "Democracy is in absolute contradiction with capitalism."[48]

Over the years, Castañeda has moderated his views, as is apparent from *Limits to Friendship: The United States and Mexico* (1988), which he co-authored with Robert Pastor;[49] *Utopia Unarmed: The Latin American Left After the Cold War* (1993);[50] and his article "Ferocious Differences," in the July 1995 *Atlantic Monthly*, in which he places heavy emphasis on cultural factors as an explanation for Mexico's problems. Castañeda now probably resides at the left edge of the democratic-capitalist consensus. As late as *Limits to Friendship*,[51] he was making a spirited defense of the same primary school textbooks that have been described to me by a prominent Mexican editor as "presenting Mexicans as victims of the United States, anticapitalist, and anti-entrepreneurial." New textbooks without the ideological skew started to be introduced during the Salinas administration.

But however much his views may have moderated in recent years, Castañeda's influence in Mexican, Latin American, and U.S. intellectual circles (he was a senior associate at the Carnegie Endowment for International Peace in Washington from 1985 to 1987 and has been a frequent speaker at American universities) was pernicious for relationships between Mexico (and Latin America more generally) and the United States. How could a constructive relationship be possible between a "victim" and an "exploiter"? Castañeda's destructive influence was magnified through a program of U.S. studies he introduced at the Autonomous University of Mexico.

Lorenzo Meyer teaches at the prestigious and influential Colegio de México and is a prolific writer. His orientation is less ideological and more nationalistic. While his views on the United States have also moderated with time, his earlier writings reflect the belief that Mexico has suffered from its economic relationships with the United States.[52] He concludes his section of *México Frente a Estados Unidos* with an explanation of Mexico's foreign policy wholly inconsistent with Salinas's NAFTA initiative:

> Whatever the form—support of nationalistic revolutions in Central America, Third Worldism, the search for markets in Europe and Asia, the Charter of Economic Rights and Obligations of nations, the North-South Dialogue, the denuclearization of Latin America . . . Mexico's foreign policy . . . had as its ultimate motive the conquest and defense of a minimum independent space that would permit Mexican nationalism, nourished by more than a century and a half of international conflict, to survive the subjugating presence of the neighboring United States of America.[53]

I might add that when I spoke at the Colegio de México late in 1995, Meyer served, graciously, as the commentator. His opening comment: "Fifteen years ago, Harrison's presentation would not have been possible here."

Adolfo Aguilar Zinser is another influential intellectual of the left, formerly of the PRI and now an independent in the Mexican legislature. The views he expressed at a 1983 symposium on nonalignment sponsored by the Mexican and Yugoslav governments are representative of Mexico's intellectual mainstream for several decades.[54] He describes the Monroe Doctrine as "defin[ing] . . . the exclusive zone of influence of a country no longer in search of colonies but of hegemonies."[55] "Moreover, the United States considered the American Continent as its own, the economic resources and potential development of which would naturally and, according to the relentless law of enterprise-oriented gains, flow into its economic arsenal to the benefit of its limitless expansion."[56] He refers to the Caribbean Basin Initiative, through which the United States offered special trade preferences to Caribbean Basin countries, as "a tardy political, economic and military stratagem for preventing any escape from the U.S. strategic border and security system imposed already for decades."[57] He labels the Cuban Revolution "successful," the Sandinista Revolution in Nicaragua "triumphant."[58] And he castigates the United States for not supporting the desperate adventure of the Argentine generals and admirals (several of whom were imprisoned during the administration of Argentine president Raúl Alfonsín) to conquer the Falkland Islands.[59]

To be sure, the views of Castañeda, Meyer, Aguilar Zinser, and many other Mexican intellectuals, which posed so great an obstacle to intimate, constructive relationships between Mexico and the United States, found considerable echo in U.S. intellectual circles, where the dependency/imperialism explanation of Latin America's underdevelopment swiftly became the conventional wisdom. The Harvard historian John Womack, an expert on Mexico, participated in a 1971 discussion with Octavio Paz and others that Paz incorporates into *El Ogro Filantrópico*. Among Womack's contributions:

> [I]f the United States maintains its current economic and political organization, with its armed forces so autonomous and corrupt . . . the preservation of Mexico's sovereignty will require closed and authoritarian politics in Mexico. . . . [T]he way the United States is today seriously limits the possibility of new liberties for the Mexicans. . . . [T]he best way for [Americans] to help Mexico is to dedicate themselves with renewed impetus to a profound democratic reform [of the United States] with the goal of installing some kind of socialism.[60]

Some Exceptions

Some Mexican intellectuals, a small minority until recent years, have argued against national foreign and economic policies based on dependency, nationalism, and statism. An example is Luis Pazos, whose voice on behalf of open economic and political systems—democratic-capitalism—has become increasingly influential in the 1990s. And even in the heyday of Mexico's anti-American, socialist nationalism two decades ago, at least one Mexican, Edmundo O'Gorman, had the courage to argue that Mexico's real problems were not the consequence of Yankee imperialism—although he has few kind words for U.S. foreign policy—but of Mexico's Ibero-Catholic cultural traditions. In *Mexico: The Trauma of Its History*, O'Gorman first points to the dramatic contrast between the evolution of the former British and former Spanish colonies in the New World, as I noted earlier in this chapter. He explicitly describes both colonial Spain and the Roman Catholic Church as "the traditional enemies of progress."[61] He then proceeds to challenge "the spiritual superiority of the Latin American vis-à-vis the North American,"[62] the superiority that Rodó and his myriad followers have asserted. And he labels the dependency explanation for Latin America's problems as scapegoating: "the real culpability for the failure of the Mexican program of liberal regeneration is the Mexican himself."[63]

O'Gorman's indictment of Mexican nationalism after World War II is searing. In his view, Mexicans are guilty of

> an unbalanced glorification of what is Mexican: their heroes were superhuman; the Mexican never had to admit error; official announcements were infallible; disasters were transformed into successful enterprises; everything made in Mexico was well made, and popular crafts were elevated to the highest esthetic levels. More than ever before they recurred to imperialist perversity to explain failures and deficiencies resulting from causes so obvious as the corruption, apathy, ineptitude or the ignorance of those really responsible, and as frosting on the cake they initiated the most radical flight from reality by trying to link the national destiny to the Third World, that curious entity that defines itself by what it isn't, while promoting a new species of nationalism that alienates us [from the wellspring of our Western culture].[64]

O'Gorman concludes with a plea to Mexicans to seek their salvation in the mainstream of Western culture and the "universal civilization" that flows from that culture.

WHITHER MEXICO?

Mexico in the mid-1990s is a country in deep crisis. The peso has collapsed, and without a bailout package put together by the United States, the collapse could easily have become free-fall. Interest rates and inflation are in excess of 35 percent as of this writing, many businesses have failed, and unemployment has soared. The PRI's control of politics is unraveling, as evidenced by the Chiapas uprising; the assassinations of Luis Donaldo Colosio, Salinas de Gortari's chosen successor, and José Francisco Ruiz Massieu, Secretary General of the PRI; the jail-ing of Salinas de Gortari's brother Raúl as a suspect in the murder of Ruiz Massieu (Raúl's former brother-in-law), and the subsequent disclosure that Raúl had deposited upward of $100 million in Swiss and other foreign banks. Within the PRI itself there are at least two factions: the "dinosaurs," exemplified by wheeler-dealer Carlos Hank González, who are reluctant to yield the monopoly powers the PRI has enjoyed for so long; and the reformers, apparently led by President Ernesto Zedillo, who has appointed an opposition Partido de Acción Nacional (PAN) leader as attorney general, has permitted PAN gubernatorial candidates to win several governorships, and has announced that he will not continue the tradition of naming his successor.

It is now apparent to most Mexicans that their problems are homemade, that blaming the United States is neither reasonable nor helpful. Mexicans understandably resent the U.S. tutelary posture with respect to the Mexican government's management of the economy. But many Mexicans believe that this is the consequence of the mismanagement of Salinas de Gortari, who has become a far more unpopular figure than Uncle Sam. During a ten-day speaking trip in five Mexican cities in November and December 1995, I found intense interest in probing the link between Ibero-Catholic culture and Mexico's acute problems.*

As I have noted in earlier chapters, profound crises are often crucial turning points in a cultural as well as a historical sense. The horror of the Spanish Civil War contributed to the emergence of a more tolerant, flexible citizenry and, forty years later, democracy in Spain. The Allende-Pinochet trauma forcefully reminded the Chileans of the costs of extremism and the value of their pluralist traditions. The collapse of the Ottoman Empire and the near-conversion of Turkey into a Greek colony made Mustafa Kemal's cultural revolution possible.

In Mexico's current crisis, in which it is apparent both that the country has failed to create a modern society and that the one-party monopoly is collapsing, two broad scenarios suggest themselves:

1: An irreversible process of political and social reform occurs, led by President Zedillo, including a vigorous campaign to root out corrup-

---

*The only exception was a discussion at the Colegio de la Frontera Norte (COLEF), near Tijuana, where the faculty and graduate students present were still largely committed to the dependency/imperialism/victim view.

tion, consolidate the independence of the judiciary, and assure the independence of the electoral authorities and the media. The economy recovers, albeit slowly; unemployment declines, but the economy still is unable to generate enough jobs for the million annual new entrants into the job market. Opposition parties make major inroads in the legislative elections of 1997; the PRI presidential candidate in the year 2000 is chosen in open convention; and an opposition party wins the presidency either in 2000 or 2006.

2: Zedillo is unable to resolve the immense economic and political problems he has inherited, including continuing deep economic recession, the abuses and intrigues of his predecessors, revelation of the extent to which corruption has been institutionalized, the profound involvement of drug traffickers in that corruption, and the generalized debility of Mexican institutions. He is overthrown, or assassinated, with the complicity of powerful elements of the PRI, perhaps in collaboration with the military. An authoritarian government is installed in the wake of widespread bloodshed. A similar outcome with a longer fuse might result from Zedillo, under pressure from the PRI dinosaurs, sliding back into the old ways of party control, including the rigging of elections.

I think the first scenario is more likely but do not foreclose the second. The longer-term consequences of the second scenario are a compelling argument to avoid it at all cost: pariah status in the Western Hemisphere and elsewhere; the probable expulsion of Mexico from NAFTA; extreme and prolonged economic difficulties; the likelihood of the emergence of a popular opposition movement leading to a civil war.

But Mexico also counts on several assets that enhance the likelihood of the first scenario. Most Mexicans are disgusted and embarrassed by the revealed reality of the Mexican "system." The educated middle class is substantial, and much of it is committed to democracy and the free market. Many of Mexico's business leaders realize that their interests are better served by a transition to genuine pluralism and a truly free market. The values of the United States increasingly compete with traditional Ibero-Catholic values, particularly in more progressive northern Mexico, the symbol of which is the dynamic city of Monterrey. Protestantism, with small but increasing numbers of congregants, provides some challenge to the Catholic monopoly and promotes many of the universal progress values. Many of the intellectuals

may still harbor resentment of the United States, but they are generally committed to democracy and are unlikely to press for resocialization
of the economy.

In sum, there is reason to believe that the cultures of the United
States, Canada, and Mexico are converging, a conclusion documented
by the surveys of Ronald Inglehart, Miguel Basáñez, and Neil Nevitte.[65]

The United States made a major error in embracing Mexico, governed by a corrupt one-party system with little respect for the law, in
NAFTA. The United States is paying for that error through the
employment and trade disadvantages that accrue to it as a result of the
massive devaluation of the peso, also with the $20 billion it has made
available to stabilize the Mexican economy. Latin America will also
pay for the error: the process of extending NAFTA to other hemispheric countries is on hold, and the ten-year time frame that was
established at the Miami Summit of the Americas in 1994 will surely
be stretched out.

But Mexico is the beneficiary of the U.S.'s error. It was kept from
an economic free-fall by the bailout package, and its economic recovery will be facilitated by the advantages conferred on it by a much
cheaper peso. (The reverse of that is, of course, lower U.S. exports to
Mexico, higher imports from Mexico, and a loss of American jobs.)
Perhaps most important, for both political and economic reasons, the
U.S. after NAFTA has a substantially increased stake in Mexico, and it
will do everything it can to assure that the first scenario materializes.

I only hope that, as Mexico works its way out of the crisis, it does
not lose sight of the cultural factors that in large measure explain it; and
that, through initiatives like a sweeping reform of the education system,
Mexico works to reinforce the progressive values and attitudes on
which its future stability and prosperity depend.

9

Trade and Investment: From "Imperialism" to Integration?

NAFTA is intended to encompass an array of economic relations beyond trade in goods and services, such as investment, transportation, communications, border relations, environmental and labor matters, just to name a few.
—SIDNEY WEINTRAUB, NAFTA—What Comes Next?

Hemispheric integration is far from a free lunch and far from certain to be the panacea it is often made out to be.
—ROBERT A. BLECKER AND WILLIAM E. SPRIGGS, Trade Liberalization in the Western Hemisphere

The purpose of this chapter is not to debate the pros and cons of the North American Free Trade Agreement (NAFTA) or a possible Western Hemisphere Free Trade Agreement (WHFTA). I believe that, in the long run, it is in the interest of the United States, Canada, and Latin America to move toward a closer integration of economic relationships through reduction and ultimately elimination of tariff and nontariff barriers to trade in the Hemisphere, as well as facilitation of foreign investment. To be sure, the United States has already taken major steps toward opening up its market to Latin America in the Generalized System of Preferences (1976) and the Caribbean Basin Initiative preferences (1984).

The Canadian-U.S. Free Trade Agreement (CUFTA), now folded into NAFTA, appears to be realizing the benefits for both countries that its proponents forecast. Mexico is likely to benefit more than the United States from NAFTA, particularly after the massive peso devaluations of 1994–95, and Latin America more than the United States from a WHFTA, particularly from assured access to the U.S. market. As a proportion of their total trade, Latin America is likely to be a smaller trading partner for the United States than the United States is for Latin America for some time to come. Among other benefits of WHFTA, a formalized trade and investment agreement between Latin America and the United States/Canada would increase the probability of irreversibility of Latin America's sweeping political and economic reforms of recent years. If Latin America sustains higher levels of growth and achieves better distribution of the fruits of that growth through democratic capitalism, it is likely to become an increasingly important trading partner for the U.S. and recipient of U.S. investment. Canada, which has historically traded little[1] with and invested little in Latin America, could also benefit substantially from a prospering Latin America.

My purpose here is threefold: (1) to place current economic relationships in the Hemisphere in better perspective in the wake of the hyperbole that surrounded the NAFTA debate in the United States; (2) to explore the implications for expanded trade and investment of the cultural differences, underscored by the post-NAFTA Mexican crisis, that go so far in explaining the striking contrast between Latin America, on the one hand, and the United States and Canada, on the other; and (3) to consider what #1 and #2 imply in terms of a pragmatic strategy to advance the process of integration.

THE WESTERN HEMISPHERE IN ECONOMIC PERSPECTIVE

When Mexico's then-president Carlos Salinas de Gortari proposed to President George Bush in 1991 that Mexico join with the United States in a free trade agreement, he jettisoned a long-standing Mexican—and Latin American—economic strategy that Isaac Cohen has labeled "defensive nationalism."[2] The strategy was rooted in the turmoil of the world market in the 1930s and 1940s[3] and nurtured by the widespread view after World War II that Latin America's underdevelopment was the consequence of exploitation, above all by the United States. Defensive nationalism was the strategy that naturally flowed from dependency theory, and it translated into import substitution and avoidance of the world market, on the one hand, and limits and controls on—and, in the extreme, nationalization of—foreign investment. Partly as a consequence, as table 9.1 shows, exports play a relatively

Table 9.1

VALUE OF EXPORTS AS A PERCENTAGE OF GNP/GDP

Country	1978 (GNP)	1993 (GDP)
United States	7	7
Japan	12	9
Canada	21	30
Germany	24	20
United Kingdom	26	22
Argentina	13	5
Brazil	7	9
Chile	16	21
Mexico	7	9

Source: World Bank, World Development Report 1980, 1995.

small role in the economies of Argentina, Brazil, and Mexico (as it does in the United States and Japan, too), particularly by contrast with Canada and some European countries. The table also indicates the impact of Chile's opening up to the world market since the mid-1970s and, to a lesser degree, Mexico's opening up in the 1980s.

Salinas's pragmatic initiative was presented at a time of high receptivity in the United States as a result of (1) a chronic, large, and growing U.S. trade deficit; (2) the snail's pace of worldwide trade liberalization negotiations under the General Agreement on Tariffs and Trade (GATT); (3) an increasingly dynamic European integration movement with a host of new aspirants following the collapse of the Soviet empire; (4) initiatives toward economic integration in East Asia, led by Japan but quite possibly with the involvement of the biggest dragon of them all, China; and (5) growing concern about the heavy flow of immigrants from Mexico, coupled with the belief that rapid economic growth in Mexico would stem the flow.

The political stakes in both the United States and Mexico were high (less so in Canada, which had already bitten the bullet in signing CUFTA). Salinas tied his own prestige and that of the PRI to a successful negotiation, and Presidents Bush and Clinton both went out on a limb in support of the enabling legislation. Some hyperbole by advocates was the inevitable result.

HYPERBOLE NO. 1:
"A NAFTA embracing 363 million people; a WHFTA embracing over 700 million people (compared to 345 million in the European Community)."

The numbers are accurate for 1990, but misleading. Of the NAFTA total of 363 million, 86 million, or almost a quarter, are Mexicans, with per capita purchasing power one-tenth or less of that of a Canadian or American. In terms of an effective market for U.S. exports, then, 86 million Mexicans convert into perhaps 8 million, about the population of Sweden.[4] Similarly, 433 million, or 61 percent, of the WHFTA total of 710 million are from Latin America and the Caribbean. Given the fact that Mexico's per capita income is above the Latin American average, those 433 million might convert into an effective market of 35 million, less than the population of Spain.

Thus, the *effective* population of NAFTA in 1990 would be 285 million, of WHFTA 312 million, both substantially below the European Community (now "Union") total.[5]

HYPERBOLE NO. 2:
"NAFTA created a $6 trillion economy (1990 GDP data)."

It is true that when one adds the 1990 GDP of the United States, Canada, and Mexico, the total is $6.2 trillion. However, the United States, with 250 million people, accounts for $5.4 trillion, or 87 percent of the total; Canada, with 27 million people, for $570 billion, or 9 percent; and Mexico, with 86 million people, for $238 billion, or but 4 percent of the total.[6]

HYPERBOLE NO. 3:
"With its new, open policies, including sharp reductions in tariffs, and resultant economic growth, Mexico has become the third most important market for U.S. exports."

As table 9.2 demonstrates, Mexico has been our third most important market at least since 1985, and while its imports from the United States had grown impressively in recent years—and are greater than

Table 9.2

U.S. TRADE DATA 1985–94
($ BILLIONS)

U.S. Exports to	1985	1990	1991	1992	1993	1994	1995
World	$219.2	$393.0	$421.9	$447.5	$464.9	$512.4	$583.9
Canada	52.9	83.0	85.1	90.2	100.2	114.3	127.0
Japan	22.2	48.6	48.1	47.8	47.9	53.5	64.3
Mexico	13.6	28.4	33.3	40.6	41.6	50.8	46.3
UK	11.1	23.5	22.1	22.8	26.4	26.4	28.8
All LA/Carib. (incl. Mex.)	30.7	54.1	63.5	75.7	78.5	92.6	90.7
Mexico as % total U.S	6%	7%	8%	9%	9%	10%	8%
LA/Carib. as % total U.S.	14%	13.8%	15%	16.9%	16.9%	18%	15.5%

U.S. Imports from							
World	$343.6	$491.3	$483.8	$525.1	$574.9	$657.9	$743.4
Canada	68.9	91.2	90.9	98.2	110.5	128.8	145.1
Japan	68.2	89.6	91.2	95.5	106.2	117.5	123.6
Mexico	18.9	29.5	30.4	33.9	38.7	48.6	61.7
All LA/Carib. (incl. Mex.)	46.4	62.4	61.0	66.5	72.7	86.3	100.8
LA/Carib. as % total U.S.	13.5%	12.7%	12.6%	12.7%	12.6%	13.1%	13.6%

Source: U.S. Department of Commerce data adapted by U.S. Agency for International Development in "United States Merchandise Trade with Developing Countries," July 1995; Foreign Trade Division, Bureau of the Census 1995 preliminary estimates.

imports from the U.S. of all other Latin American countries—even in the record year of 1994, the value of Mexican imports from the U.S. was less than half that of the value of Canadian imports from the U.S. In fact, U.S. exports to Canada, a country with a population of 30 million, are substantially greater than our exports *to all of Latin America and the Caribbean*, with a population of 450 million, just as our imports from Canada are substantially larger than our imports *from all of Latin America and the Caribbean*. In 1995, of course, Mexican imports from the United States dropped by almost 10 percent.

HYPERBOLE NO. 4:
"NAFTA will significantly reduce illegal immigration from Mexico."

This assertion can only be true in the very long run—two or three decades. The gap in well-being between Mexico and the United States is vast: the poverty line in the United States is the upper-middle class in Mexico. It is not only a question of salary and benefit levels about ten times greater in the United States. Social services, including schooling for children and free medical services, are infinitely better north of the border. The treatment of illegal immigrants by the Border Patrol and law-enforcement authorities in the United States is highly benign by contrast with the treatment of poor, unconnected Mexicans by the Mexican police and courts. Simply by giving birth north of the border, a Mexican woman automatically produces a U.S. citizen, which makes it easier for the parents to obtain public services and facilitates their legal entry.

Mexico's population is growing more than twice as fast as that of the United States. Mexico's population today is about one-third that of the United States. In 2025, it will be almost one-half, and because of the youthfulness of the Mexican population, Mexico's labor force will be *more than* one-half that of the United States. The Mexican labor force is growing by more than a million persons annually, substantially more than even a dynamic Mexican economy can absorb. "For the foreseeable future, then, the assumption of an infinitely elastic supply of labor at a relatively constant real wage is a reasonable first approximation for Mexico . . . average Mexican real wages are unlikely to rise substantially for a long time to come—especially if Mexican workers have to compete with even lower-wage workers from other Latin American countries in a WHFTA."[7]

To the extent that worker incomes do improve in Mexico, the result could be an *increase* in illegal immigration as it becomes easier to accumulate the stake necessary to get to the border, survive there for some period, and pay agents for false documentation and assistance crossing the border.

HYPERBOLE NO. 5:

"The productivity of American workers is far higher than that of Mexican workers. Therefore, Americans need not worry about good-paying jobs migrating south."

Productivity reflects a combination of worker skills, capital/technology per worker, and management. Particularly if the work to be done requires training and practical experience rather than years of education, leaps in productivity can be achieved by adding capital/technology (usually in the form of equipment) and efficient management. While it is true that average productivity is much lower in Mexico than in the United States,

> it can be highly productive in sectors where foreign capital has brought in up-to-date technology and management. In domestic corn production, for example, Mexico's productivity is very low. But in sectors such as electronics and automobiles, its productivity has in recent years been converging on that of the U.S. rapidly. As Mexico's productivity has approached America's in these industries, Mexico's wages have remained far lower. Mexico has acquired an enormous competitive advantage in unit labor costs (wages relative to productivity).[8]

HYPERBOLE NO. 6:

"Latin America is a major recipient of U.S. direct investment."

In 1991, U.S. direct investment abroad totaled $1.7 trillion. Europe accounted for the lion's share with $909 billion, or 54 percent. (The total for the U.K., the largest single recipient, was $347 billion.) Asia and the Pacific accounted for $328 billion, or 19 percent. The total for Canada was $203 billion, or 12 percent, more than twice as much as all of Latin America, which totaled $97 billion, or 6 *percent of total U.S. investment abroad.*[9]

Foreign direct investment in the United States totaled $1.8 trillion in 1991, slightly exceeding U.S. investment abroad as of that year. Japan was the leader at $439 billion, or 25 percent of the total. The U.K. followed at $290 billion (17 percent), with Canada third at $233 billion (13 percent), *a greater amount than the U.S. had invested in Canada* ($203 billion). Total direct Latin American investment in the United States was $27 billion, less than 2 percent of the U.S. total.[10]

AND THE BIG QUESTION MARK: WILL THE NEW ECONOMIC POLICIES ASSURE ACCELERATED GROWTH?

With the exception of Cuba, and to a much lesser extent Venezuela, all Latin American countries have junked the statist, import substitution policies of the past several decades in favor of the free-market, free-trade policies that the IMF, World Bank, and U.S. government have advocated. Latin America could not ignore the compelling export-driven miracles of South Korea, Taiwan, Hong Kong, and Singapore that have carried those countries into, or very close to, the First World; the more recent export-driven high growth rates of Thailand, Malaysia, Indonesia, and China; Chile's rapid and sustained export-driven growth; and increasing evidence that import substitution and state intervention were leading Latin America down a dead-end street.

But, as Paul Krugman has observed, "the widespread belief that moving to free trade and free markets will produce a dramatic acceleration in a developing country's growth represents a leap of faith."[11] With the exception of Chile, which got a head start and has been sustaining an annual growth rate of about 6 percent, there is no solid evidence in Latin America yet that the new policies significantly accelerate growth, let alone miracles. Krugman observes, "Although capital flows into Mexico reached more than $30 billion in 1993, the country's rate of growth over the 1990–94 period averaged only 2.5 percent, less than population growth [*sic*]. . . . Argentina grew at an average annual rate of more than 6 percent after the stabilization of the peso. But even optimists admitted that this growth had much to do with the extremely depressed state of the economy before the reforms. . . . Across Latin America as a whole, real growth in the period 1990–94 averaged only 3.1 percent per year."[12]

As I argued in *Who Prospers?* the East Asian miracles reflect the Confucian/Tao values of work, frugality, education, and merit, all linked to an orientation toward the future and the entrepreneurial function. The same values are relevant to the experiences of Thailand, Malaysia, and Indonesia, where the Chinese minorities have played a vastly disproportionate role in economic growth. Those values have not been nurtured by Ibero-Catholic culture. As an example of the contrast, savings rates of the East Asian countries approximate 35 percent of GDP, roughly twice that of Latin America, where "savings rates have been the world's lowest since the 1960s."[13] To be sure, Chile has increased savings to 25 percent of GDP through an enforced pension program, but no other Latin American country has yet reproduced the Chilean achievement.

With democratically elected governments running the show in almost all countries, and with most of them living in a politically volatile mixture of social injustice and lack of discipline, the people and the politicians will not wait forever for the promised improvements in growth and equity. Politicians and intellectuals of the left increasingly sneer at *neo-liberalismo* economic policy, although they have little to offer in the way of alternatives. Some of them have cited the Mexican crisis as evidence of the failure of the new economic policies.

The Mexican crisis has surely not made things any easier. Among other costs, it has, understandably, made the United States and Canada gun-shy about expanding NAFTA. Senator Daniel Patrick Moynihan recently said of the possibility of expanding NAFTA, "I am not sure we are ready for more adventures."[14] Latin American disenchantment with the slow pace of follow-up on the bold declarations in Miami at the end of 1994 has opened space for Brazil to challenge the United States through its promotion of MERCOSUR.[15]

If the new, open policies fail to generate rapid growth by the end of the 1990s, it is likely that in at least some countries, the new economic policies will lose credibility and become a victim of building political pressures. Democracy could be another victim, although this is a good deal less likely than it was in prior decades.

INTEGRATION AND CULTURE

In theory, it should be possible for free trade to occur among countries very different in their levels of development and their political institutions—and in their value systems. The basic mechanism of free trade is the elimination or harmonizing of tariffs and nontariff barriers. But, as Sidney Weintraub has stressed, free trade does not operate in a vacuum. It is inevitably linked to other economic issues, above all exchange rate, fiscal, and monetary policy, but also foreign investment and wage policy; administrative issues like the efficiency and honesty of customs operations; and even broad political issues like the independence of the judiciary and the degree of corruption in government. In the case of Europe, economic integration has promoted political integration, symbolized by the European Parliament.

Latin America has experimented extensively with ambitious integration schemes since World War II: the Latin American Free Trade Association (LAFTA), involving ten South American countries and Mexico, which was established in 1960 and restructured as the Latin American Integration Association (LAIA) in 1980; the Central American Common Market (CACM), also established in 1960; the Andean Group (ANCOM), established in 1969; and the Southern Cone Common Market (MERCOSUR), established in 1991. A large number of bilateral trade agreements have also been negotiated (for example, Chile and Mexico in 1991).

Weintraub, who is a strong supporter of NAFTA, describes these integration initiatives as "a crazy-quilt of cross-memberships and nests of small arrangements within larger agreements," and notes, "[d]espite the invigoration and proliferation of economic integration schemes, intraregional trade . . . is not extensive."[16] Trade between Argentina and Brazil has grown rapidly since MERCOSUR was established, but it is too early to conclude that MERCOSUR will achieve the sustained substantial expansion of intraregional trade that has eluded the other schemes.

I believe that the same factors—policy and institutional, to be sure, but even more important, cultural—that explain national underdevelopment in Latin America also become obstacles to integration schemes. The CACM is a case in point. Robert Pastor states that "the CACM fell victim to civil wars in Central America."[17] In fact, the CACM ran out of steam long before the Sandinista Revolution and the FMLN insurgency in El Salvador of the late 1970s, even before the 1969 "Soccer War" between El Salvador and Honduras. As Isaac Cohen explains, the early years of the CACM did not exact any significant sacrifices of the Central Americans, in part because the U.S. government was providing substantial support for integration.[18] After the early, "easy" momentum was spent, in the late 1960s, the Central Americans were unwilling to make shorter-term sacrifices for longer-term gains, and the level of trade stagnated. Integration was not stalled by political upheaval but by a lack of will.

A further dimension of the CACM problem is also relevant to this discussion: the striking differences between Costa Rica, on the one hand, and Guatemala, Honduras, El Salvador, and Nicaragua, on the other.[19] Democracy is firmly rooted in Costa Rica, incipient and fragile in the others. Costa Rica's per capita income is roughly double that of El Salvador and Guatemala, three times that of Honduras, and six times that of neighboring Nicaragua.[20] Costa Rica enjoys 93 percent adult literacy; literacy is 73 percent in El Salvador and Honduras, 55 percent in Guatemala.[21] Due process in the judicial system is a substantial reality only in Costa Rica.

Many Costa Ricans understandably, if wrongly, fear that the CACM will drag Costa Rica down to a lower common denominator. They worry that their high wages relative to the rest of Central America will leave them at a competitive disadvantage. They are concerned about substantial continuing immigration from Nicaragua. And they understandably tend to see themselves as much more like Chile, Uruguay, and even the United States than their Central American partners. Costa Rica's psychology with respect to the CACM is thus similar to the psychology of the United States and Canada with respect to WHFTA.

FOLLOWING IN EUROPE'S FOOTSTEPS?

Twice since the end of World War II, the United States has announced major initiatives in the Western Hemisphere that reflect Western Europe's experience. The trigger for the Alliance for Progress, proclaimed by the Kennedy administration in 1961, was the 1959 Cuban Revolution, followed by rapidly expanding Cuban-Soviet ties. But the model for the U.S. response was the enormously successful Marshall Plan, which helped to rebuild Western Europe and revive its economic dynamism in a decade. The Alliance for Progress planners concluded that if Europe could be revitalized from total devastation to peace and prosperity in ten years with the dedication of massive U.S. resources, the Alliance would assure that Latin America would be well on its way to prosperity, with democracy consolidated, within a decade.

Within a few years, it had become apparent that the Alliance's ten-year time frame was wildly optimistic. In 1966, Teodoro Moscoso, the architect of Puerto Rico's Operation Bootstrap and the first U.S. coordinator of the Alliance for Progress—and at the outset highly optimistic about the prospects of the Alliance—said, "The Latin American case is so complex, so difficult to solve, and so fraught with human and global danger and distress that the use of the word 'anguish' is not an exaggeration. The longer I live, the more I believe that, just as no human being can save another who does not have the will to save himself, no country can save others no matter how good its intentions or how hard it tries."[22]

George Bush announced his Enterprise for the Americas initiative in mid-1990, prompted by the several motives mentioned in this chapter. The initiative was formalized with the signing of NAFTA in 1993 and the Summit of the Americas Declaration of Principles in December 1994. The latter contained the statement, "We further resolve to conclude the negotiation of the Free Trade Area of the Americas no later than 2005, and agree that concrete progress toward the attainment of this objective will be made by the end of this century."

Once again, a ten-year period of transformation, about what it took to consolidate the early European Common Market. And once again the probability that, in the Latin American context, the ten years was highly optimistic, even had the Mexican crisis not occurred. Weintraub noted shortly before the Miami summit, "Progress toward free trade in the hemisphere is likely to be slow for reasons centered in the political and economic situations in both the United States and Latin America. . . . Other than Mexico and Chile, few LAC [Latin American and Caribbean] countries are ready and economically able to open their markets to free trade with the United States."[23] The political problems in the United States were symbolized by the extremely close congressional vote on NAFTA, an initiative that Senator Moynihan now labels an "adventure."

As was apparent from the Alliance for Progress, Latin America is not Western Europe. European political and economic institutions at the national level are rooted in a far more progressive value system, one that lends itself to economic and even political integration schemes. But, with few exceptions, democracy is not consolidated in Latin America, and with the possible exception of Chile, neither is modern capitalism. Largely because of a European initiative in the 1980s, a Central

American Parliament exists today. But how could it function effectively when democratic ideas and institutions are incipient and fragile in four of the five member countries, and high levels of mistrust exist between neighboring countries? In fact, the Central American Parliament is an expensive debating society and social club. As Robert Pastor observes, "Theories developed using the Western European experience suggest that increased economic interaction does not lead to integration and political community *unless* there is an increase in trust and of shared experiences that reinforce positive feelings toward each other."[24]

But Pastor then goes on to suggest that it is time to think about a Western Hemisphere parliament: "If the premise is accurate—that a Western Hemisphere economic area will mean that domestic agendas will become the subject of international negotiations—then a forum will be needed to debate norms and policies on such issues."[25] Given the cultural and institutional chasm that still separates Canada and the United States from Latin America, for years and perhaps decades to come, a Western Hemisphere parliament might have even less relevance to the real world than does today's Central American Parliament.

The United States ignored at great cost one lesson of the Western European integration experience: the European policy that any candidate nation have impeccable democratic credentials. Had we applied that policy, Mexico would not have been given serious consideration, and Chile would probably have been the first Latin American free-trade partner of Canada and the United States.[26]

LATIN AMERICAN "STEREOTYPES"

I have known Sid Weintraub for more than two decades. He is among the most distinguished economists the Department of State has produced, and he has also had the experience of directing a USAID mission. He knows Latin America, having served in Mexico and Chile and having worked on Latin American problems for many years in Washington. As Dean Rusk Professor of International Affairs at the Lyndon B. Johnson School of Public Affairs at the University of Texas and occupant of the William E. Simon Chair in Political Economy at the Center for Strategic and International Studies in Washington, he is the United States's foremost expert on NAFTA, which he has supported vigorously.

When, in 1983, I completed the manuscript of *Underdevelopment*

Is a State of Mind, I sent a copy to Sid for his comments. He was very skeptical of the thesis, but he thought it was worthy of consideration. He even helped me try to find a publisher, a daunting process for someone without a publishing track record, on which I almost gave up several times. His reaction was that of most economists: culture is not important; what is important is getting the economic signals right. As I pointed out earlier in this book, that position flies in the face of the fact that some ethnic groups do better than others in multicultural societies in which the economic signals are available to all.

In 1994, before the collapse of the Mexican peso and the onset of Mexico's prolonged crisis, Weintraub published *NAFTA—What Comes Next?* He wrote it after NAFTA came into effect on 1 January 1994, a time when Rudiger Dornbusch and others were predicting continuing prosperity for Mexico.[27] In a section of Weintraub's book entitled "The Cultural Dimension," he has this to say:

> The people of the United States know little of Mexican history. And it was obvious during the debate on NAFTA that the interest groups and politicians also knew little. The debate was based on *stereotypes*: Mexicans are corrupt; they have no social consciousness; the country is non-democratic; the president is a dictator for six years; human rights are completely disregarded there and Mexicans cannot be expected to pay much heed to their environment unless prodded by U.S. sanctions of one kind or another. Much of the anti-immigrant fervor assumed that all—or most—Mexicans would flee to the United States if given half an opportunity.[28]

Today, most informed Americans—and many informed Mexicans[29]—might conclude that events have demonstrated that those were not stereotypes but largely accurate descriptions of what the crisis has revealed about Mexico and its culture. As I argued in chapter 8, whatever the economic policy errors made by the Salinas de Gortari and Zedillo administrations, at the heart of the Mexican crisis is a failed revolution, a failed dynasty, and above all, a failed culture.

WHERE DO WE GO FROM HERE?

The ten-year schedule for WHFTA announced at the Miami summit at the end of 1994 is a dead letter, the victim of the Mexican crisis. It is not just the emergency $20 billion bailout package that has provoked reactions like Senator Moynihan's use of the word *adventure*. The value of the peso against the dollar is as of this writing less than half what it was when NAFTA went into effect at the outset of 1994, and the new rate substantially nullifies the increases in U.S. exports to Mexico that NAFTA supporters promised, at the same time making Mexican exports to the U.S. significantly cheaper—at least for the time being. The $15 billion deficit in 1995 is not only painful for us in terms of our balance of payments and the strength of the dollar. It also implies significant costs in terms of the hundreds of thousands of jobs lost to Mexico, the concern at the heart of the AFL-CIO's opposition to NAFTA.

Moreover, Mexico's recovery is likely to be slow and painful, and the optimistic NAFTA trade projections are unlikely to be realized for some time. Meanwhile, the Tequila effect of the collapse of the peso on other Latin American countries—and indeed on the "emerging markets" in general—has been disruptive, particularly in terms of its negative impact on capital flows to the region and capital flight from the region, at least in the short run.

With the possible exception of Chile, which has weathered the Tequila effect without significant impact, it is unlikely that the U.S. Congress will be interested in considering new NAFTA partners for some years to come in the wake of the Mexican "adventure." Moreover, it is uncertain that the new free-market, outward-looking policies in Latin America will endure, particularly if they fail to produce high growth and employment generation in the next few years. And Latin America's disappointing experience with integration schemes during the past several decades, the apparent dynamism of MERCOSUR notwithstanding, leaves some big question marks. Finally, as we have been so forcefully reminded by the Mexican crisis, a wide cultural and institutional North/South gap exists, the apparent recent convergence of political institutions, economic policies, and values and attitudes notwithstanding. Yet, as I said at the outset of this chapter, it is in the long-term interest of the United States, Canada, and Latin America to facilitate a freer flow of commerce within the Hemisphere.

Sidney Weintraub's recognition of factors that argue for gradualism in Western Hemisphere economic integration leads him to an approach that makes a lot of sense to me: focus on the subregional arrangements and work to strengthen them as the building blocks of a subsequent WHFTA.[30] The lessons learned, the institutions built, and the people trained at the subregional level will be indispensable resources for the construction of a Hemisphere-wide free-trade arrangement. In subregional groupings, national economies can move toward international competitiveness without the wholesale bankruptcies that would result from a cold-turkey plunge into the world market. The success of subregional groupings would demonstrate to the United States and Canada a degree of maturity that would be reassuring for the prospects of the broader scheme. Conversely, failure of the subregional groupings would make a compelling case against proceeding with a WHFTA.

The subregional building block approach implies a much longer time frame than the participants at the Miami summit envisioned. And it caters to Brazil's ambitions to preempt the U.S. in South America. But, as the Mexican case reminds us, the economic integration of the Western Hemisphere poses problems that cannot be solved by the prescriptions of distinguished economists alone. The problems that impede effective integration run much deeper than economic policy, to the very essence of what makes societies work—or not work.

10

Narcotics: A Grotesque Distorting Mirror of Both Cultures

[T]he American people were aware that this situation was not simply a public policy crisis, but a profound moral crisis. There was a sense that the substance of American society was at stake. The drug crisis raises questions not only about our productivity and efficiency, but about our national character and our fitness to lead the world. Had our ancestors fought valiantly for liberty only to see it squandered in crack houses and back alleys? Was blood spilled at Gettysburg and in the Argonne and at Normandy to make the world safe for bongs and cocaine parties and marijuana smoke-ins? Were our great cities becoming the world portrayed in Lord of the Flies? Were we descending into barbarism and into a world governed only by appetite and instinct?
—GOVERNOR BOB MARTINEZ, DIRECTOR OF THE U.S. OFFICE OF NATIONAL DRUG CONTROL POLICY, 1991

Latin America as a whole is sliding into the drug war. Argentina and Brazil can see their future in Bolivia. Bolivia sees its own [future] in Peru, Peru in Colombia, and Colombia in Lebanon. It's an endless cycle.
—IBÁN DE REMENTERÍA OF THE ANDEAN COMMISSION OF JURISTS, 1991

One of the strongest north-south links in the Western Hemisphere today is highly pernicious: the drug trade. Widespread narcotics consumption in the United States both reflects and aggravates the erosion of the traditional Anglo-Protestant value foundation upon which America's success is based. Production and trafficking in Latin America have exposed the weakness of nascent democratic institutions and the traditional Ibero-Catholic value system on which those institutions rest so precariously.

The market in the United States is vast. While estimates of consumption vary widely, let's use numbers that appear in a 1995 U.S. Office of National Drug Control Policy report: perhaps nine million Americans use marijuana once a month or more, and, after years of decline, the number is now increasing; 1.3 million use cocaine once a month or more; and 600,000 are addicted to heroin.[1] The same office estimated in 1989 that annual drug sales in the United States totaled $110 billion, more than twice the total profits of the Fortune 500 companies.[2]

The relationship between drug trafficking/use and crime is intimate and powerful. In 1993, criminal arrests in the United States totaled about 14 million, of which more than 1 million, or 8 percent, were arrests for drug-abuse violations. More than 60 percent of the 90,000 people incarcerated in federal prisons were drug offenders. Large but unknown percentages of the 860,000 people incarcerated in state prisons in 1993 committed crimes that were drug-related—either motivated by the need to obtain money to satisfy a habit or perpetrated in a state of narcotic intoxication.[3] Four-fifths of the noncitizens who are in jail are there for drug-related crimes, the vast majority having engaged in the retail sale of drugs on city streets.[4]

While narcotics are consumed in Latin America, chiefly by the urban poor, and that consumption is growing, it is tiny by comparison with the market in the United States. Latin American production and trafficking respond to international demand, above all in the United States. Peru, Bolivia, and Colombia account for almost all of the world's coca production, Colombia for most of the processing of coca into cocaine. Most opium poppies are cultivated in Asia, particularly Afghanistan, but both Mexico and Colombia produce small amounts. Mexico is the world's largest producer of marijuana, but Colombia is also an important producer (as is, by the way, the United States, which is the source of about one-third of the marijuana consumed in the United States). Jamaica is a smaller but nonetheless significant producer.

Colombia is, of course, the country most extensively involved in narcotics traffic, principally cocaine. Mexico is also a major player. But today, virtually every country in Latin America and the Caribbean is in the narcotics business, either as a way station for the flow of product to

the United States or as a site of laundering of the billions of drug profits. That includes Chile: "Because of [its] proximity to cocaine producing countries and miles of unprotected borders, it has become an important transit route . . . to the United States, Europe and Asia. . . . [I]t [is]
an easy place to launder drug money . . . drug use within Chile is rising
sharply."[5]

Narcotics plays a salient role in the economies of Colombia, Peru,
and Bolivia:

> In the mid-1980s, South American cocaine traffickers probably
> earned between $5 and $6 billion annually from international sales
> in the U.S. market. Perhaps $1.5 to $2 billion flowed back to the
> cocaine-producing countries. Viewed in terms of repatriated dol-
> lars, cocaine exports are equivalent to an estimated 10 to 20% of
> Colombia's legal exports, 25 to 30% of Peru's, and 50 to 100% of
> Bolivia's. . . . Cocaine is almost certainly the most important
> export in Peru and Bolivia, although in Colombia it probably earns
> less than coffee and petroleum.[6]

Among other favorable economic consequences of the industry,
the recent success of Bolivia and Peru in stabilizing exchange rates and
prices has been much facilitated by narcotics earnings. Writing five
years ago, Francisco Thoumi, a Colombian economist, cited estimates
that the "narco-capitalists" could account for as much as one-third of
Colombia's wealth and "could eventually become the dominant economic group within Colombia."[7] By 1996, that prophecy may have
been realized, as we can appreciate from the influence the narco-capitalists obviously exert on the executive (including the police and the
military), legislative, and judicial branches of the government.

The employment implications of the narcotics trade are profound.
In 1990, *Newsweek* estimated that "as many as 1.5 million Colombians,
Peruvians, and Bolivians are involved in growing coca, smuggling coca
paste, or producing finished cocaine."[8] The estimate applies to people
directly employed; a vast additional number are indirectly involved
through the selling of goods and services to the industry. Lee estimates
that 350,000 to 400,000 Bolivians—5 to 6 percent of the population—
are directly employed in coca production, transportation, and processing.[9] As many as 279,000 Peruvians are directly and indirectly
employed—4.5 percent of the labor force.[10]

Note that most of these estimates are for coca/cocaine only and do not reflect production and trafficking of marijuana and opiates.

Producing, processing, and transiting countries have reaped handsome economic benefits, as have, in lesser degree, the many other countries that have felt the impact of laundering operations. But the costs in terms of the undermining of the institutions of democracy—and particularly the administration of justice—have been enormous and constitute a fundamental threat to the consolidation of those institutions and a major impediment to the reinforcement of the modernizing values on which Latin America's progress depends. Demand in the United States has made all this possible.

THE PATHOLOGY OF NARCOTICS IN THE UNITED STATES

There is in human nature a current that seeks the escape, suppression of reality, and intoxication that narcotics and other psychotropic substances furnish. John Irving captured one eddy of this current in his novel *The Cider House Rules*,[11] in which Dr. Wilbur Larch, a humanitarian, altruist, and wise and admirable physician, frequently escapes his daily life by inhaling ether. The use of mind-altering substances has been common in cultures as different as China, where widespread opium use in the nineteenth century contributed to the debilitation of the Middle Kingdom, and pre-Columbian Mexico, where peyote, derived from cactus, was an important element of religious ritual.

It is tempting for me to relate the narcotics epidemic in the United States that began in the 1960s to the erosion of traditional values that dates from the same moment in history. And indeed there is, I believe, an important link between the two. But the contemporary epidemic is not the first in our history, and the impulse in human nature to escape is also relevant. The first epidemic occurred in the latter part of the nineteenth century, a time we associate with a robust national culture solidly anchored to the Protestant ethic. At that time, opiates, introduced chiefly by the Chinese laborers who were imported to help build railroads, were widely available over the counter or from mail-order catalogs.[12] Addiction to opiates, particularly morphine, grew to 4.59 people per 1,000 in the 1890s, the equivalent of more than a million people in today's population.

The high incidence of addiction led to increasingly stringent controls, including a section in the Pure Food and Drug Act of 1906 that required identification of narcotic content on labels. The United States acquired another opiate problem when the Philippine Islands became a U.S. possession following the Spanish-American War. Use of opium had been common in the Chinese population of the Philippines; it was prohibited on moral grounds by the American authorities, and the United States took the lead in organizing an international campaign against narcotics, much as it has in the past three decades. The sweeping Harrison Bill, which imposed rigorous controls, was passed in 1914.

Cocaine was commonly used in soft drinks until 1900. That includes Coca-Cola, which presumably derives the first half of its name therefrom. At one point in the late nineteenth century, cocaine had been considered a wonder drug, but its malign properties were apparent by the end of the century, and it was subsequently treated as comparably obnoxious to the opiates.

The reduction in opiate and cocaine consumption as a result of strict laws and public support fell far short of total abstinence. "In the early 1920s, most of the crime in New York City was blamed on drug use."[13] Between 1912 and 1925, narcotic treatment clinics operated in, among other places, New York, New England, and Florida. They faded away thereafter, principally because of financial problems but also because of a decline in drug usage.

Marijuana was introduced by Mexican agricultural workers, half a million of whom came to the United States in the 1920s. It was most commonly used in the West and Southwest. Legislation to tax the sale of marijuana was passed in 1937, but the Federal Bureau of Narcotics' principal weapon against marijuana was a public education campaign that highly exaggerated its adverse effects: "The substance was described to the public as a danger at least equal to cocaine or morphine, and the penalties for its illegal use or possession were severe."[14] Widespread use of marijuana did not begin until the 1960s.

It is difficult to avoid the conclusion that the drug epidemic that broke out then was related to the values of the users, mostly, at the outset, educated youths who would become known as the Sixties Generation. The Kennedy assassinations; racist violence in the South and the assassination of Martin Luther King, Jr., accompanied by the consciousness raising of whites as to the condition of blacks; the possibility of nuclear holocaust; and above all the unpopular war in Vietnam were the immediate causes of the cultural revolution, subsequently reinforced by Watergate. The cultural revolution transformed the order, patriotism, self-restraint, complacency, and conformity of the 1950s into the anarchy, disgust with America, impatience, hedonism, dissatisfaction, and conformity (to a very different set of values) of the 1960s. The symbol of escape in the fifties was the glamorous martini, in the sixties, iconoclastic pot.

I argued in *Who Prospers?* that two more fundamental forces were also at work: the unprecedented prosperity and power of the United States, which had effectively delinked work from survival; and the growing influence of television, with its relentless, easy message of instant gratification and cheap thrills.

While the Sixties Generation played an important and constructive role in the racial and gender revolutions, and while it clearly influenced the withdrawal of the United States from Vietnam (for the wrong reasons, I believe), the United States has paid a very high cost for its excesses. The level of trust, of one another and of our institutions, has dropped precipitously in recent decades, and the Sixties Generation, who wrongly saw the Vietnam War as evidence that the United States was an evil, imperialist power, has contributed to this decline, as, to be sure, did the government's less-than-candid handling of the war, and Watergate.[15] Another serious cost was the infatuation of the intellectual community with another manifestation of "Yankee imperialism," dependency theory, which helped to drive a wedge between Latin America and the United States for a quarter of a century, as I have described in earlier chapters.

The Sixties Generation, which merges into the Now Generation, also contributed to our loss of focus on the future, the erosion of the work ethic, and the loss of sense of community. But perhaps the most destructive feature of its legacy is narcotics. With the exception of marijuana, the use of which has increased in the past few years after a prolonged decline, middle-class use of narcotics has fallen off steadily, principally as a result of vigorous education and enforcement programs. But drug use by the urban underclass, the heirs of the 1960s' drug legacy and overwhelmingly black and Hispanic, has increased, with terrible consequences, most tragically in the loss of thousands of young lives in the endless drug-inspired shootings and stabbings. The generational symbols of the glamorous martini and iconoclastic pot have been succeeded by lethal crack cocaine.

The nightmare of the ghettos, which indeed does evoke William Golding's *Lord of the Flies*, is in important part a cultural phenomenon. Sixties nihilism and hedonism and the Now Generation's materialism reinforce the anomie of those blacks—a minority, to be sure—who have not found their way into the national mainstream and whose values and attitudes still reflect the slavery experience, perpetuated by the isolation of Jim Crow and ghetto segregation. Hispanics bring a different culture, a different kind of anomie to the ghetto, but with similar tragic consequences. The alienation and anomie of the ghetto stimulate the escape impulse in human nature and nurture drug abuse, much as the alienation and anomie of the Indian reservations so often lead to alcohol abuse.

Bob Martinez may have been guilty of hyperbole in the epigraph at the outset of this chapter, but at a time when skepticism surrounds the American Dream, dissipating the idea of progress; a time of declining trust in one another, our leaders, and our institutions; a time of intensifying divisiveness along racial and ethnic lines, the persistence of large-scale use of narcotics and other psychotropic substances is surely a cause for grave concern.

THE NARCOTICS MALIGNANCY IN LATIN AMERICA

Narcotics is a serious problem in the United States that is in part fed by the deterioration of traditional values and institutions. But it is a good deal more than a problem in Latin America: it vastly magnifies the traditional Latin American problems of abuse of power and corruption, and it consequently poses a grave threat to incipient democratic institutions. Several aspects of traditional Ibero-Catholic culture magnify the threat of narcotics, particularly the strength of individualism and familism and the resulting weakness of the sense of community; the underdeveloped sense of justice and fair play; and an ethical code that lacks rigor.

The threat in Colombia is especially worrisome. I spent several days speaking in Bogotá in February 1995 and left staggered by the extent to which the narcotics malignancy had spread throughout the society. The best-known symbol of the sickness is President Ernesto

Samper, who, as of this writing, is under pressure to resign because of strong evidence that he knowingly accepted large sums of money from narco-traffickers during his campaign. But all of Colombia's public institutions have been profoundly affected, as Douglas Payne, Freedom House's Latin American expert, has stressed in an article entitled "Narco-democracy":

> The Cali Cartel has bought a good part of the Colombian state: judges, prosecutors, the police and the military. The Cartel's influence in Congress led to the prohibition of extradition of Colombians to the United States—the only thing really feared by the narco-traffickers—in the new constitution promulgated in 1991. In 1993, the lawyers of the Cartel virtually dictated reforms of the penal code that enabled the narco-traffickers to surrender themselves and confess to a lesser drug violation, thereby receiving a two-thirds reduction of their sentence and immunity from prosecution for other drug offenses.[16]

Colombia's rich tradition of violence is sustained today not only by the narco-traffickers but also by some 10,000 guerrillas, most of whom long ago shed their Marxist-Leninist ideology for the financial benefits of banditry and kidnapping—*The Economist* estimates total ransoms at $350 million between 1991 and 1994[17]—and who effectively control a significant percentage of Colombia's mountain and jungle regions. The narco-traffickers have cooperated with some of the guerrillas, and indeed some of the guerrillas have become narco-traffickers.

Narcotics money seems to touch every aspect of Colombian life. Some elements of the media have been bought. As I mentioned earlier in this chapter, the narcotics industry has become a—possibly *the*—dominant force in the economy. Extensive construction of urban buildings, particularly luxury apartments and condominiums, which are in oversupply, is widely believed to be a form of money-laundering. So is the acquisition of rural land.

And the narcotics problem overwhelms the diplomatic dialogue between Colombia and the United States. U.S. ambassador Myles Frechette frequently appears as the butt of columns and cartoons, particularly in connection with the annual, congressionally mandated State Department certification that a country has either "cooperated fully with the United States, or taken adequate steps on its own, to achieve full compliance with the goals and objectives of the 1988

United Nations Convention Against Illicit Traffic in Narcotic Drugs and Psychotropic Substances."[18] Colombia has not been certified recently but had received a waiver based on "vital national interests" that has made it possible for the United States, for example, to vote for loans to Colombia from the World Bank and Inter-American Development Bank. That waiver was not exercised in the certification process early in 1996.

The United States has also been dissatisfied by the antinarcotics programs of Bolivia, Paraguay, and Peru, all of which have also received "vital national interest" waivers. And in each of those countries, the diplomatic dialogue is strongly focused on narcotics.

Mexico: Approaching a Point of No Return?

Mexico is the primary transshipment point for Colombian cocaine on its way to the United States. Mexico is the largest exporter of marijuana to the United States. And it also produces and exports heroin. Mexico was certified in the State Department's March 1995 *International Narcotics Control Strategy Report*, but the language of the report leaves the reader wondering whether the certification may not have been influenced by a combination of Mexico's NAFTA membership, the collapse of the peso, and the Clinton administration's problems in selling the $20 billion bailout package:

> the results of [Mexico's anti-drug] campaign were mixed, with cocaine seizures falling to the lowest level of Salinas's tenure . . . and few major traffickers arrested and prosecuted. Narco-corruption remains a serious impediment to effective drug law enforcement. Eradication of opium poppy and cannabis also declined substantially. . . . Money laundering, particularly the large-scale conversion of cash from the United States, remains a major problem in Mexico, which [the government of Mexico] has not yet effectively curbed. . . . Anti-corruption actions, as well as efforts to build strong anti-drug institutions, were undermined by narco-influence (and money).[19]

The 1995 report has good things to say about Carlos Salinas de Gortari's intentions and efforts in the narcotics campaign while noting disappointing results. As we observed in chapter 8, later in 1995, with Salinas a pariah because of his role in the collapse of the economy, his brother, Raúl Salinas de Gortari, was jailed as a suspect in the murder of José Francisco Ruiz Massieu, Secretary General of the PRI and Raúl's former brother-in-law. This was followed by the disclosure that Raúl had deposited upward of $100 million in Swiss and other foreign banks that was widely assumed to be the profit of money laundering or subornation, or both.

The 1995 report goes on to laud the narcotic policy statements of the then recently inaugurated president, Ernesto Zedillo. But a year later, in early 1996, Mexican progress on suppression of narcotics production and trafficking was limited, and there was some reason to doubt the commitment of the Zedillo government. Billionaire trafficker Juan García Abrego was picked up by Mexican authorities on 14 January 1996 and extradited to the United States. But the circumstances of his arrest—at a night spot near Monterrey that he was widely known to frequent—suggest that the impunity he was confident he had purchased had been lifted and that he was a sacrificial lamb the Mexican government offered up under pressure from the United States government.

A few days after García Abrego was turned over to U.S. authorities in Houston, the *New York Times* published a report that tended to confirm this interpretation:

> The [Mexican] Government today portrayed [García Abrego's] arrest as an early trophy in a scorched-earth campaign against "crime, corruption and impunity." But academics, journalists and opposition politicians, while granting that Mr. García Abrego's arrest and expulsion were important achievements and the fruit of patient detective work, argued that they were just as much a result of Mr. Zedillo's decision to mollify the United States. [I note that this occurred shortly before the 1996 certification announcement.]
>
> Other drug lords will continue to enjoy the impunity of which Mr. García Abrego was so suddenly stripped, the analysts said, and the river of drugs flowing into the United States from Mexico will continue unhampered. Rival Mexican traffickers with their own armies and payrolls of Government officials began to eclipse Mr. García Abrego a year ago, they said.
>
> "Every administration has its favorite trafficker," said Peter Lupsha, a professor at the University of New Mexico who studies the drug trade. "García Abrego was the favorite of the last administration. This administration has a new favorite."[20]

Andrew Levison reached a similar conclusion in an article published in the *Atlanta Journal-Constitution* and the *Christian Science Monitor* and added, "[Mexico offers] vast isolated areas controlled by powerful and unaccountable regional bosses, poorly trained and unmotivated police forces accustomed to accepting petty bribes, public officials with a tradition of accepting payments for the support and protection of private ventures, and highly sophisticated networks for transporting drugs and smuggling them across the border."[21]

Those who viewed the delivery of García Abrego to U.S. authorities as the offering of a sacrificial lamb at the time of the annual certification by the State Department were subsequently proved to be correct. Less than two weeks before the 1 March 1996 certification date, the *New York Times* published an article headlined, "Clinton Urged to Cite Mexico for Drug Flow." While there was no consensus among the several federal agencies concerned with the certification, the *Times* noted that "[s]ome Federal drug enforcement experts fear that Mexico may be only a few years away from a point of no return when drug cartels have so deeply penetrated the country's criminal justice and political systems that anti-drug and anti-corruption efforts have little chance of success."[22] On 1 March, Mexico was certified, if not enthusiastically.

The centrality of corruption as a way of life in Mexico, starting with the colonial period and reaching extraordinary levels during the almost seventy years of control by the PRI, particularly with the wealth generated by oil and narcotics, is highlighted in chapter 8. Mexico is not atypical. There are few Latin American countries where money cannot easily buy politicians, judges, and the media. Costa Rica has better defenses against corruption than most, particularly in its judiciary. But the taint of corruption has frequently reached the highest levels of the Costa Rican government in recent decades. The fugitive financier Robert Vesco was permitted to live in Costa Rica for many years because of his relationship with prominent Costa Rican politicians, particularly former president Daniel Oduber. Rumors of corruption have swirled around several other Costa Rican presidents, including José Figueres, the leader of the 1948 revolution that preserved democracy and one of Latin America's best-known democratic political figures.

Today, drug money is present in disturbing quantities in most Latin American countries. The National Narcotics Intelligence Consumers Committee August 1995 report focuses on Colombia,

Mexico, Peru, and Bolivia, but it also highlights trafficking and money laundering in Guatemala, Costa Rica, El Salvador, Honduras, Nicaragua, Panama, the Dominican Republic, Argentina, Brazil, Chile, Ecuador, Paraguay, and Venezuela. The potential for corruption implicit in the narcotics industry is vast in the Big Four: Colombia, Mexico, Peru, and Bolivia. It menaces the survival of the relatively recent democratic experiments in Peru and Bolivia and the longer-standing but still very fragile democratic institutions of Colombia. And it heavily burdens Mexico as that troubled country tries to work its way out of an authoritarian system susceptible to corruption that has dominated it throughout its history, particularly in the latter decades of this century.

THE NARCOTICS IMPEDIMENT TO A HEMISPHERIC COMMUNITY

Short of a major decline in narcotics demand in the United States, which does not appear imminent, the drug problem is sure to be a continuing major irritant in north-south relationships in the hemisphere. (*North*, by the way, includes Canada, which also has a significant narcotics consumption problem, although the Canadian market is a small fraction of the American.) Based on the limited success to date of U.S. efforts to force Latin American governments to curb production; the susceptibility of Latin American institutions to corruption; and the many hundreds of thousands of raw-material producers who benefit from the economics of coca, marijuana, and opium poppy production, and the many other hundreds of thousands who service them, it would be highly optimistic to expect a breakthrough on the supply side for the foreseeable future. With respect to crop substitution programs, former Bolivian Minister of Agriculture José Guillermo Justiniano has observed: "The standard of living of Andean campesinos is comparable to the lowest levels in Africa . . . it is difficult to imagine that coercive measures against campesinos could ever have positive results. Peasants producing coca have nothing to lose. As long as coca provides a family livelihood, they will protect their coca crop at all costs."[23]

The narcotics problem is thus likely to continue to dominate the diplomatic dialogue between the United States and several Latin American countries and continue to be a frequent subject of controversy with many others. It could easily bar serious consideration in the U.S. of extension of NAFTA to a number of countries, as perhaps it should have in the case of Mexico. And the pressure exerted on governments by the United States will have inevitable costs in terms of resentment by the weak of the exercise of power by the strong. It will be viewed by many Latin Americans as demeaning and a new kind of "imperialism," no matter how reasonable and responsible such pressure may look from our side. It will, for the foreseeable future, continue to be a major impediment to the forging of a real hemispheric community.

There are no easy solutions. During my speaking trip to South America in 1995, I was asked several times about legalization of consumption in the United States, a broad version of which could, with a stroke of the pen, substantially resolve Latin America's problems, converting the producers and traffickers into legitimate farmers and businessmen. While there is enough similarity in the effects and risks of alcohol and marijuana to warrant consideration of their being treated similarly, legalization, or decriminalization of consumption, of cocaine, the opiates, and strong chemical psychotropic substances poses, in my view, an unacceptable threat to the foundations of a society that are already under stress from the erosion of the universal progress values and intensifying divisiveness along racial and ethnic lines.

I see no alternative to persisting with a strategy centered on "prevention: the promotion of education, counselling and awareness in all elementary and secondary schools, in community organizations, in the media, in the workplace."[24] We have a better chance of winning the war on the demand side through education than we do on the supply side through coercion, although I think we must persist with both.

11

Immigration: The Latinization of the United States?

Migration should be viewed as a bridge between two nations that are destined to come closer despite their governments' worst intentions. Across this bridge, the Mexican culture and Spanish language will journey north, and American political attitudes and consumer tastes will go south. But the growing bonds connecting people and families in both countries will remain more significant than ideas or commodities that are traded. These new bonds mean that, over time, the United States may be dealing with Mexico less as a neighbor and more as a relative.

–ROBERT A. PASTOR, Limits to Friendship

The problem in which the current immigration is suffused is, at heart, one of numbers; for when the numbers begin to favor not only the maintenance and replenishment of the immigrant's source culture, but also its overall growth, and in particular growth so large that the numbers not only impede assimilation but go beyond to pose a challenge to the traditional culture of the American nation, then there is a great deal about which to be concerned.

–Dallas Morning News AND Washington Post COLUMNIST RICHARD ESTRADA, LETTER TO AUTHOR

Latin America is the largest single source of legal and illegal immigration into the United States. Of the almost 20 million foreign-born who participated in the 1990 census, about 7.6 million, or 38 percent, were born in Latin America, and of those, 4.3 million were Mexican-born.[1] The 1990 census shows 21,900,000 foreign- and U.S.-born

Hispanics (8.8 percent) out of a total of 248,710,000. The real total is almost surely substantially larger, above all reflecting avoidance of the census by illegal immigrants, the majority of whom are from Latin America, the large majority of those from Mexico. The Urban Institute estimates that 6.3 million Mexican-born immigrants lived in the United States in 1994 (compared with the 4.3 million reported in the 1990 census).[2] Leon Bouvier, a demographer associated with the Center for Immigration Studies, has estimated (conservatively, in his view) that the number of Mexicans who have migrated legally and illegally to the United States since 1960, plus their offspring, is about 10 million.[3]

The effects of so vast a flow of immigrants from Latin America are prodigious and diverse. Coupled with high Hispanic fertility rates, the flow is transforming the ethnic structure of American society, above all in the states of California (where Hispanics account for 28 percent of total population), Texas (28 percent), Florida (14 percent), and New York (13 percent). Early in the next century, Hispanics will overtake blacks as the largest minority in the United States. By 2030, Hispanics are projected by the Census Bureau to account for 18.9 percent of the American population, blacks 13.1 percent. Hispanic populations are projected to rise to 36.5 percent of the total in California, 40.2 percent in Texas, 21.4 percent in Florida, and 15.9 percent in New York in 2020.[4]

The flow is significant in a cultural and economic sense for the sending countries, particularly Mexico, as well as for the United States. Through their experience in the United States, most immigrants are likely to develop a greater sense of the possibilities of life; of influence over their destinies; of what responsible democratic government can do to promote the well-being of people, justice, and opportunity. Many no doubt encounter discrimination and exploitation in the United States. But it pales by comparison with the extreme discrimination, exploitation, and hopelessness they encounter in their own countries. They communicate this new world view to their families and friends back home. Many of the immigrants, particularly the Mexicans, pay visits, often extended, to their native villages, towns, and cities. In many cases, they leave indigent and return affluent. Some resettle, buy property, and set up enterprises. But whether they remain in the United States, which the large majority do, or return to their native countries, their traditional world view is altered, and their expectations, including their expectations of government, are elevated. How much their values and attitudes change is an overriding issue that I shall discuss later in this chapter.

The immigrants also develop a more objective, probably more favorable view of the United States than what they may have learned in their country of origin. (As we have noted, Mexican primary- and secondary-school textbooks reflected until recently the anti-American, anticapitalist nationalism that was Mexico's conventional wisdom for many decades.) This may have contributed, albeit in a minor way, to the decline of anti-gringoism in Latin America.

Highly significant economic benefits for sending countries attend the emigration of large numbers of their citizens. A combination of high population growth rates and sluggish economies has produced high levels of unemployment, symbolized by the ubiquitous and thinly disguised (and sometimes menacing) begging that one constantly encounters in Latin American cities in the form of shoeshiners, windshield washers, parked-car watchers, package carriers, and, in depressed Mexico City late in 1995, circus-style clowns at major intersections. Immigration to the United States represents, at least for Mexico, the Dominican Republic, Haiti, El Salvador, and, albeit in a different political context, Cuba, a crucial escape valve. I mentioned Leon Bouvier's estimate that about 10 million Mexican-origin people live in the United States as a consequence of immigration since 1960. Try to imagine conditions in Mexico today if those ten million people were south of the border, not north of it.

Another highly significant—and infrequently mentioned—economic benefit that attends immigration for the countries of origin is the remittances sent home by emigrants. Sharon Stanton Russell, an immigration expert at Massachusetts Institute of Technology, recently calculated that officially reported remittances from Latin American and Caribbean immigrants in the United States to their countries of origin totaled $5.7 billion in 1991 and 1992.[5] But as she emphasizes, "[t]he actual figures are undoubtedly higher, since substantial fractions of remittances flow through informal channels and to countries that have not reported their balance of payments to the IMF [which is the source of her data]." Russell's tables show $3 billion to Mexico in 1991. An executive of Western Union, which transfers a significant percentage of the remittances, told me in 1995 that Western Union estimates the current flow to Mexico at $5–6 billion annually, constituting the third-largest source of dollar income for Mexico, behind petroleum exports and tourism.

Russell's data show $468 million for El Salvador in 1991. The U.S. Embassy in El Salvador recently estimated remittances at $858 million in 1992 and $962 million in 1994 based on Salvadoran Central Bank data.[6] Citing the University of California migration specialist Raul Hinojosa, the *Washington Post* estimated that remittances to El Salvador in 1993 totaled $2 billion, more than El Salvador's total exports. The remittances "allowed the Salvadoran government to revise the national budget and reduce import tariffs to zero."[7] One hears estimates that Salvadoran immigrants may number one million, although the 1990 census shows 465,000 born in El Salvador, which would suggest a significant number of illegal immigrants. If the one million is correct, that would amount to about $1,000 per immigrant per year in remittances. The outflow of remittances to Latin America and the Caribbean could thus exceed $10 billion annually.

The impact, particularly economic, within the United States of immigration has been the subject of intense debate in recent years as immigration has become an increasingly hot political issue, symbolized by the 59 percent support that anti-immigration Proposition 187 received in the California elections of 1994. The immigration issue has begot some odd bedfellows: in favor of high levels of immigration, the *Wall Street Journal* and the *New York Times*, Edward Kennedy and Jack Kemp, and William Bennett and Fidel Castro; opposed, Patrick Buchanan and Eugene McCarthy, *National Review* and *Forbes* editor Peter Brimelow and former Democratic governor of Colorado Richard Lamm.

Among the most respected immigration analysts is George Borjas, formerly at the University of California in San Diego and now at the John F. Kennedy School at Harvard, who was born in Cuba and migrated to the United States as a child soon after the Cuban Revolution. Borjas recently drew nine demythifying conclusions about immigration based on a careful assessment of recent research, including his own.[8] I cite them here because I believe they are among the most reliable findings on immigration available, and I want to focus the balance of this chapter on a central immigration issue—acculturation—that receives less attention than the economic issues:

Myth 1: By historical standards, immigration today is not all that high. While the foreign-born accounted for 14 percent of the population in 1910 compared to 8 percent in 1990, the flow of immigrants in the 1990s, which Borjas estimates at 13 million (legal and illegal) will be 50 percent higher than the flow of 8.8 million in the peak years 1900–1910.

Myth 2: Immigrants do well in the labor market. "Most of the immigrants now entering the United States . . . are less skilled workers who have little hope of reaching economic parity with native workers during their lifetimes."[9] Borjas mentions that in 1990, immigrants arrived with an average of 11.9 years of schooling compared to 13.2 years for natives, a datum that underscores the vital need to disaggregate global immigration data by national source and ethnicity. As Borjas observes: "There are huge differences in educational attainment, earnings, and welfare propensities among groups of different national origins. . . . In 1990, immigrants from France and Germany earned about 25 percent more than natives . . . those from El Salvador and Mexico 40 percent less than natives."[10] Recall from chapter 8 that more than 35 million Mexicans over the age of fifteen—more than a third of the population—have not completed primary school. (The World Bank lists a 13 percent illiteracy rate for Mexico in 1990.)[11] The vast majority of Mexican immigrants, particularly those who enter illegally, come from the lower strata of Mexican society, which suggests that for many, *the average number of years of education may be four or less.*[12]

Myth 3: Immigrants use welfare less than natives do. In 1990, 8.3 percent of newly arrived immigrants received public assistance, such as Aid to Families with Dependent Children and Supplemental Security Income, compared with 7.4 percent of natives. Moreover, earlier arrivals experienced an upward trend in welfare usage: 5.5 percent of the cohort that entered during 1965–69 received welfare. Almost 10 percent of the same cohort received welfare in 1990. Once again, the overall data need to be disaggregated. There is a strong presumption that immigrants from Japan, Korea, and China (many via Taiwan and Hong Kong) will seek welfare far less frequently than immigrants from Latin America.

Myth 4: Immigrants pay their way in the welfare state. Borjas, after reviewing the complex of factors that must be considered in the calculation, concludes that there is a substantial shortfall between what immigrants contribute in taxes and the services they receive when the services, beyond welfare and education, that all of us receive and pay for (such as defense, highways, national parks) are factored in.

Myth 5: Refugees and illegal aliens are the source of the immigration problem. Especially because so many legal immigrants enter on the basis of family preferences rather than skills, legal immigration is also a problem.

Myth 6: Immigrants do not hurt the earnings of native workers. Contrary to his earlier findings,[13] Borjas now believes that about one-third of the growing income gap in the 1980s between high school dropouts and those who completed high school is the consequence of the heavy flow of relatively unskilled immigrants.

Myth 7: Americans gain a lot from immigration. Those citizens who benefit from immigration are likely to be affluent, for example, those who hire unskilled workers and those who hire domestic help. Borjas has calculated that "native workers lose about $133 billion a year, or 1.9 percent of GDP in a $7 trillion economy, mainly because immigrants drive down the wages of competing workers."[14]

Myth 8: Immigrants are more likely to be entrepreneurs, and these entrepreneurs are very successful. The gross data show that immigrants are slightly less entrepreneurial than natives. But once again, disaggregation is important: 18 percent of Koreans are self-employed, but only 5 percent of Mexicans are (the average for natives is 7 percent).

Myth 9: The melting pot works fast. Borjas examines the evidence and concludes: "It might take up to four generations for the ethnic differences in economic status . . . to disappear."[15] But he again stresses the importance of disaggregating by national origin.

LATIN AMERICANS AND THE MELTING POT

If Latin America's problems are chiefly the consequence of traditional Ibero-Catholic culture, then immigrants from Latin America are bringing with them, obviously in varying degrees, those values and attitudes. To be sure, people who decide to emigrate are more likely to be achieving risk-takers than those who remain at home.[16] But when immigration flows from a neighboring country, the difficulties, risks, and hardships are reduced, diluting the risk-taker self-selection phenomenon.

The perpetuation of the traditional values and attitudes will tend to reproduce in the United States patterns of behavior that evoke the political, economic, and social pathologies of Latin America. Thus, particularly when the numbers of immigrants are great, it is indispensable not only for the welfare of the immigrants themselves but also for the welfare of the broader society that the more progressive mainstream values of the United States, rooted in Anglo-Protestant traditions now widely secularized, substantially displace the traditional Ibero-Catholic values. Failure of the melting pot to work for these immigrants will result in an enduring and rapidly growing ethnic underclass, prone to see itself as a victim of discrimination, susceptible to calls to ethnic unity and separatism, and a major aggravant to the worrisome problems we already face in building an all-embracing national community at a time of intensifying racial divisiveness.

The absorption of mainstream American values by Latin American immigrants need not mean the eradication of Latin culture or the suppression of the Spanish language, although the acculturation patterns of other immigrant groups, for example, the Italians, suggest that the language may be substantially lost after a few generations. But other aspects of Italian culture persist, including strong emphasis on the family, attachment to the Catholic Church, and the rich culinary traditions that have contributed so much to what is now "American" cuisine. Displacement of the traditional Ibero-Catholic values does not require massive defections to Protestantism, since the Catholic Church in the United States today operates within, and for the most part reinforces, the secularized value system—although the growing numbers of Latinos in the United States who have converted to Protestantism, particularly fundamentalist sects, is worth noting.[17] (This may reflect, of course, the growing number of conversions that are occurring in Latin America.)

The crucial question is whether, in the massive immigrant flow from Latin America to the United States and its concentration in a few states, Latinos are following other immigrant groups, including the Italians and Irish, also Catholic, into the melting pot.[18] The acculturation problem of the contemporary immigrants may be made more difficult by the erosion of traditional American values—for example, work ethic, frugality, community—in the broader society in recent decades. That erosion notwithstanding, American culture today is substantially more conducive to democratic politics, economic creativity, social justice, and fair play than is the Latin culture in which the immigrants have been nurtured.

I have selected five factors that will suggest both the condition of immigrants and, by implication, their values and attitudes: education, income and poverty, use of welfare, political participation, and crime. Of particular relevance and concern is the question of what happens to the U.S.-born second, third, and subsequent generations. In the case of Latin American immigrants, and particularly in the case of Mexicans, who are by far the most numerous, the evidence of the degree of acculturation is not encouraging. Unfortunately, the data are incomplete, particularly across the generations; moreover, limitations of data leave no alternative but to draw on data organized by different groupings, that is, "Hispanic," "Latino," "Mexican."

Education

Education is the principal engine of progress for members of a society, whether natives or immigrants. A general correlation exists between the amount of education and the degree of economic success. For example, in 1980, the average number of years of education completed by U.S.-born males of Chinese (14.9 years), Japanese (13.7 years), and Korean (13.8 years) antecedence was well above the non-Hispanic white average of 12.9 years. Their family income was $9,000 to $13,000 more than the non-Hispanic white average of $26,535.[19]

Some progress has been made over the years by Hispanic-Americans, for example with respect to the percentages that have completed high school and university educations. But the educational achievement is generally quite low by comparison with national averages and other ethnic groups. In 1991, 12.5 percent of the Hispanic population over twenty-five had completed less than five years of schooling (for those of Mexican antecedence, the figure was 15.9 percent; Cuban antecedence 7.7 percent), compared with 1.6 percent of non-Hispanics. Almost 49 percent of Hispanics over twenty-five had not completed high school (56.4 percent of those of Mexican antecedence, 39 percent of Cuban antecedence), compared with 19.5

percent of non-Hispanics. Slightly less than 10 percent of Hispanics had completed four or more years of college (6.2 percent of Mexicans), compared with 22.3 percent of non-Hispanics.[20]

To be sure, these data, particularly with respect to early dropout and high school completion, are distorted by the continuing heavy flow of immigrants, legal and illegal, many of them young, most of them from Mexico. To the extent that recent young immigrants are reflected in the data, what we are seeing is more a picture of the condition of education in sending countries, above all Mexico, than in the United States. A recent RAND Corporation analysis of the 1990 census data showed that more than 70 percent of Mexican immigrants in California had not completed twelve years of school.[21] While this was an improvement over 1960 data, when 89 percent had not completed twelve years, the 54 percent figure is the highest of those countries of origin listed. Mexico is also the lowest in terms of percentage of immigrants with more than sixteen years of school (6 percent).

Recent young immigrants represent but a fraction of the total, but the overall picture remains disconcerting, with Hispanic high school dropout rates in the vicinity of 30–35 percent between 1972 and 1991, although with some improvement in 1992 and 1993.[22]

Also disconcerting are data that Linda Chavez, the author of *Out of the Barrio*,[23] has developed that show an aggravation of the problem of noncompletion of high school from the second to the third generation of Mexican-origin males. The data show that 72.4 percent of the first generation (Mexican-born) fail to complete high school. This drops to 22 percent in the second generation, but increases to 29.2 percent in the third generation.[24]

This kind of troubling pattern is today usually explained by factors like "poor facilities and inadequate teaching staff; discrimination, racism, and low expectations; lack of Latino role models among school personnel; inadequate resource allocation; and the lack of appropriate programs to meet language needs and involve parents."[25] The people making these judgments rarely ponder the condition of education in Mexico and other Latin American countries. If they did, they might perceive that the problems they face with respect to Hispanic underperformance in education are linked to the underdevelopment of education in Latin America, which in turn reflects the traditional Ibero-Catholic undervaluation of education, particularly for the masses.

I would suggest that the principal reason that significant numbers of third-generation Americans of Mexican extraction are dropping out is because the value system they have acquired, principally at home, does not attach a high priority to education. Joan Moore observed in 1970 that "Jewish and Japanese children . . . march off to school with enthusiasm. Mexican and Negro children are much less interested. Some sort of cultural factor works here."[26] Some may answer that most Jews and Japanese are in the upper-middle class and that a class phenomenon is being misread as a cultural phenomenon. But there was a time, early in this century, when Jews and Japanese were lower-middle and low class; their children still marched off to school with enthusiasm.

Income

Hispanics as a category are earning substantially less than American whites—about 70 percent of white mean family income in 1991. Moreover, whether we measure family, household, or individual income, we find a small deterioration of the Hispanic position since 1980. Hispanic families below the poverty line had increased from 23.2 percent in 1980 to 26.5 percent in 1991, while white families increased from 8 percent to 8.8 percent. Hispanic individuals below the poverty line increased from 25.7 percent in 1980 to 28.7 percent in 1991, while white individuals increased from 10.2 percent to 11.3 percent.[27]

Just as "immigrants" needs to be disaggregated in order, for example, to appreciate the dramatic differences between immigrants from East Asia and Latin America, so too does "Hispanics." We find 25 percent of Mexican and 13.8 percent of Cuban families below the poverty line in 1990, the latter a good deal closer to the white average of 8.1 percent. Similarly, in 1990, 29 percent of Cuban males enjoyed an income of more than $25,000 compared with 21.1 percent of Mexican males—and 40.8 percent of white males.[28] The reader will have noted similar contrasts between Mexican and Cuban performance in education. But we must remember that most of the Cubans who fled Castro's revolution, particularly in the early years, were middle class, educated, and upwardly mobile, in sharp contrast to most Mexican immigrants.

We see some evidence of the same troubling generational pattern with respect to income that we noted with education: a significant improvement from the first to the second generation, but some decline from the second to the third.[29]

With respect to occupational distribution, data for Mexican-Americans in California show a majority of workers in the unskilled, farm, and semiskilled categories: the three categories account for 81 percent of the Mexican-born, 55 percent of the U.S.-born, and 39 percent of all Californians; conversely, 19 percent of Mexican-born, 45 percent of U.S.-born, and 61 percent of all Californians work in white-collar categories.[30] Once again, the dynamic across generations is worrisome. A study of Mexican-Americans in Oxnard, Santa Barbara, and Santa Paula, California, concludes:

> While social assimilation . . . increases from the first to the second generation, it tends to level off thereafter. Economic assimilation proceeds similarly: dramatic mobility takes place for second-generation [Mexican-Americans] who become integrated into the stable blue-collar labor force, while white-collar jobs continue to remain out of reach for the vast majority of those from succeeding generations.[31]

This summary of income patterns is generally consistent with the patterns noted by Leo Grebler, Joan W. Moore, and Ralph C. Guzman in their classic 1970 study, *The Mexican-American People*;[32] also with the data that appear in Peter Skerry's more recent *Mexican Americans*. It is also consistent with Borjas's findings with respect to low levels of entrepreneurship among Mexican immigrants. Once again, the data are skewed downward by the heavy continuing flow of poor, unskilled, and uneducated immigrants from Latin America, particularly Mexico.

The RAND study of the 1990 census data for California contains a table of recent immigrant earnings as a percent of native earnings that shows Japanese, Koreans, and Chinese at 76 percent of native earnings on entry into the United States and 103 percent ten years later, while Mexicans start at 52 percent of native earnings and have *declined* to 47 percent ten years later.[33] The report concludes, "immigrants of Mexican origin command the lowest earnings, are less likely to complete high school, and have experienced the lowest rate of economic progress."[34]

One of the great virtues of the RAND study is that it disaggregates by country of origin and extent of education. Mexicans in general come to the United States with far less education than other groups, except Central Americans and Vietnamese, and their below-average economic performance in part reflects that education shortfall. But, as the RAND study points out, "even if immigrants had completed the same number of years of school as natives, a significant gap would remain between Mexicans and natives."[35] Among the several explanations that the RAND study adduces is "unexplained cultural differences in attitudes towards work."[36]

Welfare

George Borjas and Stephen Trejo's analysis of 1970 and 1980 census data led them to conclude that more-recent immigrants make more extensive use of welfare programs than do earlier immigrants. Welfare use increases with time of residence in the United States. And the financial impact of immigrant use of welfare is substantial: immigrant households that arrived between 1975 and 1980 would receive a lifetime total of $11.2 billion compared to $6.5 billion for an equal number of native households.[37]

The 1970 census showed a lower percentage (5.5 percent) of immigrants receiving welfare than natives (6 percent). But the 1990 data shown a sharp increase in immigrant participation: 8.3 percent versus 7.4 percent of natives.[38] Disaggregating the immigrants by country of origin shows wide variations in welfare utilization: the average for Europeans is 6.4 percent (interestingly, by far the highest national group is the Spaniards, at 13.4 percent); the average for China, Japan, and Korea is 6.6 percent; the average for Ibero-American countries is 12.1 percent. The highest welfare usage is by Vietnamese, at 29.3 percent, and Dominicans, at 25.8 percent. Among Mexicans, who constitute the largest national group, 12.4 percent receive welfare.[39] The RAND report is in conflict: in California, Mexicans and Central Americans are described as "infrequent users of welfare (less than 5%)."[40]

Hispanic Americans: A Statistical Sourcebook disaggregates 1986 welfare data by cash assistance, food stamps, and people whose welfare participation accounted for 50 percent or more of income for one month or more.[41] The data show that 18.2 percent of Hispanics had received cash assistance, compared with 6.2 percent of whites; 25.8 percent of Hispanics had received food stamps, compared with 9.9 percent of whites; and 19.6 percent of Hispanics had depended on welfare for more than 50 percent of their income, compared with 6.4 percent of whites. Borjas found that almost 30 percent of female-headed Mexican immigrant families were receiving welfare in 1980.[42]

Contributing to disproportionate Hispanic use of welfare is the disproportionate incidence of single Hispanic mothers. In 1993, Hispanics accounted for 10.3 percent of the total population but 21.1 percent of single mothers.[43] In California, "[t]he highest incidence of teen-age pregnancy is in the Hispanic community, which makes up 35 percent of the teen-age population but 59 percent of teen-age births."[44]

Additional intergenerational trend data with respect to participation of Hispanics in welfare programs would be very helpful in assessing this aspect of acculturation. I have been unable to find any.

Political Participation

"Naturalization is the most visible manifestation of Americanization." Those are the words of the late Barbara Jordan, then Chair of the U.S. Commission on Immigration Reform, that appear in her summary of the commission's 7 June 1995 interim recommendations on legal immigration reform. Of the almost 20 million foreign-born who participated in the 1990 census, almost 8 million—41.5 percent—had become American citizens. But disaggregation is again revealing. Almost 66 percent of European immigrants were naturalized, 54 percent of Canadians, and 41 percent of Asians. But only 26 percent of Latin American immigrants had naturalized, and the figure for Mexicans, by far the largest national group, was 22.6 percent.

In the past few years, and particularly in the wake of the large vote in favor of California's Proposition 187, immigration has become one of the hottest political issues, and sweeping immigration reforms curtailing both illegal and legal immigration are under consideration in the Congress. Some of the reforms that have been discussed would deny Medicare and other benefits to noncitizens, which has contributed to a rush to naturalize. In response, the Mexican government is promoting an amendment to the Mexican Constitution that would permit Mexicans who naturalize in the United States to retain Mexican nationality rights, including ownership of land. In an interview with Sam Dillon of the *New York Times* late in 1995, the Mexican Foreign Minister stated that the initiative "is designed to stress our common language, the culture, the history." But Dillon notes that some observers believe that the Mexican goal is to "enable Mexican-Americans to help defend Mexican interests in the United States."[45] The consequences for the acculturation of Mexican immigrants in the United States would clearly be negative: the effect of the legislation would be to perpetuate an emotional and cultural bond to Mexico.

Sidney Verba, Kay Lehman Schlozman, and Henry E. Brady demonstrate in *Voice and Equality* that the political participation of Latino citizens lags behind that of non-Hispanic whites and blacks: 73 percent of whites, 65 percent of blacks, and 52 percent of Latino citizens vote; 52 percent of whites, 38 percent of blacks, and 27 percent of Latino citizens belong to political parties.[46] A similar pattern prevails with respect to participation in secular, nonpolitical activities, including organizational affiliation, work for such organizations, charitable work, and charitable contributions. I would argue that these patterns are echoes of the familism, limited sense of community, fatalism, authoritarianism, and paternalism that have posed potent obstacles to the flourishing of democratic institutions in Latin America. They doubtless also reflect the limited practical experience of immigrants from Latin America in the workings of democracy.

In *Mexican Americans*, Peter Skerry emphasizes an aspect of Mexican-American political comportment that he finds troubling: the prominence of organizations, above all the Mexican American Legal Defense and Educational Fund (MALDEF), that do not have a mass following but emphasize race/ethnicity consciousness and resentments and present themselves as representing the interests of Mexican-Americans. The result is "a politics without organization and with weak or nonexistent ties between leaders and 'members' or 'constituents.'"[47] (MALDEF was created by and is supported by the Ford Foundation.) MALDEF evokes, disturbingly, traditional Latin American politics, and Skerry concludes:

> In essence, this approach is profoundly antipolitical. It teaches those without political power that it can and should be bestowed on them by elite benefactors, whether Anglo or Latino. This approach also transforms Mexican-American leaders into one more voice of principled disharmony and rigidly defined abstract rights, resistant to compromise in the political arena. In the name of politics, we now have a new source of discord—of antipolitics.[48]

Crime

My data on Hispanic involvement in crime are fragmentary and inferential. I believe that the absence of comprehensive data on Hispanic involvement in crime may reflect a politically correct reluctance to expose behavioral patterns of a "victim minority" that might strengthen anti-Hispanic, anti-immigration attitudes. The political correctness problem has been operative in Canada, too, according to several informed Canadians with whom I spoke in the fall of 1995. Peter Brimelow observes: "News about immigrant crime is firmly in the unfit-to-print category. Researchers find that official figures on immigrant and ethnic crime patterns are rarely collected. Cities like New York, Chicago and San Francisco have even instructed their employees not to cooperate with INS [the Immigration and Naturalization Service]."[49]

Brimelow cites the following data:

• Criminal aliens accounted for more than 25 percent of the federal prison population in 1993 (that doesn't include naturalized criminals).

• In 1990, foreign-born criminals comprised 18 percent of the inmates passing through the Los Angeles County Jail Inmate Reception Center.

• When INS was permitted access to an Orange County, California, courthouse in 1989, it discovered that 36 percent of convicted criminals, many of them repeat offenders, were illegal aliens.[50]

These data do not, of course, tell us the extent of Hispanic involvement in crime. What we know is that Hispanics are the largest immigrant group and that, within that group, Mexicans are by far the most numerous. We also know that Hispanics, principally Mexicans, disproportionately migrate to California. Linda Thom, who works for Santa Barbara County, recently presented California-wide 1993 arrest data that show Hispanics accounting for 44 percent of felony arrests and 43 percent of misdemeanor arrests.[51] (Hispanics account for 28 percent of California's population.) Former Colorado governors Richard Lamm and John Love wrote in 1988 that Hispanics, mostly of Mexican origin, accounted for 11 percent of the total population of the state but 25 percent of the prison population.[52]

We also know that Colombians and Mexicans dominate the wholesale distribution of cocaine within the United States and that

Cubans, Dominicans, and Mexicans are prominently involved in retail distribution.[53]

Political correctness taboos notwithstanding, Citizenship and Immigration Canada, the Ottawa counterpart to INS, has published 1991 data that show a disproportionate incarceration rate for immigrants from Latin America. The rate for Canadian natives was 10.7 per 10,000, 14 per 10,000 for immigrants born in Latin America. The study observes that "immigrants from the Caribbean [particularly Jamaica] and South and Central America may experience problems in the integration process generally. They have relatively high rates of unemployment, low incomes and low rates of home ownership."[54]

Once again, intergenerational data would be very helpful. It may be that participation in crime declines in subsequent generations.

IN SUM

What I have just presented is not comprehensive, and there are glaring gaps, particularly with respect to intergenerational performance. The subject of acculturation of Latin American immigrants should be studied in depth and warrants several books, rather than a chapter. But the data I have presented do strongly suggest that the melting pot is not working efficiently for Hispanic immigrants, and that the United States confronts a serious political, economic, and social problem in the rapid growth of its Hispanic population. Obviously, the melting pot *is* working well for *some* Hispanic-Americans, particularly the Cubans and South Americans, most of whom arrived with middle-class antecedents and relatively high levels of education.

The melting pot problem is aggravated above all by the vast flow, as Richard Estrada has argued. But it is also made more difficult by the Hispanic leadership, particularly in MALDEF and similar institutions, whose vision is of a multicultural, "salad bowl" America with a Hispanic—and particularly Mexican—"community," a principal objective of which is the perpetuation of Hispanic culture and the Spanish language. That vision reinforces the "victim" emphasis of the leadership, which looks to "concessions" from the Anglo majority as the principal means of overcoming the gap in well-being and progress between the Hispanic and the white components of the society. The vision evokes the Latin American obsession, until recent years, with dependency and imperialism and the erstwhile belief of Latin American leaders that they could solve their problems only by levering concessions from the United States.

The extent to which Hispanics have been discriminated against in the United States can be legitimately debated. My own opinion is that Chinese and Japanese immigrants have suffered at least comparable discrimination and greater persecution. Yet they are among the most successful ethnic groups in our society, with education, income, and general achievement levels far above national averages. Their essentially Confucian value system, in several respects similar to the Protestant ethic, has facilitated their entrance into the melting pot, as well as their success.

The enjoyment by native-born Hispanics of affirmative action benefits can also be legitimately debated. (I explained in *Who Prospers?* that I had been an early proponent of affirmative action for blacks but believe that its costs, particularly its contribution to divisiveness in our increasingly polarized society, now exceed its benefits.) But, as James S. Robb points out in *Affirmative Action for Immigrants—The Entitlement Nobody Wanted*, affirmative action benefits also absurdly accrue to legal immigrants—and doubtlessly, in practice, to illegal immigrants with bogus documents—the moment they cross the border![55] We have no moral or legal obligation to extend these benefits, which are not available to a majority of American citizens, to immigrants, but the Immigration Reform and Control Act of 1986 effectively made it illegal to deny them affirmative action benefits.

We were compellingly reminded of the potential costs of biculturalism and bilingualism in the 1995 referendum on sovereignty for Quebec, which was defeated by the narrowest of margins and may presage a majority for separation from Canada within the next several years. Linda Chavez has argued that bilingual education is "at its heart a program to help maintain the language and culture of Hispanic children,"[56] a view shared by former bilingual teacher Rosalie Pedalino Porter, author of *Forked Tongue*.[57] Richard Estrada believes that the language problem in the U.S. Southwest may be greater than in the case of Quebec:

> For Quebec ... does not lie contiguous to France ... the Southwest, on the other hand, shares a 2,000-mile-long border with a Spanish-speaking country of at least 85 million people, hun-

dreds of thousands of whom yearly move to the United States, or who reside with one foot in one country, the other in the other. The twin factors of geographic contiguity and rate of immigration must give pause. No one can witness the growth of Spanish-language media in this country and fail to believe that things are headed in the direction of a parallel culture. And that is the point: bilingualism has generally militated against assimilation. It has promoted a parallel culture instead of a subordinate one.[58]

I am reminded of a billboard I saw in Santa Monica, California, in the fall of 1995 that read, "L.A.'s #1 NEWSCAST IS IN SPANISH."

One of the obstacles to Hispanic participation in the melting pot and the upward mobility it implies is less than complete mastery of English. In my view, the overriding objective of bilingual education should be the mastery of English at the earliest possible time. Most younger children pick up languages so rapidly that bilingual programs for them normally need not last more than a year. Longer programs may be necessary for teenagers who are being exposed to English for the first time, but even they can finish high school with substantial mastery of English if that is the principal objective of the bilingual program. There is considerable evidence that for many of the Hispanic teachers and school administrators involved in bilingual education, the objective is perpetuation of the Spanish language and Hispanic culture.[59] But there is also evidence that Hispanic parents support it, too.[60]

There is a simple answer for those Hispanic children (or their parents) who want to preserve their Spanish-language skills and enhance their knowledge of their country of origin: elective courses that teach the Spanish language, and (in English) Spanish and Latin American history. A primary or secondary school does not need a bilingual education program to offer such courses.

It helps neither Hispanic-Americans nor the broader society when the condition of Hispanics is interpreted as chiefly the consequence of discrimination. Discrimination against Hispanics doubtlessly has made their progress more difficult, particularly in the nineteenth and first half of the twentieth centuries. But I want to repeat that the discrimination they faced was probably no more flagrant than that faced by Chinese and Japanese immigrants. Moreover, my sense, shared by the prominent Mexican-American intellectual Rodolfo de la Garza, is that anti-Hispanic discrimination has declined significantly.[61]

If the condition of Hispanics is *not* chiefly the consequence of discrimination, then one cannot avoid the conclusion that culture is an important factor, a conclusion that is reinforced by the contrast in progress between the United States and Canada on the one hand and Latin America on the other. I fully appreciate that culture is both difficult and painful to deal with, but if we fail to do so, the result is likely to be misguided policies and further deterioration of the fabric of our society. We have a graphic lesson of the consequences of a significant minority remaining outside the melting pot in the case of blacks.

We must heed Richard Estrada's warnings that the size of the immigration flow from Latin America, above all Mexico, threatens both the successful adaptation of the immigrants and the coherence of our society. It also threatens the well-being of poorer citizens, many of whom are black and Hispanic.

The *Wall Street Journal* must recognize that large numbers of unskilled, uneducated immigrants—which translates into cheap labor—confound the high-priority objective of steadily increasing real incomes for American workers, not to mention the costs in social divisiveness. Michael Porter makes the point compellingly in *The Competitive Advantage of Nations*:

> The principal economic goal of a nation is to produce a high and rising standard of living for its citizens. . . . A rising standard of living depends on the capacity of a nation's firms to achieve high levels of productivity and to increase productivity over time . . . cheap labor [is not a] meaningful definition of competitiveness. . . . The ability to compete *despite* paying higher wages would seem to represent a far more desirable national target.[62]

The *New York Times* must recognize that the United States is today a very different, far more densely populated country than it was when Emma Lazarus wrote the words "Give me your tired, your poor, your huddled masses yearning to breathe free . . ." that appear on the Statue of Liberty; that many of the social problems we face, particularly in New York City and including that one-third of black citizens who still live in poverty, are in part the consequence of high levels of immigration; that the composition of the current heavy immigrant flow is very different from the late nineteenth and early twentieth centuries; and that some national and ethnic groups acculturate much more quickly than others to American mainstream values and the democratic-capitalist institutions that reflect them.

Many people on the right and left who are pro-immigration argue that we can't, in any event, control immigration across the 2,000-mile Mexican-American border. That is a canard that has been disproven recently in El Paso and San Diego. Silvestre Reyes, former head of the El Paso Border Patrol, designed and executed a strategy based on deterrence of entry by tight spacing of Border Patrol agents—he calls it Operation Hold the Line—rather than apprehending illegal immigrants after they have entered. "There is some dispute as to whether Reyes had support in this effort from Washington,[63] but no dispute that the experiment has been largely successful and wildly popular with the population of El Paso, itself heavily Mexican-American."[64]

Reyes's success and the personal interest of Janet Reno led to a substantial beefing up of the Border Patrol's capabilities in the Tijuana area south of San Diego. The terrain is quite different from El Paso, where the Rio Grande is the border, and the Border Patrol strategy has been to reinforce its capacity to locate and apprehend illegal immigrants, the vast majority of whom cross at night. An infrared remote sensing system has been installed that, along with several lines of mobile Border Patrol agents and a computerized finger-printing system, has resulted in a dramatic reduction of the flow.* In both the El Paso and Tijuana cases, the result has been to divert at least part of the flow to more remote areas, which some pro-immigrationists argue proves that you can't stop the flow. Reyes's response is that twenty-four-hour-a-day presence of Border Patrol agents on the 10 percent (200 miles) of the border that is not forbidding desert, plus remote sensing and helicopter surveillance, will substantially seal the border. "If they make a three-day trek into the desert and get caught, it's very demoralizing," Reyes added.[65]

For decades, Mexican governments have tacitly supported illegal immigration both as a means of reducing Mexico's adverse ratio of new

---

*I visited the Tijuana defense system the evening of 6 December 1995 with Marco Ramírez, Border Patrol public information officer, and Nancy LeRoy of the U.S. Consulate in Tijuana. While the terrain is clearly more difficult than the terrain at El Paso, I nonetheless believe that the "Hold the Line Approach" can work there if enough resources are dedicated to it. Apprehension and deportation are expensive and less efficient than deterrence, particularly since the ultimate sanction (after many repeated apprehensions)—indictment for a felony—leads to expensive prison terms paid by the U.S. taxpayer.

labor market entrants to jobs created and also as a means of increasing the flow of dollar remittances from Mexican immigrants. Some Mexicans also see heavy Mexican immigration into the United States as a gradual process of irredentism. We have missed two golden opportunities to elicit Mexican government cooperation to curb the illegal flow: the NAFTA negotiations and the negotiation of the 1995 bailout package. That cooperation should become a high-priority focus of the diplomatic dialogue between the two countries. Some progress has been made toward repatriation of deportees to their towns and cities of origin, which are often in the south of Mexico, rather than to the border. But the Mexican government should also enforce an existing Mexican law that prohibits border crossings at other than legal ports of entry, which could result in patrols on both sides of the border.[66]

Our immigration policy must be responsive to the needs of our own society, and particularly our poorer citizens, not the failures of other societies. The recent disaggregation of performance of immigrants by country of origin makes it clear that some immigrant groups—for example, the East Asians—are doing much better than others—for example, the Mexicans—with respect to education, upward mobility, and acculturation. An immigration policy based on country of origin is not feasible, but one that emphasizes education, skills, and financial resources is. Reductions in legal and illegal immigration are supported by a large majority of Americans—including large numbers of blacks and Hispanics—and until the number of citizens and legal immigrants in poverty declines significantly, reductions, coupled with an immigration policy that stresses education, skills, and financial resources, should be pursued.[67] And bilingual education programs should be reshaped to emphasize mastery of English, consistent with the vision of a national community that embraces all of us.

12

Conclusion: Democracy and the Free Market Are Not Enough

Let's now offer some answers to the questions posed in the introduction.

Q. Is the Partnership for Development and Prosperity—the successor to the Enterprise for the Americas Initiative George Bush announced in 1990—destined to follow the Alliance for Progress, and Franklin Roosevelt's Good Neighbor Policy, into the cemetery of frustrated good intentions, of Pan-American dreams?

A. Not necessarily. The world of 1996 is very different from the world of 1961. There is no viable ideological alternative that seriously challenges democratic-capitalism. Latin America's progress in the past three decades has been disappointing, but it at least appears to recognize that "defensive nationalism" has been very costly to its progress and that close relationships with the United States are in its interest. But it is going to take a good deal of time—decades—to knit anything like the intricate fabric that binds Canada and the United States—or the Western European nations—together.

Q. Can a coherent, functional, durable community that will transform the dream into reality be constructed with building blocks so different: to the north, the United States and Canada, prosperous First World countries with centuries-old democratic roots and institutions; to the south, Latin America's poor Third World countries whose centuries-old political traditions and institutions are for the most part authoritarian and who, in most cases, are today experimenting with democratic institutions and free-market economic policies for the first time?

252

A. It is because the gap between the participants—in prosperity, in institutional strength, in human resources, and ultimately in values and attitudes—is so wide that the forging of a community will be a slow, painstaking process and a good deal more difficult than the forging of the community in Western Europe, much as the Alliance for Progress was a good deal more difficult to bring to a successful conclusion than was the Marshall Plan.

Q. *Why, as we approach the end of the twentieth century, are Canada and the United States, their own problems notwithstanding, a half-century or more ahead of Latin America with respect to the sturdiness of their democratic institutions, the level of prosperity enjoyed by the average citizen, and the access of the average citizen to education, health services, opportunity for advancement, and fair treatment in the legal system? What explains the Latin American traditions of authoritarianism, abuse of power, suppression of economic creativity, and social injustice?*
A. While a number of other factors are relevant, including geography, climate, policies and institutions, and sheer luck, the most important explanation for the progress of Canada and the United States and the underdevelopment of Latin America is the contrast between Anglo-Protestant and Ibero-Catholic culture.

Q. *Why has it taken so long for Latin America to arrive at the conclusion that intimate, open relationships with the United States are in its own best interests?*
A. Several factors come into play: the resentment of the more successful by the less successful; feelings of inferiority and impotence in Latin America; ideological conflicts sharpened by the cold war; cultural conflicts that impede effective communications; and, most concretely, large numbers of intellectuals in Latin America, the United States, and Canada committed to the costly myth that the United States is an irresponsible, avaricious, imperialist power that has gotten rich exploiting poor countries.

Q. *Finally, what might be done to enhance the prospects for a genuine, dynamic community in the Hemisphere?*
A. Much of what follows attempts to answer that question.

THE ROOT OF THE PROBLEM

About twenty years ago, I heard a story that was exquisitely relevant to the Western Hemisphere of that moment—and for many years thereafter—but is today decidedly anachronistic. The story is about three Latin American men: one is a conservative, the second a liberal, and the third a Marxist-Leninist. Each returns home early one afternoon to find his wife in bed with another man. The conservative glowers and says, "You are both guilty," pulls out a pistol, and shoots them both. The liberal trembles and says, "I am guilty," pulls out a pistol and shoots himself. And the Marxist-Leninist runs downtown and throws rocks at the American Embassy.

Today, one rarely hears that Latin America's problems are the consequence of "Yanqui imperialism." Mexico's leap into the embrace of the United States and Canada is a symbol of the demise of dependency theory. Left-fringe, anti-U.S. activists of two decades ago like the Mexican writer Jorge Castañeda today find themselves participants in the democratic-capitalist consensus, although in the growth-versus-equity debate, they come down more on the equity side. As I mentioned in chapter 8, Castañeda recently published an article in *The Atlantic Monthly* that focuses on cultural factors to explain Mexico's problems.[1] Such an explanation would have been regarded as heresy and treason in Latin American—and American—intellectual circles twenty years ago.

Indicative of the receptivity of contemporary Latin Americans to cultural interpretations of Latin America's problems was a symposium held in Costa Rica 28–30 June 1996 under the auspices of the Central American Business Administration Institute (the Spanish acronym is INCAE).* The symposium was dedicated to the role of culture in political, economic, and social development, and participants included several writers mentioned in this book: Hernando de Soto, Michael Novak, Carlos Alberto Montaner, Mariano Grondona, Claudio Véliz, David and Bernice Martin, Maria Lucia Victor Barbosa, Ronald Inglehart, Miguel Basañez, and Marita Carballo; as well as Octavio Mavila and Alfonso Esguerra, who will be mentioned later in this chapter; Luis Ugalde, S. J., the rector of the Catholic University of Caracas;

---

*INCAE was founded in 1964 with the help of Harvard University's Graduate School of Business Administration, with which INCAE has retained ties over the decades. See pages 77–78.

and myself. Eleven Latin American countries were represented. While the question of what if anything can be done to strengthen progressive values and attitudes was debated vigorously, all of the participants believe that culture is a central causal factor behind Latin America's generally precarious political institutions, the gap in prosperity between it and the nations of the First World, and its widespread pattern of social rigidity and inequality.

It was precisely twenty years ago that the Venezuelan writer and journalist Carlos Rangel, little-known outside his own country, published a book that argued that Latin America's real problems were grounded in Ibero-Catholic culture.[2] Rangel, who, with his wife, Sofía Imber, co-hosted Venezuela's leading morning television show, had studied at Bard College and New York University and had served in the Venezuelan foreign service. The reader can imagine the impact in intellectual circles at that time of a book that argued:

> It was Latin America's destiny to be colonized by a country that . . . was at the time beginning to reject the emerging spirit of modernism and to build walls against the rise of rationalism, empiricism, and free thought—that is to say, against the very bases of the modern industrial and liberal revolution, and of capitalist economic development.[3]

> . . . Latin America's history bears witness to the failure of Catholicism, in contradistinction to Protestantism, or, at least, to the defeat of the Catholic ethic by the Protestant ethic, which shaped the development of the United States. . . . The North American Protestant society appears more Christian, or perhaps less anti-Christian, than Latin American Catholic society. It demands of its followers a pattern of social behavior that dictates reasonably good faith in daily affairs and in interpersonal relations and requires socially constructive action even of those in opposition.[4]

Receptivity to Rangel's views—and to my *Underdevelopment Is a State of Mind*, which refers extensively to his ideas—has increased over the years. Recall from chapter 8 the comment the prominent Mexican intellectual Lorenzo Meyer made after I spoke at the Colegio de México late in 1995: "Fifteen years ago, Harrison's presentation would not have been possible here." For several years now, Latin American (and American, Canadian, and European) intellectuals have had to ask themselves, "If dependency theory is essentially a scapegoating myth, how else can Latin America's tortured history, its underdevelopment, be explained?" One easy, and superficial, alternative is bad policies and weak institutions. But the bad policies and weak institutions have persisted for almost two centuries. They have to be symptoms of a fundamental underlying weakness, as Tocqueville would have argued. And that weakness is traditional Ibero-Catholic culture and its incompatibility with modernization.

In the early years following the publication of his book, Rangel was treated by most Latin American intellectuals as a traitor, a pariah. But with the collapse of communism in Eastern Europe, the decisive defeat of the Sandinistas in the 1990 Nicaraguan elections, Chile's return to the democratic ranks and its dynamic economic performance, and the new democratic-capitalist consensus in Latin America, Rangel, who died by his own hand in 1988, is now widely regarded as a courageous visionary by many prominent Latin American thinkers. Mario Vargas Llosa, Carlos Alberto Montaner, Mariano Grondona, and Claudio Véliz, for example, share Rangel's view, and the best-selling *Manual of the Perfect Latin American Idiot* is dedicated to him and Jean François Revel. An American who applauded Rangel's wisdom and courage was Puerto Rican Teodoro Moscoso, the first U.S. coordinator of the Alliance for Progress. Moscoso wrote in 1988, "I have long admired [this] outstanding Latin American thinker who has been saying ['Let's stop blaming the North Americans for our own failures'], but who has been ignored in the U.S. and denounced as a 'lackey of American imperialism' by his Latin American peers."[5]

Recognition that Latin America's problems are rooted in the Latin American mind, not in the evil designs of foreign devils, is a crucial first step toward fundamental change. Among other positive consequences, it has contributed to Latin America's rejection of socialism and authoritarianism and its willingness to experiment with the democracy and capitalism that Latin America's intellectuals and politicians of the left had sneered at for so long as "exploitation of the masses," "Wall Street manipulated," "Yanqui intervention."

But are democracy and the free market enough to assure Latin America of the transformation it seeks from the Third World to the First World? Can Latin America confidently assume that, because it has adopted the political system and economic policies of the First World, it is now inevitably destined to join the ranks of the prosperous democracies?

The new democratic-capitalist consensus in Latin America is an extremely important and positive development. While democratic capitalism is very late in arriving in Latin America, the new consensus can greatly facilitate modernization. But it is not, in itself, sufficient to assure modernization for reasons that Tocqueville very correctly perceived: the new institutions and policies will not work as they should if the people who function within them possess values and attitudes that are incompatible with democracy and the free market.

I am reminded of the American interventions in Nicaragua in 1912 and the Dominican Republic in 1916, both motivated by concern that the chaotic political and financial circumstances in each (and in Haiti, which we occupied in 1915) would invite a hostile, most likely German, presence near the newly opened Panama Canal. In each case, the Americans concluded that the absence of professional military and police forces was the principal destabilizing factor. The occupying U.S. Marines thus accorded a high priority to the training of constabularies committed to the idea of professionalism and civilian control within a democratic political environment. But those ideas, central as they were to the culture of the United States (and Canada), were alien to the national cultures, and after the Americans left the Dominican Republic in 1924 and Nicaragua in 1933, the "professionalized" constabularies became the launching pads of the Trujillo and Somoza dictatorships.

Democratic forms and open economic policies are a major step forward for Latin America, and they are likely to promote the values and attitudes that are necessary for their successful functioning. But a good deal more is necessary before Latin America can be confident of the irreversibility of democracy and free-market policies, to say nothing of purposeful, sustained, and rapid movement toward First World status and intimate relationships with the United States and Canada.

SOME RECENT CASES IN POINT

If we look at the three countries—Colombia, Venezuela, the Dominican Republic— with the longest democratic continuity in Latin America after Costa Rica, it is difficult to be optimistic about democracy's capacity to transform Latin American societies. In each of the three, democratic forms have operated for a decade or more than they have in Spain. Yet political stability is not consolidated in any of the three; distribution of wealth, land, and income is still highly inequitable; and due process in the courts is routinely corrupted by money and politics.

Democracy, at least in a formal and particularly electoral sense, has been practiced in Colombia since 1958. But the violence that characterized Colombia's history has continued, initially given impetus by the Cuban revolution and gradually reverting to traditional banditry and general lawlessness. The enormously lucrative narcotics industry has profoundly magnified the traditional corruption of the political and judicial systems.

Venezuela has functioned within democratic forms since 1959. Yet its political fragility, social injustice, and widespread corruption are underscored by two coup attempts in this decade, impeachment proceedings against one ex-president (Carlos Andres Pérez), and criminal proceedings against another (Jaime Lusinchi). Under President Rafael Caldera, who has governed with some of the traits of a caudillo, it is one of the few countries in Latin America today that had backed away from free-market, privatization policies, although Caldera appeared to be shifting course toward the consensus in 1996.

The Dominican Republic has functioned within democratic forms for three decades. But with the enormous influence Joaquín Balaguer has exercised over politics since he defeated Juan Bosch in the 1966 elections that followed the Dominican Revolution and U.S. intervention, the country's political development has been stunted, and acute social problems have persisted. The symbol of the failure of "caudillo democracy" to transform the Dominican Republic is the heavy flow of immigrants to the United States. Many of them are illegal, their entry facilitated by the proximity of the Dominican Republic to Puerto Rico.

In these cases, and in almost all other Latin American countries except Costa Rica, Chile, and Uruguay, an observation made by Freedom House's Douglas Payne is apt: "Judicial systems are less about justice than providing protection for those who can pay for it and punishing those who cannot."[6]

The destiny of free-market economic policies is also uncertain, particularly in light of the anti-entrepreneurial Ibero-Catholic tradition (as we have noted, Brazil and Chile are exceptions) and the cozy government-oligarchy economic arrangements that have prevailed throughout Latin America's history. Joseph Schumpeter spotlighted the entrepreneur as the real engine of development, but he had in mind the entrepreneurial geniuses—Henry Ford and the like. As Japan and the East Asian dragons have demonstrated, economic growth depends more on the creativity, work ethic, and frugality of the common citizen. Traditional Ibero-Catholic culture has not nourished those values. Nor has it created the climate of trust and confidence that facilitates economic efficiency and creativity.

Spain is a case in point. It was at about the same level of prosperity as Argentina, Chile, Uruguay, and Cuba at the end of World War II. Today it is in the First World, with a per capita GNP of $13,590, almost twice that of Argentina, Latin America's most prosperous nation according to the World Bank (but about two-thirds of the Western European average).[7] However, Spain's economic growth has been far slower than that of the East Asian dragons: its per capita GNP grew at a rate of 4.7 percent between 1960 and 1979, compared with 7.4 percent for Singapore, 7.1 percent for South Korea, and 7.0 percent for Hong Kong (the rate for Japan during that period was 9.4 percent).[8] Between 1980 and 1993, the rate for Spain was 2.7 percent, compared with 8.2 percent for South Korea, 6.1 percent for Singapore, and 5.4 percent for Hong Kong.

Unlike the dragons, whose growth has been driven principally by internal savings and entrepreneurship, Spain's growth has been heavily dependent on outside factors: tourism; the remittances of Spanish sojourner workers in Western Europe, particularly in the fifties and sixties; and foreign investment and management, facilitated by Spain's accession to the European Community in 1986. Spain's scant entrepreneurial tradition in part explains its extremely high—over 20 percent—unemployment and the dependency on government, particularly in the form of direct employment and pensions, of something like half the Spanish population.

We also have to ponder the inability of the free market in Latin America to assure adequate trickle-down of prosperity to the poorer classes. Without a well-developed sense of community and justice, and without effective democratic institutions, Latin America has produced some of the most inequitable societies in the world as measured by income distribution and distribution of wealth, land, and opportunity. The Brazilian economy has been among the fastest-growing in the world in this century.[9] Between 1965 and 1980, Brazil experienced annual growth rates averaging almost 10 percent. Yet among those countries in the world reporting income distribution patterns, Brazil is the most inequitable, with Chile and Mexico not too far behind. The top 10 percent of Brazilians account for more than 50 percent of income. The average figure in the advanced democracies is 25 percent.

The final case in point is Puerto Rico. Carlos Alberto Montaner makes the point tellingly:

> In 1998, the American occupation of Puerto Rico will be 100 years old. In that century, Puerto Rico has enjoyed democracy, increasing self-government, an independent judiciary, a state of law, a market economy, and the largest transfer of financial resources in world economic history—$7 billion in 1995. The result: the per capita income of the Puerto Ricans is one-half of the per capita income of the poorest state in the United States. At the same time, the Puerto Ricans who migrate to the United States constitute the poorest Hispanic minority despite having the highest level of education, greater mastery of English, and all of the advantages of citizenship.[10]

PROMOTING PROGRESSIVE CULTURAL CHANGE

Culture changes. It is not a genetic phenomenon. It is learned, acquired, starting at birth, and it has a powerful momentum, in part because child-rearing practices change very slowly. Many forces can shape cultural values and attitudes: religion, art, the media, war, economic hardship, affluence, the education system, policies, among others. Some of the most dramatic changes in national cultures have been the result of strong, visionary leadership, particularly in the wake of a major threat or defeat: for example, the youthful Meiji leadership that transformed Japan following the collapse of the tradition-bound Tokugawa Dynasty, a collapse precipitated in part by the intimidating visits of American warships under Commodore Perry; and Mustafa Kemal Atatürk's vision of a modern, westernized Turkey built on the rubble of the Ottoman Empire after its collapse in World War I.

The case of *la Madre Patria*—Spain—is particularly relevant. An important part of the foundation for the rapid transition to democracy following the death of Franco in 1975 was forged in the suffering of the Spanish people in the extremist violence of the Civil War of the 1930s.

Further impetus was given to the transformation by Franco's reluctant decision at a moment of economic crisis in the late 1950s to open up the Spanish economy to the rest of the world, above all to Western Europe and the United States. Until that moment, he had pursued a policy of self-sufficiency that was wholly consistent with José Ortega y Gasset's characterization of the Spanish national character: "The perfect Spaniard needs nothing. More than that, he needs nobody. This is why our race are such haters of novelty and innovation. To accept anything new from the outside world humiliates us. . . . To the true Spaniard, all innovation seems frankly a personal offense."[11]

I have identified ten cultural factors usually present, albeit in varying degrees, in the successful countries of the West and East Asia, as well as high-achieving ethnic immigrant groups like the East Asians and Jews: future orientation, work ethic, frugality, education, merit, community, a rigorous ethical code, justice, diffused authority, and secularism. What can be done to reinforce these values and attitudes on which Latin America's modernization so much depends, recognizing that modernization itself is an important—but far from the only—reinforcing device? Obviously, the solutions to so enormous a problem require mobilization of the entire society.

The indispensable starting point is broad recognition that the traditional values present an obstacle to progress. That consensus is difficult to achieve because it requires the capacity for objective introspection and attribution of failure to internal factors that touch on the most sensitive questions of self-image and self-respect. As Carlos Alberto Montaner has said, "Only if we confront the truth, without fear, with humility, and with the purpose of seeking change, will it one day be possible for us to attenuate or end our underdevelopment. It is useless to hide our heads in the sand and deny the obvious in the name of a false nationalistic pride. . . . [W]e are responsible for our own failures, no one else, and it's useless to seek alibis and scapegoats."[12]

But that starting point is a good deal easier to reach today than it was during the heyday of dependency theory.

Atatürk said to his fellow Turks after World War I, "We must be of the West!" The Argentine educator, writer, and statesman Domingo Faustino Sarmiento had said to his compatriots fifty years earlier, "We must be the United States!"—with far less impact. Both leaders shared a vision of a modern democratic society based on the adoption of the values and institutions of successful countries. The message of the Meiji leadership to the Japanese people was similar, although they had the advantage of a culture, predominantly Confucian, that emphasized several of the values central to the success of the West.

The Role of Political Leadership

Vigorous, intelligent political leadership with a vision of a modern democratic society can be a powerful engine of cultural change, be it in the public declarations of leaders, their personal conduct and style, or their policies and programs, especially those that attack corruption, emphasize merit, and open up opportunities for those theretofore denied access. I want to repeat my belief that democracy and the free market are key, not only because they break down centuries-old barriers to participation but also because they can play an important role in changing the way people see themselves, their neighbors, their society, their chances for a better life. Democracy serves as an indispensable brake on abuse of political, economic, and military power, while the economic pluralism and dynamism of the free market nourish political pluralism, as we have seen in the cases of Japan, Spain, South Korea, and Taiwan. (With respect to Latin America's traditions of militarism, I note in passing that most Latin American countries, and that includes Chile, have not achieved full civilian control of their military institutions.)

But neither democratic institutions nor the free market will function well if the participants do not bring the requisite values, attitudes, and preparation to them. Those economists who argue that the market works the same way in all cultures are patently wrong: the widely differing economic performance of ethnic groups—for example, the Koreans and the Puerto Ricans—in a multicultural society like the United States demolishes that position.

It is, however, true that some policies and programs can generate widespread benefits and reinforce progressive values. Examples are the savings incentives established by the Chilean government and efforts to regularize land and other property holdings so that they are readily negotiable in markets, an initiative promoted by Hernando de Soto in recent years.[13]

Political leadership has at its disposal perhaps the most powerful engine of cultural change: the education system. Sweeping educational reform is of the highest priority throughout Latin America. It is within the capacity of all Latin American countries to assure that all school-age children receive a complete primary education, and a good proportion of them a complete secondary education, during the next twenty years. The elimination of illiteracy, and the functional illiteracy that is inevitable when a person completes only two or three grades, will put an end to a chronic condition in Latin America that has perpetuated the traditional value system.

But the necessary educational reform does not stop there. It seeks to transform the traditional authoritarian, rote pedagogy into one that encourages creativity, participation, and problem solving. It inculcates the values of democratic-capitalism, particularly the importance of education, the work ethic and self-discipline, merit, community and cooperation, association, fair play. It teaches how democratic societies work and the role of the individual in a democratic society. And it emphasizes the building of character. Montaner says, "Education has to do with character. It has to do with discipline, respect for norms of behavior, intellectual honesty, the quest for excellence, making good on commitments, punctuality, scientific curiosity, problem solving, and the rest of the virtues that characterize the most advanced peoples of the earth."[14]

Montaner's words evoke the Human Development Institute (the Spanish acronym is INDEHU), established in Peru in 1990 by Octavio Mavila, a businessman in his seventies who has represented Honda for several decades. After visiting Japan many times on business, he came to the conclusion that the only truly significant difference between Japan and Peru was that Japanese children learned progressive values and attitudes while Peruvian children learned values and attitudes that were obstacles to progress. With the help of the Peruvian government and the private sector, INDEHU has introduced the Ten Commandments of Development in high school courses that have been attended by more than two million Peruvian youngsters. The "Commandments" are order, cleanliness, punctuality, responsibility, achievement, honor, respect for others, respect for the law, work, and frugality.

Political leadership can also promote the decentralization of government in an area of the world where an exaggerated centralization has been the mode since earliest colonial times. Robert Putnam makes the point in *Making Democracy Work* that decentralization in Italy has not only encouraged grassroots participation but has also led to some positive changes in values and attitudes, for example, with respect to the possibility of influencing one's own destiny.

The Role of Intellectuals and the Media

Intellectuals and the media have a key role to play in progressive cultural change. Spain's transformation owes much to the tradition of social criticism starting with Cervantes and including, among others, José Ortega y Gasset, Miguel de Unamuno, Salvador de Madariaga, and Fernando Díaz-Plaja. In the Latin American context, Carlos Rangel was very much in the same tradition.

Today, the media, above all television, offer an immensely important resource for cultural change. Media encouragement of an introspective explanation of Latin America's condition can go a long way toward neutralizing the impact of the several decades during which "dependency"/"Yankee imperialism" explanations filled the media. Mariano Grondona's highly popular prime-time weekly television talk show in Argentina is a model of what the media can do to hold a mirror up to a society.

Little scholarly research has been done on the relationship between culture and progress (or the lack of progress) because it is so politically incorrect. The social sciences are still strongly influenced by two schools of thought that clash with cultural interpretations of why some countries and ethnic groups do better than others. Most anthropologists are wedded to cultural relativism, which asserts that all cultures are equal—comparative value judgments are taboo—and since culture is the bailiwick of the anthropologists, other social scientists have also come under the influence of cultural relativism. Most economists would prefer to believe that the market overrides cultural differences, evidence to the contrary notwithstanding.

The reader can appreciate the extreme sensitivity of cultural analysis from an encounter I had with a professor of political science at Carleton University in Ottawa in 1994. I had explained my views on the roots of Latin America's problems when she concluded the conversation—and any further contact between us—with, "You know, that's the kind of theory that led to the slaughter of six million Jews."

The relationships among culture, institutions, policies, and progress are highly complicated; cause and effect run in both directions. Sorting out those relationships and analyzing them requires the involvement of anthropologists, sociologists, psychologists, economists, and political scientists, particularly those comfortable working in an interdisciplinary environment. We need to know much more about the transmission of values and attitudes from generation to generation, also the principal acculturating forces: the home; the school; the church; the media, particularly television; the workplace; peers. We have to understand how humans, most especially children, acquire either progress-prone or progress-resistant values. Particularly in the early years of life, the home is the source of acculturation, and we need to understand much better how values and attitudes are transmitted to infants and small children through child rearing. And we have to use this improved understanding of child rearing to better prepare young adults for their role as parents.

Research on transmission of values and attitudes, and parenting, obviously has relevance for all countries, including the United States. I am reminded of the observation of a friend who taught kindergarten in the Maryland suburbs of Washington, D.C. Black children from the Washington ghetto were bused to her school, and a pattern soon emerged in their performance. In her words, "They arrived in kindergarten already programmed for failure in school." Her words evoke the observation of Joan Moore (see chapter 11) that "Jewish and Japanese children . . . march off to school with enthusiasm. Mexican and Negro children are much less interested. Some sort of cultural factor works here."[15]

Cultural Change in the Workplace

Tomás Roberto Fillol, an Argentine, was a student at Massachusetts Institute of Technology when he wrote his master's thesis, *Social Factors in Economic Development*. It starts with an analysis of Argentine culture that anticipates my analysis in *Underdevelopment Is a State of Mind*, emphasizing focus on the present; an aversion to work; an excessive individualism and familism that is the enemy of the larger community; inherited status and connections rather than merit; a zero-sum world view that presumes that my gain is at your expense; relationships permeated by authoritarianism and submission symbolized by the *caudillismo* of Juan Perón. He concludes his analysis with the observation that "steady, long-run economic development will hardly take place in Argentina unless there is a simultaneous change in the value orientation profile of the people."[16]

Notwithstanding the centuries-long persistence of the Hispanic culture that impedes Argentina's progress, Fillol believes that changes are possible that can improve Argentina's chances for a more prosperous future. He points to the workplace as a setting in which changes can be introduced that will ultimately reverberate throughout the culture, including the family. Traditional management in Argentina—in private enterprise and in government—reiterates the authority/submission pattern that the Argentine encounters at home, in the school, and in the church. It deprives the Argentine of a sense of accomplishment and, as a result, self-esteem. It magnifies the sense of insecurity and inspires rage, which the Argentine is likely to vent on his children.

Modern participatory management, of the kind we now associate with Japanese industry, can precipitate cultural change, in Fillol's view. The manager who explains rather than commands, who encourages communication in his organization, who encourages and rewards initiative, can create an environment in which

> workers feel they are recognized by their superiors; responsibilities and a certain degree of autonomy are . . . delegated by all levels of management; all levels of personnel identify with their jobs, the enterprise, and its goals; workers willingly cooperate with each other and with all levels of management in the pursuit of personal, but common, advantages; individuals are free to discuss problems arising from their jobs with superiors and workmates and willingly take advantage of such opportunities.[17]

Fillol is skeptical that workers in enterprises that are so managed will experience transformation of their values and attitudes. "But their anxiety, their rancor, their rage and forced suppression of it during working hours may have considerably declined. . . . Above all, people will not have to discharge their anxiety, rage, and aggression on their subordinates and especially their children."[18] The real payoff in cultural change will, he believes, appear in subsequent generations.

Changing the mentality of the private sector should also extend to a more highly developed sense of social responsibility on the part of businessmen. The traditions of philanthropy, in contrast to charity, are underdeveloped in Latin America, reflecting, I would argue, the alienation of the individual from the broader society by Ibero-Catholic culture—the underdeveloped sense of community. The narrow concentration of wealth in all Latin American countries should facilitate the mobilization of very substantial amounts of money from the private sector for education, health, housing, small-business promotion, and other longer-term projects that will both promote growth and improve equity. The vast potential of philanthropy has attracted the interest of, among others, Alfonso Esguerra, a Colombian radiologist who taught at Yale and who now dedicates a good part of his time promoting the idea and practice of philanthropy in Colombia.

Association

The traditions of association in Latin America are scant, similar to the condition of southern Italy that Banfield and Putnam have described. This phenomenon reflects the excessive individualism and familism that characterize Latin American societies—the absence of a sense of community. Clearly, the idea of association and its benefits needs to be inculcated in children, particularly in the home and in the school.

The functioning of the advanced democracies is facilitated by the existence of private organizations that intermediate between the government and the individual. The consolidation of democracy depends in part on the emergence of organizations such as *Poder Ciudadano* and *Ciudadanos en Acción* in Argentina. The citizen, the intellectuals and educators, the media, the churches, the private sector, and the government all have a role to play in the promotion of associations.

SOME ASSETS THAT MAY HELP

It has taken almost two centuries, but Latin America appears finally to be rejecting the political authoritarianism and economic mercantilism that it inherited from Spain and Portugal—and that both those countries have finally turned away from in the past few decades. Democracy and capitalism are fragile, but as the experiments persist, they get stronger and closer to irreversibility.

It would be rash to assert that the irreversibility of democracy has been achieved. In several countries—El Salvador, Nicaragua, Guatemala, for example—the wounds of recent civil strife and violence have not healed, and the military institutions still play a dominant political role. Colombia, above all, but also Bolivia, Peru, and Mexico are threatened by the vast financial resources and consequent corrupting political influence of the narco-traffickers. Even in Chile, the military still enjoys a degree of autonomy that is inconsistent with democratic standards.

But the defenses at the national, regional, and international levels against military takeovers are all stronger than they once were. While it was much easier to force the Haitian military from power after the ouster of Jean-Bertrand Aristide than it would be to reverse a *golpe de estado* by the Venezuelan military (which almost happened twice in the early 1990s), any *golpista* is going to confront the indignation, and perhaps loss of trade concessions, or even embargoes, of the members of the Organization of American States. Today, the overthrow of an elected government also assures the contempt and enmity of the First World.

In chapter 9, I observed that the free-market experiments are not consolidated except in Chile. The free-market proponents have promised high levels of growth and employment, and if those do not materialize within the next few years, the pressures to relax austerity, arrest and perhaps reverse privatizations, and increase tariff protection may reach levels that threaten in the first instance the survival of the open economic policies, in the second, democracy itself.

But political pluralism and the free market do open up opportunities for those heretofore denied access, and they are important assets both because of the potential benefits they offer for stability and development, and for the contribution they can make to progressive cultural change.

I have made repeated references to *traditional* Ibero-Catholic culture. But the changing culture of Latin America has also witnessed— and been influenced by—a changing, more this-worldly and pluralist Catholic Church that could be an asset for progressive cultural change. Some of the new Catholicism has found its expression in Marxist-based liberation theology, which Michael Novak has correctly and effectively challenged in *Will It Liberate?* as a detour from true democracy, to say nothing of the obstacle it poses to capitalism.[19] Novak, who was one of the early critics of dependency theory, argued prophetically in *The Spirit of Democratic Capitalism* that dependency theory was not only essentially a myth; it also obscured the crucial and negative role traditional "Latin Catholic" culture has played in Latin America.[20]

Novak has argued in two recent books that some progressive currents of Catholicism are increasingly making themselves felt. In *This Hemisphere of Liberty—A Philosophy of the Americas*, he discusses the traditions of "Catholic Whiggism"—the commitment to liberty, tradition, and modest (in contrast to utopian) progress going back to St. Thomas Aquinas in the thirteenth century.[21] And in *The Catholic Ethic and the Spirit of Capitalism*, he traces the Catholic currents, admittedly not mainstream, that have paralleled the Weberian Protestant ethic, especially in recent times.[22]

The rise of Protestantism, mostly evangelical, is probably also an asset, although it will be some time before its usefulness to economic growth and the consolidation of democracy becomes fully apparent. The research of David and Bernice Martin indicates that Protestants in Latin America conform in many respects to the Weberian model: as Bernice Martin observes, "[w]ork is a good thing, not a punishment;"[23] they eschew machismo, alcohol, drugs, and promiscuity; they are widely known and respected for their honesty (and are prized as domestic servants for that virtue). In one major respect, the Latin American Protestant diverges from the Weberian model. Bernice Martin observes that "the general culture of Latin America does not have a strong ascetic streak; self-denial is not valued in and for itself."[24] That self-denial, of course, is the engine of Weberian capital accumulation.

But the fact remains that something like 10 percent of Latin Americans—perhaps 50 million or more people—are Protestant, the movement continues to grow, and the Catholic monopoly has been shattered. That, coupled with the work ethic, discipline, and sobriety of the converts, is surely a force for progress.

Finally, the United States and, increasingly, Canada are assets for Latin America, particularly now that Latin Americans are more open to intercourse with the United States, more aware of the potential benefits that can accrue to them from the full range of constructive relationships: political, economic, social, cultural, diplomatic. The heightened acceptability of the United States brings with it the heightened acceptability of democracy and capitalism.

IMPLICATIONS FOR U.S. POLICY

What the Mexican crisis has demonstrated is that there is no such thing as an instant community, the kind trumpeted at the Miami summit. To say this is not to say that a Western Hemisphere community is an unrealizable dream. But it does imply a slow process and a good deal of patience and restraint on the part of the United States, based on the recognition that a wide cultural and institutional gap still exists between Latin America and the United States and Canada. The convergence of recent years has operated principally at the institutional level, particularly with respect to democratic forms and economic policies. But in most countries, the forms need to be converted into the living substance of democracy, and that depends on cultural change. The economic policies will need time to make their benefits widely felt, and it is uncertain that the fragile politics will hold together long enough to permit that to happen. Moreover, the entrepreneurship and savings shortfalls in Latin America suggest that economic miracles may be a good deal more difficult to bring to pass than in East Asia.

For some time to come, the United States and Canada are going to find themselves a good deal more compatible, more comfortable, with one another, with Europe, and even with East Asian countries than with Latin America. I mean that in the sense of the way business is transacted, of the way legal and administrative institutions function, of a diplomatic dialogue of equals. The Latin American private and public sectors will be moving toward First World norms, but that movement will be slow. And the diplomatic dialogue between the United States and Latin America will be burdened for some time to come by the long-standing tutelary posture of the former with respect to the latter over such issues as narcotics, economic performance, and human rights.

The United States should resist its historical tendency to announce great initiatives (for example, the Alliance for Progress, the Enterprise for the Americas Initiative) and work quietly and persistently for step-by-step progress in the consolidation of democratic institutions, the opening up of markets, and the integration of hemispheric economies. With respect to economic integration, U.S. policy makers should follow Sidney Weintraub's counsel for a patient policy that supports subregional groupings as building blocks—and schools—for a subsequent regional integration scheme. This should not negate the possibility of expanding NAFTA to individual countries with demonstrably solid democratic institutions and effectively functioning open economic policies, like Chile.

IMPLICATIONS FOR THE WORLD BANK, THE INTER-AMERICAN DEVELOPMENT BANK, THE U.S. AGENCY FOR INTERNATIONAL DEVELOPMENT, AND OTHER AID DONORS

The multilateral and bilateral donor institutions have shied away from the issue of cultural values and attitudes in part because of the professional biases of the economists and anthropologists, in part because of the political and psychological sensitivities evoked by the mere idea that some cultures provide a better environment for human progress than others. That avoidance of culture over the "development decades" since World War II has been very costly. The answers to the problems of the areas that have most resisted progress—Africa, most Islamic countries, South Asia, Latin America—are not just the framing of good policies and the building of modern institutions. What the experience of the last half-century tells us is that those good policies and modern institutions will be very difficult to put in place, and once in place may not function well, if the people who design and implement the policies and those who staff the institutions are not imbued with progressive values and attitudes. For example, planning will not work well when the focus of the planners is on the present or past; market policies will not work well in the absence of entrepreneurs (who will not, by the way, magically appear in response to market signals, as Spain, and Latin American immigrants in the United States, have demonstrated); and institutions of justice will not function well where mistrust is rife, people do not identify with other people in the society, and the ethical code is flexible.

The donor institutions should encourage Latin American and other Third World countries to consider the impact of traditional values on progress, including support for value and attitude research; analysis of traditional child-rearing practices and their implications for the inculcation of progressive values; and analysis of school curricula and pedagogical practices in terms of their impact on values and attitudes. The donors should also support public and private initiatives aimed at reinforcing progress-prone values, including civic education; support of democratic institutions, including an independent judiciary; decentralization of government; nongovernmental organizations that promote effective parenting, political participation, community mobilization, and philanthropy; and media programs.

Of highest importance is a campaign to end illiteracy, including, in the first instance, the completion of primary school by all school-age youngsters, to be followed by a mass expansion of secondary education with the goal of a high school diploma for all. Curriculum and pedagogy reforms illuminated by research activities should be integrated into this program, as well as civic education and ethics.

High priority should also be accorded to the development of quality universities that produce first-rate professionals, including the social scientists and administrators needed for the research and programs mentioned here. High priority should also be attached to university programs that not only teach modern methods of business management but that also promote entrepreneurship and inculcate ethics.

In Sum

A genuine Western Hemisphere community is possible and is worth working toward. But it will take more time and effort on the part of many actors than most of its promoters have appreciated, and it is obviously not a substitute for the relationships of the United States–Canada community with other parts of the world, above all Western Europe and East Asia. The realization of a genuine Western Hemisphere community will depend on the speed with which the values that make democracy and the free market really work displace the traditional values that largely explain why, as we approach the end of the twentieth century, Latin America lags so far behind Canada and the United States.

Notes

INTRODUCTION: DREAM OR REALITY

1. The reference is to Jerome Levinson and Juan de Onis, *The Alliance That Lost Its Way: A Critical Report on the Alliance for Progress* (Chicago: Quadrangle Books for the Twentieth Century Fund, 1970). Levinson and de Onis largely blamed the United States for the failure of the Alliance because it didn't do enough, a view that clashes with the conclusion of Teodoro Moscoso, first U.S. Coordinator of the Alliance, that "just as no human being can save another who does not have the will to save himself, no country can save others no matter how good its intentions or how hard it tries." Events of the past thirty-five years tend to confirm Moscoso's judgment. Moscoso quote is from Teodoro Moscoso, "The Will to Economic Development," in L. Ronald Scheman, ed., *The Alliance for Progress—A Retrospective* (New York, Westport, and London: Praeger, 1988), p. 86.

2. "Summers on Mexico: Ten Lessons to Learn," *The Economist*, 23 December 1995–5 January 1996, pp. 46–48.

3. The World Bank's *World Development Report 1994*, table 30, pp. 220–21, shows Chile's top 10 percent of income earners claiming 48.9 percent of total income in 1989, exceeded only—among all the world's countries reporting income distribution data—by Brazil's 51.3 percent. *World Development Report 1995* shows the top 10 percent with 45.8 percent of the income (1992), following Brazil, Zimbabwe, Guatemala, and Tanzania.

4. Legal immigration from Latin America between 1960 and 1990 totaled about 6 million. The demographer Leon Bouvier roughly estimates illegal immigration from 1965 to 1995 at 4.5 to 5 million (telephone interview with author, 5 February 1996).

1. THE ROOTS OF THE DIVERGENCE

1. I am omitting Haiti from this discussion because its history is unique: a former French slave colony that has substantially preserved its African culture. Haiti is the subject of two chapters in my *Underdevelopment Is a State of Mind—The Latin American Case* (Lanham, Md., and London: The Center for International Affairs, Harvard University, and University Press of America, 1985).

2. Anthony P. Maingot, *The United States and the Caribbean—Challenges of an Asymmetrical Relationship* (Boulder and San Francisco: Westview Press, 1994), p. viii.

3. The subtitle of the English edition of Carlos Rangel's milestone 1976 book *The Latin Americans* is *Their Love-Hate Relationship with the United States* (New York and London: Harcourt Brace Jovanovich, 1977).

4. Rangel, *The Latin Americans*, p. 67.

5. The World Bank's *World Development Report 1994* shows the United States with a GNP per capita of $23,240, Canada with $20,710. The Latin American average is $2,720, roughly one-eighth that of the average of Canada and the United States. (Income distribution in Canada and particularly the United States is at the inequitable end of that of the advanced democracies but is still substantially more equitable than that of Latin America.) At a growth rate of 3 percent per capita—a very optimistic figure—it would take about seventy years for per capita income to multiply eight times.

6. See World Bank, *World Development Report 1994*, table 30, pp. 220–21.

7. For a discussion of the new economic paradigm in Latin America, see David E. Hojman, "The Political Economy of Recent Conversions to Market Economies in Latin America," *Journal of Latin America Studies* 26 (1994): 191–219.

8. Magnus Blomström and Patricio Meller, eds., *Diverging Paths* (Washington, D.C.: Inter-American Development Bank, 1991).

9. For an explanation of Costa Rica's democratic evolution, see Harrison, *Underdevelopment Is a State of Mind*, chap. 3.

10. Alexis de Tocqueville, *Democracy in America* (London: David Campbell Publishers/Everyman's Library, 1994), p. 320.

11. Charles de Secondat, Baron de Montesquieu, *The Spirit of the Laws* (Cambridge, U.K., and New York: Cambridge University Press, 1989).

12. Ellsworth Huntington, *Civilization and Climate* (New Haven, Conn.: Yale University Press, 1915). For a more recent argument on the impact of climate on culture, see Thomas Sowell, *Race and Culture: A World View* (New York: Basic Books, 1994).

13. José Enrique Rodó, *Ariel* (Cambridge, U.K.: Cambridge University Press, 1967).

14. Lucian W. Pye, with Mary W. Pye, *Asian Power and Politics—The Cultural Dimensions of Authority* (Cambridge, Mass., and London: Belknap Press of Harvard University Press, 1985), p. 4.

15. Douglass C. North, *Institutions, Institutional Change, and Economic Performance* (Cambridge, U.K.: Cambridge University Press, 1990), pp. 3–4. For another policy/institutional explanation with dependency overtones, see John H. Coatsworth, "Notes on the Comparative Economic History of Latin America and the United States," in Walther L. Bernecker and Hans Werner Tobler, *Development and Underdevelopment in America* (Berlin and New York: Walter de Gruyter, 1993), pp. 10–30.

16. North, *Institutions, Institutional Change, and Economic Performance*, p. 102.

17. Keith Rosenn, "Federalism in the Americas in Comparative Perspective," *Inter-American Law Review* 26, no. 1 (Fall 1994), p. 4.

18. This conclusion is the central theme of Claudio Véliz's *The New World of the Gothic Fox—Culture and Economy in English and Spanish America* (Berkeley, Los Angeles, and London: University of California Press, 1994).

19. Tocqueville, *Democracy in America*, chap. 18.

20. Ibid., p. 300. Tocqueville also concludes, presciently, that secularization of Catholic societies will make them more susceptible to democracy (p. 301).

21. Ibid., pp. 322–23.

22. Ibid., p. 299.

23. Ibid., p. 320.

24. Ibid., pp. 231–32.

25. George Foster, *Culture and Conquest: America's Spanish Heritage* (Chicago: Quadrangle Books, 1960), p. 3.

26. Rangel, *The Latin Americans*, p. 6.

27. Interview with author, 12 February 1996.

28. In Véliz, *The New World of the Gothic Fox*, pp. 190–91.

29. In Rangel, *The Latin Americans*, pp. 27, 29.

30. Anthony Pagden, *Spanish Imperialism and the Political Imagination* (New Haven, Conn.: Yale University Press, 1990), pp. 139–40.

31. In Rangel, *The Latin Americans*, p. 6.

32. Domingo Faustino Sarmiento, *Facundo: Civilización y Barbarie* (Buenos Aires: Espasa-Calpa Argentina, 1951), p. 103; my translation.

33. Salvador Mendieta, *La Enfermedad de Centro-América* (Barcelona: Tipografía Maucci, 1936), pp. 60, 115; my translation.

34. Talcott Parsons, *Toward a General Theory of Action* (Cambridge, Mass.: Harvard University Press, 1957), p. 15.

35. See Max Weber, *The Protestant Ethic and the Spirit of Capitalism* (New York: Scribner's, 1950); *The Religion of China* (New York: Macmillan, 1951); and *The Religion of India* (Glencoe, Ill.: Free Press, 1958).

36. Talcott Parsons, *The Social System* (Glencoe, Ill.: Free Press, 1951).

37. Florence Kluckhohn, *Variations in Value Orientations* (Evanston, Ill: Row Peterson, 1961).

38. See, for example, the introduction to Jack M. Potter, May N. Díaz, and George M. Foster, *Peasant Society—A Reader* (Boston: Little, Brown, 1967).

39. Edward Banfield, *The Moral Basis of a Backward Society* (Glencoe, Ill.: Free Press, 1958).

40. Mariano Grondona, *Toward a Theory of Development* (unpublished).

41. Daniel Etounga-Manguelle, *L'Afrique—A-t-Elle Besoin d'un Programme d'Ajustement Culturel?* (Ivry-Sur-Seine: Editions Nouvelles du Sud, 1990).

42. These are the words of a former chief rabbi of Great Britain in J. H. Hertz, ed., *The Pentateuch and Haftorahs* (London: Soncino Press, 1961), p. 196.

43. David McClelland, *The Achieving Society* (Princeton, N.J.: D. Van Nostrand, 1961).

44. Robert Putnam, *Making Democracy Work—Civic Traditions in Modern Italy* (Princeton, N.J.: Princeton University Press, 1993). The quotation is from the dust jacket.

45. Francis Fukuyama, *Trust—The Social Virtues and the Creation of Prosperity* (New York: Free Press, 1995).

46. José Ortega y Gasset, *Invertebrate Spain* (New York: Norton, 1937).

47. Weber, *The Protestant Ethic and the Spirit of Capitalism*, p. 117.

48. Personal communication, October 1995.

49. Putnam, *Making Democracy Work*, p. 107.

50. Quoted in *The New Republic*, 7 July 1986.

51. Thomas Sowell, *Ethnic America* (New York: Basic Books, 1981), p. 88.

52. Richard Herrnstein and Charles Murray, *The Bell Curve* (New York: Free Press, 1994), p. 275.

2. CANADA AND THE UNITED STATES

1. "All Things Considered," National Public Radio, 16 October 1995.

2. John Herd Thompson and Stephen J. Randall, *Canada and the United States: Ambivalent Allies* (Montreal and Kingston, London, Buffalo: McGill-Queen's University Press, 1994), p. 246.

3. Seymour Martin Lipset, *Continental Divide—The Values and Institutions of the United States and Canada* (New York and London: Routledge, 1990).

4. Ibid., p. 1.

5. Ibid.

6. Ibid.

7. Thompson and Randall, *Canada and the United States*, p. 15.

8. For a breakdown of the two countries' contrasting psychology/ideology, see Michael A. Goldberg and John Mercer, *The Myth of the North American City* (Vancouver: University of British Columbia Press, 1986), p. 14.

9. Lawrence E. Harrison, *Who Prospers? How Cultural Values Shape Economic and Political Success* (New York: Basic Books, 1992), p. 235.

10. In Thompson and Randall, *Canada and the United States*, p. 83.

11. Lipset, *Continental Divide*, p. 4.

12. Ronald Inglehart, Miguel Basañez, and Neil Nevitte, *The North American Trajectory* (Hawthorne, N.Y.: Aldine De Gruyter, 1996).

13. Thompson and Randall, *Canada and the United States*, chap. 1.

14. Quoted from a 27 December 1845 editorial in the New York *Morning News* by Julius W. Pratt in *A History of United States Foreign Policy* (Englewood Cliffs, N.J.: Prentice-Hall, 1965), p. 110.

15. Thompson and Randall, p. 48.

16. Ibid., p. 42.

17. Ibid., p. 60.

18. Pratt, *A History of United States Foreign Policy*, p. 213.

19. Thompson and Randall, *Canada and the United States*, p. 72.

20. Thompson and Randall (p. 85) cite the words of the liberal postmaster general Rodolphe Lemieux: "Our theatres, sports, magazines, newspapers, are all more or less of the Yankee sort."

21. Ibid., p. 87.

22. Ibid., p. 88.

23. Ibid., p. 97.

24. Ibid., p. 98. The words are those of the Canadian historian H. L. Keenleyside, published in 1929.

25. Ibid., pp. 192–93.

26. Ibid., p. 272.

27. Ibid., p. 288.

28. U.S. Department of Commerce, *U.S. Direct Investment Abroad—Revised 1991 Estimates* (Washington, D.C.: U.S. Government Printing Office, 1994), table II.A.1.

29. U.S. Department of Commerce, *Foreign Direct Investment in the United States—Revised 1991 Estimates* (Washington, D.C.: U.S. Government Printing Office, 1994), table A–2.

30. Thompson and Randall, *Canada and the United States*, p. 8.
31. Alexis de Tocqueville, *Democracy in America* (London: David Campbell Publishers/Everyman's Library, 1994), p. 320.
32. Lansing Lamont, *Breakup* (New York and London: Norton, 1994), p. 67.
33. In Ramsay Cook, *French Canadian Nationalism* (Toronto: Macmillan of Canada, 1969), pp. 153–54.
34. Ibid., p. 68.
35. I heard Bouchard make this comment on an American television news program shortly before the referendum.
36. *New York Times*, 1 November 1995, p. 1.
37. For an insightful and moving analysis of Québecois nationalism, including its occasional anti-Semitic manifestations, see Mordechai Richler, *Oh Canada, Oh Quebec—Requiem for a Divided Country* (Toronto, London, New York: Penguin Books, 1992).
38. Canadian Heritage (a department of the Canadian government), "Ethnic Origins in Canada 1986/1991" (January 1994), shows 351,665 blacks in 1991, 158,910 "Spanish," in a total population of 26,994,045 people.
39. Richard Lamm and John Love, both former governors of Colorado, note in "Apartheid: American Style" (*Rocky Mountain News*, 18 September 1988) that Colorado's Hispanic population in 1988 was 11 percent of the total, while Hispanics accounted for 25 percent of the prison population.
40. Derrick Thomas, Citizenship and Immigration Canada (the Canadian federal government department responsible for immigration matters), "The Foreign Born in the Federal Prison Population," presented to the Canadian Law and Society Association Conference, Carleton University, Ottawa, 8 June 1993.
41. Thompson and Randall, *Canada and the United States*, p. 81.
42. For U.S. attitudes on immigration, see the 1992 Gallup Poll, pp 32–33. For Canadian attitudes, see Douglas L. Palmer (Citizenship and Immigration Canada), "Determinants of Canadian Attitudes Toward Immigration: More Than Just Racism?" (undated). The 2 November 1994 *Washington Post* reported the Canadian government's decision to reduce immigration from 250,000 in 1994 to 215,000 in 1995.
43. Personal communication, 12 September 1995. Thompson and Randall use *narcissism* in the same sense (*Canada and the United States*, p. 245).
44. Thompson and Randall, *Canada and the United States*, p. 217.
45. Ibid., p. 237.
46. Preface to John M. Kirk, "Back in Business: Canada-Cuba Relations After 50 Years," Canadian Foundation for the Americas, *The FOCAL Papers*, 1995.
47. Ibid.

3. LATIN AMERICA AND THE UNITED STATES

1. For a discussion of the new economic paradigm in Latin America, see David E. Hojman, "The Political Economy of Recent Conversions to Market Economics in Latin America," *Journal of Latin America Studies* 26 (February 1994): 191–219.

2. Plinio Apuleyo Mendoza, Carlos Alberto Montaner, Alvaro Vargas Llosa, *Manual del Perfecto Idiota Latinoamericano* (Barcelona: Plaza & Janes Editores, S.A., 1996).

3. According to Angus Maddison, "Raoul [sic] Prebisch's influential 1950 manifesto (*The Economic Development of Latin America and Its Principal Problems*) proclaimed a powerful role for government in avoiding the deflationary policies of the interwar years, though his message was more *dirigiste*, more inward looking, less optimistic about the possibilities for restoring a liberal world economy than was the case in OECD countries." (Angus Maddison, *The World Economy in the Twentieth Century* [Paris: OECD, 1989], pp. 69–70.)

4. UN Economic Commission for Latin America, CEPAL Review, First half of 1976, p. 74.

5. See Lawrence E. Harrison, *Who Prospers? How Cultural Values Shape Economic and Political Success* (New York: Basic Books, 1992), chap. 3, for an elaboration of this view.

6. Maddison, *The World Economy in the Twentieth Century*, p. 19.

7. See Barrie Dyster, "Argentine and Australian Development Compared," *Past and Present* 84 (August 1979): 94.

8. Data are from World Bank annual *World Development Reports*.

9. Fernando Henrique Cardoso and Enzo Faletto, *Dependencia y Desarrollo en América Latina* (Mexico City: Siglo Veintiuno Editores, 1971).

10. Fernando Henrique Cardoso and Enzo Faletto, *Dependency and Development in Latin America* (Berkeley and Los Angeles: University of California Press, 1979).

11. Ibid., p. ix.

12. Ibid., p. 133.

13. Ibid., p. xxiv.

14. Julio Cotler and Richard R. Fagen, *Latin America and the United States: The Changing Political Realities* (Stanford: Stanford University Press, 1974).

15. Castañeda's most recent book is *Utopia Unarmed—The Latin American Left After the Cold War* (New York: Knopf, 1993).

16. Alberto Couriel, *Las Empresas Internacionales* ("The International Enterprises") (Montevideo: Tierra Nueva, 1974), p. 6.

17. Jaime Wheelock Román, *Imperialismo y Dictadura*, 3d ed. (Mexico City, Madrid, Buenos Aires, and Bogotá: Siglo Veintiuno Editores, 1979).

18. Ibid., pp. 192–94, passim. My translation.

19. For a history of the early years of the Central American Common Market, see Isaac Cohen Orantes, *Regional Integration in Central America* (Lexington, Mass.: Lexington Books, 1972). Cohen concludes that avoidance of sacrifices and costs by the five participating countries caused the stagnation of the initiative.

20. Carlos Escudé, *El Realismo de los Estados Débiles—La Política Exterior del Primer Gobierno Menem Frente a la Teoría de las Relaciones Internacionales* (Buenos Aires: Grupo Editor Latinoamericano, 1995).

21. Ibid., p. 3.

22. Maddison, *The World Economy in the Twentieth Century*, table 1.3, p. 19.

23. *World Development Report 1995*, table 1, pp. 162–63.

24. Ibid., tables C–2, C–3, pp. 128–29; table D–1, pp. 138–39.

25. *World Development Report 1995*, table 13, pp. 186–87.

26. The sources are the World Bank's annual reports for 1980 and 1994.

27. United Nations Economic Commission for Latin America and the Caribbean, *Social Panorama of Latin America*, Washington, D.C., 1993 ed.

28. This point is documented by John Coatsworth in "Notes on the Comparative Economic History of Latin America and the United States," in Walther L. Bernecker and Hans Werner Tobler, *Development and Underdevelopment in America* (Berlin and New York: Walter de Gruyter, 1993), pp. 10–30.

29. World Development Report 1994, p. 163.

30. World Bank "purchasing power parity" statistics show Chile at $8,400 in 1993, the United States at $24,740. At the stipulated growth rates, it would take Chile fifty-six years to catch up with the United States.

31. Foreword to David Martin, *Tongues of Fire* (London: Basil Blackwell, 1990), p. vii.

32. Ibid., p. ix.

33. "Pragmatic Protestants Win Catholic Converts in Brazil," *New York Times*, 4 July 1993.

34. Martin, *Tongues of Fire*, p. 281.

35. Martin makes this point repeatedly, for example, on p. 212. It is wholly consistent with the self-view of Protestant converts with whom I've spoken in Mexico, Central America, and the Dominican Republic, also the view of Protestants by Catholics.

36. Martin, *Tongues of Fire*, p. 280.

37. I have calculated the 1960 per capita GNP levels by backtracking from

the World Bank's data in *World Development Report, 1980*. The data that follow derive from the same source.

38. Quoted in John Hooper, *The Spaniards: A Portrait of the New Spain* (New York: Viking, 1986), p. 73.

39. Francisco Andrés Orizo, *Los Nuevos Valores de los Españoles* (Madrid: Fundación Santa María, 1991), p. 211. Extensive value and attitude data are available on Spain: Andrés Orizo works with the World Values Survey, as does another distinguished Spanish political scientist, Juan Díez Nicolás.

4. THE DESTRUCTIVE ROLE OF AMERICAN INTELLECTUALS

1. Joseph Schumpeter, *Capitalism, Socialism, and Democracy* (New York: Harper Bros., 1942).

2. For a scholarly analysis of the extremes of the *dependencistas* in American universities, see Robert A. Packenham, *The Dependency Movement— Scholarship and Politics in Development Studies* (Cambridge, Mass., and London: Harvard University Press, 1992).

3. Quoted in Lawrence E. Harrison, "We Tried to Accept Nicaragua's Revolution," *Washington Post*, 30 June 1983.

4. Andre Gunder Frank, *Capitalism and Underdevelopment in Latin America* (New York and London: Monthly Review Press, 1967).

5. Ibid., p. xi.

6. Ibid.

7. Ibid.

8. Ibid., p. xv.

9. Ibid., p. 318.

10. The paper was republished, with revisions, by Sage Publications in 1971.

11. Ibid, p. 10.

12. Ibid., p. 20.

13. Ibid., p. 29.

14. Julio Cotler and Richard R. Fagen, *Latin America and the United States: The Changing Political Realities* (Stanford: Stanford University Press, 1974), pp. 259, 262. Italics in original.

15. Ibid., p. 265.

16. Ibid., p. 260.

17. Susanne Jonas and Edward J. McCaughan, eds., *Latin America Faces the Twenty-first Century* (Boulder, Colo.: Westview Press, 1994), p. 3.

18. Ibid., p. 4.

19. In Charles Truehart, "Hemisphere Builds Bridges Across Once Deep North-South Divide," *Washington Post*, 13 August 1995. Italics added.

20. "Activist's Hard Road," *Boston Globe*, 30 January 1996.
21. Piero Gleijeses, *Shattered Hope: The Guatemalan Revolution and the United States 1944–54* (Princeton, N.J.: Princeton University Press, 1991), p. 89: "Managed with ruthlessness, skill, and ambition, UFCO [United Fruit Company] earned its sobriquet: the Octopus."
22. Pablo Neruda, *Canto General*, trans. Jack Schmitt (Berkeley and Los Angeles: University of California Press, 1991), p. 179.
23. The historical information in this section comes chiefly from Stacy May and Galo Plaza, *The United Fruit Company in Latin America* (Washington, D.C.: National Planning Association, 1958).
24. Thomas McCann, *An American Company—The Tragedy of United Fruit* (New York: Crown Publishers, 1976), pp. 21–22. The same incident was similarly described in the March 1933 issue of *Fortune*, which may have been McCann's source.
25. Telephone interview with author, 1989.
26. His daughter told me this when I called on her at her home outside New Orleans in 1989.
27. *Life* magazine, 19 February 1951, 92.
28. Hernando de Soto, *El Otro Sendero* (Lima: Editorial El Barranco, 1986).
29. For a description of Communist involvement in Guatemala's banana operations, see John H. Coatsworth, *Central America and the United States—The Clients and the Colossus* (New York: Twayne Publishers, 1994), p. 68. One of the blurbs on the paperback edition was written by Jeffrey L. Gould at Indiana University and says, in part, "[The author] argues persuasively that Central America's tumultuous twentieth-century conflicts have been a direct consequence of that region's extreme economic and political dependence on the United States."
30. Stephen Kinzer and Stephen Schlesinger, *Bitter Fruit* (Garden City, N.Y.: Anchor Books, 1983).
31. Kinzer and Schlesinger extensively cite McCann's *An American Company*, which contains a detailed profile of Zemurray.
32. Kinzer and Schlesinger, *Bitter Fruit*, p. 85.
33. Stephen Kinzer, *Blood of Brothers: Life and War in Nicaragua* (New York: Putnam, 1991).
34. Kinzer and Schlesinger also cite the Stacy May/Galo Plaza study of United Fruit, which documents these conclusions.
35. Kinzer and Schlesinger, *Bitter Fruit*, p. 71.
36. Gleijeses, *Shattered Hope*, p. 90.
37. Ibid., p. 93.
38. Like Kinzer and Schlesinger, Gleijeses cites the McCann book, which contains a detailed profile of Zemurray. Zemurray's name does appear

once in *Shattered Hope*, in a footnote (p. 89) about a 1946 *Business Week* article, "Banana Split—à la Zemurray."

39. Coatsworth, *Central America and the United States*, p. 16.
40. Ibid., p. 221.
41. Ibid., p. 88. Fortuny's words are quoted from Gleijeses, *Shattered Hope*, p. 366.
42. Lawrence E. Harrison, *Underdevelopment Is a State of Mind—The Latin American Case* (Lanham, Md., and London: Center for International Affairs, Harvard University, and University Press of America, 1985), p. 162, note 3.
43. May and Plaza, *The United Fruit Company in Latin America*, p. 224.
44. Ibid., pp. 224–42, passim.

5. Argentina: First World to Third World?

1. Carlos H. Waisman, *Reversal of Development in Argentina: Postwar Counterrevolutionary Policies and Their Structural Consequences* (Princeton, N.J.: Princeton University Press, 1987), p. 405.
2. Angus Maddison, *The World Economy in the 20th Century* (Paris: Organization for Economic Cooperation and Development, 1989), passim.
3. Carlos Rangel, *The Latin Americans: Their Love-Hate Relationship with the United States* (New York and London: Harcourt Brace Jovanovich, 1977), pp. 240–41.
4. Domingo Faustino Sarmiento, *Facundo: Civilización y Barbarie* (Buenos Aires: Espasa-Calpa Argentina, 1951), p. 14. My translation.
5. Carlos F. Díaz Alejandro, *Essays on the Economic History of the Argentine Republic* (New Haven, Conn.: Yale University Press, 1970), p. 9.
6. In *Argentina: The Divided Land* (Princeton, N.J.: Van Nostrand Co., 1966), McGann notes in Argentine culture an excessive egoism and machismo; an exaggerated concern with dignity; a focus on status rather than accomplishment; disdain for manual labor; apathy; loyalty to the extended family and the *patrón* rather than to the law and the society; institutionalized corruption; and paternalistic, authoritarian relationships between managers and their employees (pp. 110–13, passim).
7. V. S. Naipaul, *The Return of Eva Perón* (New York: Vintage Books, 1981): "[Argentina] is like a sixteenth-century colony of the Spanish Empire, with the same greed and internal weaknesses, the same potential for dissension, the cynicism and sterility . . . politics have to do with the nature of human association, the contract of men with men. The politics of a country can only be an extension of its idea of human relationships" (pp.159, 166).

8. McGann, *Argentina: The Divided Land*, p. 100, quotes Garosa: "Argentines are imitative . . . habitually dissatisfied with their fellow men, their attitudes a mixture of impatience and inertia, people who are improvident, sentimental, full of self-love, and suspicious. Behind the pose of cynicism and sophistication, there is immaturity."

9. Carlos Escudé, *El Fracaso del Proyecto Argentino: Educación e Ideología* (Buenos Aires: Instituto Torcuato Di Tella, 1990).

10. Ibid., p. 206. My translation.

11. Waisman, *Reversal of Development in Argentina*, pp. 99–100.

12. Ibid.

13. Tomás Roberto Fillol, *Social Factors in Economic Development* (Cambridge, Mass: MIT Press, 1961).

14. Interestingly, southern Italy was a Spanish colony from 1503 until 1713. Of that period, the *Encyclopedia Britannica* (1957 ed., vol. 12, p. 776) says, "Spain and the Counter Reformation destroyed the free spirit of an earlier age and sapped the energies of the people."

15. Edward Banfield, *The Moral Basis of a Backward Society* (Glencoe, Ill.: Free Press, 1958).

16. Robert Putnam, *Making Democracy Work* (Princeton, N.J.: Princeton University Press, 1993).

17. Fillol makes essentially the same point when he says (*Social Factors in Economic Development*, p. 39), "we can conclude that the Argentine society has assimilated the impact of the massive immigration without undergoing a noticeable change in its value-orientation profile."

18. Escudé, *El Fracaso del Proyecto Argentino*, p. 189.

19. Ibid., p. 202.

20. Naipaul, *The Return of Eva Perón*, p. 119.

21. I happened to be in Buenos Aires when this story broke.

22. Sarmiento, *Facundo*, p. 103. My translation.

23. Naipaul, *The Return of Eva Perón*, p. 171.

24. "Emerging-Market Indicators," *The Economist*, 10 February 1996, p. 112.

25. Carlos Escudé, *El Realismo de los Estados Débiles—La Política Exterior del Primer Gobierno Menem Frente a la Teoría de las Relaciones Internacionales* (Buenos Aires: Grupo Editor Latinoamericano, 1995).

26. James L. Busey, "Costa Rica and Nicaragua Compared," *Western Political Quarterly* (September 1958): 585.

27. Marita Carballo, "Nuevas Tendencias de los Argentinos en Política" ("New Tendencies of the Argentines in Politics"), *La Nación*, 4 January 1993.

28. Ibid.

29. Marita Carballo, "Nuevas Tendencias de los Argentinos en Economía y

Trabajo" ("New Tendencies of the Argentines in Economics and Work"), *La Nación*, 5 January 1993.

30. Seminar at the Center for International Affairs, 26 April 1995.

31. World Bank, *World Development Report 1995*, p. 163.

32. Marita Carballo reports that her data show that 90 percent of Argentines identify themselves as Catholic ("La Religiosidad de los Argentinos" ["The Religiousness of the Argentines"], *La Nación*, 10 April 1993).

33. David Martin, *Tongues of Fire* (London: Basil Blackwell, 1990), p. 51.

6. BRAZIL: IS THE FUTURE NOW?

1. *World Development Report 1995*, pp. 166–67. Brazil's GNP in 1993 calculated on the basis of purchasing power parity was $5,370.

2. Angus Maddison, *The World Economy in the Twentieth Century* (Paris: OECD, 1989), table 1.2, p. 15.

3. *World Development Report 1995*, table 1, pp. 162–63.

4. Raymundo Faoro, *Os Donos do Poder* ("The Masters of Power") (Rio de Janeiro and Porto Alegre: Editorial Globo, 1958), p. 41. My translation.

5. Charles Wagley, *An Introduction to Brazil* (New York and London: Columbia University Press, 1963), p. 206.

6. In the early 1950s, UNESCO sponsored a symposium on immigration that focused on five countries: Argentina, Australia, Brazil, the United Kingdom, and the United States. The symposium was coordinated by Harvard's Oscar Handlin, and the Brazil rapporteur was Dr. Emilio Willems. The proceedings were published by UNESCO as a book, *The Positive Contribution of Immigrants* (Paris, 1955). The information in this section is drawn from the Willems chapter of that book.

7. Werner Baer, *The Brazilian Economy: Growth and Development* (Westport, Conn., and London: Praeger, 1995), p. 39.

8. United Nations Economic Commission for Latin America and the Caribbean, *Social Panorama of Latin America* (Washington, D.C.: 1993).

9. See "Fortuna Invisível" ("Invisible Fortune"), *Veja* (6 September 1995), for an analysis of the Brazilian informal sector.

10. World Bank, *Brazil: Public Spending on Social Programs: Issues and Options* (Washington, D.C., 27 May 1988), p. 1.

11. Robert Wesson and David V. Fleischer, *Brazil in Transition* (New York: Praeger, 1983), pp. 10, 11, 51.

12. This view of race in the United States is discussed in my *Who Prospers? How Cultural Values Shape Economic and Political Success* (New York: Basic Books, 1992), chap. 7.

13. José Ortega y Gasset, *Invertebrate Spain* (New York: Norton, 1937), pp. 49–50.

14. Fernando Díaz-Plaja devotes about a third of *El Español y Los Siete Pecados Capitales* ("The Spaniard and the Seven Deadly Sins") (Madrid: Alianza Editorial, 1966; reprint 1985) to *soberbia*.

15. José Oswaldo de Meira Penna, *Psicologia do Sub-Desenvolvimento* ("Psychology of Underdevelopment") (Rio de Janeiro: APEC Editora, 1972), p. 34. My translation.

16. Roberto DaMatta, *A Casa e a Rua* (São Paulo: Editora Brasiliense, 1985), p. 40.

17. Wesson and Fleischer, *Brazil in Transition*, p. 11.

18. Ibid., p. 12.

19. Ibid., p. 17.

20. Ibid., p. 18.

21. Riordan Roett, *Brazil: Politics in a Patrimonial Society* (Westport, Conn., and London: Praeger, 1992), p. 94.

22. Ibid., p. 33.

23. See Hernando de Soto, *El Otro Sendero* (Lima: Instituto Libertad y Democracia, 1986).

24. Statistics are from Baer, *The Brazilian Economy*, statistical appendix.

25. Ibid., pp. 74–75.

26. From the dust cover of Roberto Campos, *A Lanterna na Popa* (The Lantern on the Poopdeck) (Rio de Janeiro: Topbooks Editora, 1994).

27. Wesson and Fleischer, *Brazil in Transition*, p. 33.

28. Campos, *A Lanterna na Popa*, p. 1,283.

29. Wesson and Fleischer, *Brazil in Transition*, p. 35.

30. Ibid., p. 37.

31. Baer, *The Brazilian Economy*, table 6.2, p. 94.

32. Roett, *Brazil: Politics in a Patrimonial Society*, p. 28.

33. *The Economist*, 8–14 July 1995, p. 36.

34. Maria Lucia Victor Barbosa, *América Latina em Busca do Paraíso Perdido* ("Latin America in Search of Paradise Lost") (São Paulo: Editora Saraiva, 1995), p. 429. My translation.

35. Ibid., p. 430.

36. Interview with the author, Brasilia, 15 March 1995.

37. Interview with the author, Rio de Janeiro, 20 March 1995.

38. Interview with the author, Rio de Janeiro, 21 March 1995.

39. This section draws on David Martin's *Tongues of Fire* (London: Basil Blackwell, 1990), chap. 4.

40. Ibid., p. 64.

41. Ibid., p. 68. The quote is from Roger Bastide's *The African Religions of*

Brazil (Baltimore: Johns Hopkins University Press, 1977), p. 372. Martin notes that there are conflicting data with respect to the upward mobility of Protestants.

42. For example in Harrison, *Who Prospers?*

7. THE CHILEAN MIRACLE

1. World Bank, *World Development Report 1995*, pp. 220–21.
2. Forestry operations are becoming an important environmental issue in Chile; see "Chile—Forest Fire," *The Economist*, 3 February 1996.
3. Francisco A. Encina, *Nuestra Inferioridad Económica* ("Our Economic Inferiority") (Santiago: Editorial Universitaria, 1978), pp. 36–37.
4. Simon Collier, Thomas E. Skidmore, and Harold Blakemore, eds., "Chile," in *Cambridge Encyclopedia of Latin America* (Cambridge, U.K.: Cambridge University Press, 1992), p. 263.
5. Ibid.
6. Ibid., p. 264.
7. Encina, *Nuestra Inferioridad Económica*, pp. 107–9. Encina cites an estimate that there were 32,000 Chileans and children of Chilean parents in the south of Argentina in 1905.
8. Arnold J. Bauer, *Chilean Rural Society* (Cambridge, U.K.: Cambridge University Press, 1975), pp. 16, 24.
9. François Depons, *Viaje a la Parte Oriental de la Tierra Firme en la América Meridional* ("Trip to the Eastern Part of the Continent of South America") (Caracas: Banco Central de Venezuela, 1960). Cited in Luis Ugalde, S.J., Rector of Andrés Bello Catholic University, "Appreciation of Productive Work," a lecture at the Rómulo Gallegos Latin American Center, 5 October 1993.
10. Depons, *Viaje a la Parte Oriental*, p. 84.
11. Ibid., p. 85.
12. Ibid., p. 105. Note the use of the word *customs*, the same word Tocqueville used for *culture*.
13. Ibid., p. 229.
14. Markos Mamalakis, *The Growth and Structure of the Chilean Economy* (New Haven, Conn., and London: Yale University Press, 1976), p. 53.
15. Mamalakis, *The Growth and Structure of the Chilean Economy*.
16. David Martin, *Tongues of Fire* (London: Basil Blackwell, 1990), p. 51.
17. Angus Maddison, *The World Economy in the Twentieth Century* (Paris: OECD, 1989), p. 19.
18. Ibid., p. 15.
19. Magnus Blomström and Patricio Meller, eds., *Diverging Paths: Comparing*

a *Century of Scandinavian and Latin American Economic Development* (Washington. D.C.: Inter-American Development Bank, 1991), p. 41.

20. Mamalakis, *The Growth and Structure of the Chilean Economy*, pp. 210, 290.

21. Ibid., p. 293.

22. Ibid., p. 353.

23. Mark Falcoff, *Modern Chile 1970–89—A Critical History* (New Brunswick, N.J., and London: Transaction Publishers, 1989), p. x.

24. Falcoff, *Modern Chile 1970–89*, p. 76. Paul Sigmund makes the same point in *The United States and Democracy in Chile* (Baltimore and London: Johns Hopkins University Press, 1993), p. 204: "It is not accurate to describe the U.S. economic pressures, as President Allende did, as 'an invisible blockade,' and Chile was able to secure substantial aid from many other countries in Europe and Latin America, although it only received limited assistance from the Soviet Union."

25. *World Development Report 1995*, p. 162.

26. Falcoff, *Modern Chile 1970–89*, p. 81.

27. Many Allende supporters have argued that the soldiers who entered the Moneda Palace on 11 September 1973 shot him. But in the days and hours before his death, his statements strongly suggest that martyrdom was his goal, for example, "I will not resign . . . I will pay with my life for the loyalty of the people." Cited by Lois Hecht Oppenheim in *Politics in Chile—Democracy, Authoritarianism and the Search for Development* (Boulder, Colo., San Francisco, and Oxford: Westview Press, 1993), p. 91. Oppenheim had just noted (p. 90), "Although we will never know for sure, Allende's body was examined when it was exhumed for reburial in September 1990. Allende's widow, Hortensia Bussi de Allende, asked her husband's personal doctor to examine the remains so that she would be assured that it was, in fact, he. In a press conference later that day, the doctor stated that the physical evidence supported the theory that Allende had committed suicide."

28. The Argentine government announced in January 1996 the arrest of Enrique Arancibia Clavel, a former Chilean intelligence agent, for the car-bomb murder of Prats and his wife, Sofía. Many observers were convinced that Pinochet knew of the assassination. As the *New York Times* noted, "A conviction would point guilt directly at General Pinochet" ("Charges in 1974 Killing Raise Tensions in Chile," 17 February 1996).

29. Barry P. Bosworth, Rudiger Dornbusch, and Raúl Labán, *The Chilean Economy: Policy Lessons and Challenges* (Washington, D.C.: Brookings Institution, 1994), p. 5.

30. Ibid., p. 8.

31. Ibid., p. 9.

32. "Various Lobbies Pose Tough Choices for Chile as It Prepares to Join NAFTA," *Washington Post,* 25 December 1994, p. A33.

33. Mamalakis, *The Growth and Structure of the Chilean Ecomony,* p. 353.

34. Data are from World Bank, *World Development Report 1995.*

35. David Hojman, "Education, Ideology and Economic Growth in the Chilean Neo-Liberal Model," paper presented to the Annual Conference of the Society for Latin American Studies, Liverpool, U.K., 26–28 March 1994, p. 2.

36. "A Global Gauge of Greased Palms," *New York Times,* 20 August 1995, p. E–3. The study was conducted by Transparency International, "a Berlin-based watchdog organization."

37. Encina, *Our Economic Inferiority,* passim.

38. W. W. Rostow, *The Stages of Economic Growth—A Non-Communist Manifesto* (London and New York: Cambridge University Press, 1960), p. 11, note.

39. J. A. C. Mackie, "Overseas Chinese Entrepreneurship," *Asian-Pacific Economic Literature* (May 1992): 54.

40. Sigmund, *The United States and Democracy in Chile,* p. 213.

41. Personal correspondence, 25 September 1995.

42. Quoted in *The New Republic,* 7 July 1986.

43. Rudiger Dornbusch, "North-South Trade Relations in the Americas: The Case for Free Trade," in Inter-American Development Bank and Economic Commission for Latin America and the Caribbean, *Trade Liberalization in the Western Hemisphere* (Washington, D.C.: 1995), p. 46.

44. "Various Lobbies Pose Tough Choices for Chile," p. A33.

8. MEXICO: THE FAILURE OF A REVOLUTION

1. The preliminary figures of the Foreign Trade Division of the Bureau of the Census show a deficit of $15.4 billion. The economist Pat Choate estimated the job loss in an interview on CNBC on 13 March 1996.

2. The actual vote took place on 17 November 1993, and NAFTA was approved for implementation starting on 1 January 1994.

3. The estimate has been developed by Leon Bouvier, a demographer who advises the Center for Immigration Studies.

4. *The Cambridge Encyclopedia of Latin America* (Cambridge, UK: Cambridge University Press, 1992), p. 178.

5. Ibid., p. 190.

6. José Dolores Gámez, *Historia de Nicaragua* ("History of Nicaragua") (Managua: Banco de América, 1975), p. 134.

7. *The Cambridge Encyclopedia of Latin America*, p. 201.

8. Samuel Ramos, *Profile of Man and Culture in Mexico*, trans. Peter G. Earle (Austin: Texas Pan-American Series, 1962), p. 33.

9. Edmundo O'Gorman, *México: El Trauma de su Historia* ("Mexico: The Trauma of Its History") (Mexico City: Universidad Nacional Autónoma de México, 1977), p. 8. My translation.

10. David Hackett Fischer, *Albion's Seed* (Oxford, New York, Toronto: Oxford University Press, 1989), pp. 20–21.

11. Ibid., p. 21.

12. Ibid., p. 23.

13. Ibid., p. 24.

14. Ibid., p. 26. Fischer also mentions that the ratio in Brazil was 100 to 1.

15. Octavio Paz, *El Ogro Filantrópico* ("The Philanthropic Ogre") (Mexico City: Joaquín Mortiz, 1979), p. 55. My translation.

16. John Coatsworth noted this contrast in a symposium he and I attended in Atlanta in the spring of 1995.

17. Paz, *El Ogro Filantrópico*, pp. 57, 60.

18. O'Gorman, *México: El Trauma de su Historia*, p. 55.

19. Mexican sources deny that such encouragement occurred.

20. Mexican sources also deny that Mexico initiated hostilities.

21. Octavio Paz, *The Labyrinth of Solitude* (New York: Grove Press, 1961), p. 129.

22. *The Cambridge Encyclopedia of Latin America*, p. 234.

23. Jonathan Kandell dates the long-standing tradition of police corruption to the Porfiriato (*La Capital* [New York: Random House, 1988], chap. 14).

24. Paz, *The Labyrinth of Solitude*, p. 132.

25. Quoted in ibid., p. 153.

26. Ibid., pp. 152, 153.

27. The source of the 35 million figure is the Secretary of Public Education, Miguel Limón Rojas, cited in an article ("35 Millones de Mexicanos no han Concluido la Primaria" ["35 Million Mexicans Haven't Completed Primary School"]) in *El Financiero* (Mexico City), 29 November 1995. The 18 percent estimate was made by the Rector General of the Instituto Tecnológico de Estudios Superiores de Monterrey as reported in *El Occidental* (Guadalajara), 3 December 1995.

28. Kandell, *La Capital*, p. 511.

29. Alan Riding, *Distant Neighbors: A Portrait of the Mexicans* (New York: Vintage Books, 1986), p. 81.

30. Kandell, *La Capital*, p. 496.

31. Riding, *Distant Neighbors*, p. 85.

32. Kandell, *La Capital*, p. 542.

33. Keith S. Rosenn, "Corruption in Mexico: Implications for U.S. Foreign Policy," *California Western International Law Journal* 18, no. 1 (1987–88): 97.

34. Ibid., p. 103.

35. In a Senate Foreign Relations Committee hearing, Jesse Helms asserted that de la Madrid failed to get even 40 percent of the vote, based on data compiled by "de la Madrid's Military Chief of Staff." (Cited by Rosenn, "Corruption in Mexico," p. 100.)

36. From personal notes.

37. Rosenn, "Corruption in Mexico," p. 97.

38. "Drawing Lessons from the Mexican Crisis: Preventing and Resolving Financial Crises—the Role of the IMF," address by Michel Camdessus at the Twenty-fifth Washington Conference of the Council of the Americas, Washington, D.C., 22 May 1995.

39. Ibid., pp. 5–15, passim.

40. Ramos, *Profile of Man and Culture in Mexico*, p. 19.

41. Ibid., p. 23.

42. Ibid., p. 64.

43. Paz, *The Labyrinth of Solitude*, p. 82.

44. Ibid., p. 40.

45. Ibid., p. 175.

46. Carlos Escudé, *El Realismo de los Estados Débiles—La Política Exterior del Primer Gobierno Menem frente a la Teoría de las Relaciones Internacionales* (Buenos Aires: Grupo Editor Latinoamericano, 1995), p. 22. My translation.

47. Jorge Castañeda and Enrique Hett, *El Economismo Dependentista* (Mexico City, Madrid, Buenos Aires, and Bogotá: Siglo Veintiuno, 1978).

48. Ibid., p. 107.

49. Robert A. Pastor and Jorge G. Castañeda, *Limits to Friendship: The United States and Mexico* (New York: Knopf, 1988).

50. Jorge Castañeda, *Utopia Unarmed: The Latin American Left After the Cold War* (New York: Knopf, 1993).

51. Pastor and Castañeda, *Limits to Friendship,* chap. 2.

52. See Josefina Zoraida Vázquez and Lorenzo Meyer, *México Frente a Estados Unidos* ("Mexico Faces the United States") (Mexico City: El Colegio de México, 1982).

53. Ibid., p. 225.

54. Aguilar Zinser presented a paper, "Latin America in Search of Non-alignment," that appears in Luis Echeverría (President of Mexico) and Milos Minic, *Non-alignment and the New International Economic Order* (Belgrade: Ekonomika, 1983), pp. 131–40.

55. Ibid., p. 131.
56. Ibid., p. 132.
57. Ibid., p. 134.
58. Ibid., pp. 134, 138.
59. Ibid., p. 137.
60. Paz, *El Ogro Filantrópico*, pp. 138–39. My translation.
61. O'Gorman, *México*, p. 46. This and subsequent quotations are my translations.
62. Ibid., p. 15.
63. Ibid., p. 46.
64. Ibid., p. 102.
65. Ronald Inglehart, Miguel Basáñez, and Neil Nevitte, *The North American Trajectory* (Hawthorne, N.Y.: Aldine de Gruyter, 1996). As I noted in chapter 2, the authors also demonstrate that Canadian and American values are a good deal closer to each other than they are to Mexico's.

9. TRADE AND INVESTMENT

1. In 1990, Latin America was the destination of 1.57 percent of Canada's exports, compared to 72.7 percent to the United States (Robert A. Blecker and William E. Spriggs, "Beyond NAFTA: Employment, Growth, and Income Distribution Effects of a Western Hemisphere Free Trade Area," in IDB/ECLAC, *Trade Liberalization in the Western Hemisphere*, 1995, table, p. 136.
2. Isaac Cohen, "Economic Questions," in G. Pope Atkins, ed., *The United States and Latin America: Redefining U.S. Purposes in the Post–Cold War Era* (Austin, Tex.: LBJ School of Public Affairs, 1992), p. 28. Cohen is the director of ECLAC's Washington Office.
3. Sidney Weintraub points out that the United States had proposed a hemispheric free-trade area in 1889–90 that was roundly rejected by the Latin Americans ("Western Hemisphere Free Trade: Getting from Here to There," in IDB/ECLAC, *Trade Liberalization in the Western Hemisphere*, p. 336).
4. "With per capita income one-ninth of the U.S. level, and greater inequality, the ability of the average Mexican to purchase exported U.S. consumer goods must be quite minimal" (Blecker and Spriggs, "Beyond NAFTA," p. 125). That assertion was made *before* the peso crisis, which significantly reduced further the ability of the average Mexican to buy such products both because of the impact of the devaluation and the deep economic recession that followed it.

5. Source is Blecker and Spriggs, "Beyond NAFTA," p. 126, drawing on World Bank, *World Development Report 1992* data.

6. Blecker and Spriggs, "Beyond NAFTA."

7. Ibid., p. 127.

8. Ibid., p. 143.

9. U.S. Department of Commerce, *U.S. Direct Investment Abroad—Revised 1991 Estimates*, 1994, table II.A.1.

10. U.S. Department of Commerce, *Foreign Direct Investment in the United States—Revised 1991 Estimates*, 1994, table A–2.

11. Paul Krugman, "Dutch Tulips and Emerging Markets," *Foreign Affairs* (July/August 1995): 33.

12. Ibid., pp. 40–41. World Bank data show a population growth rate for Mexico of 2.2 percent in 1993.

13. Moises Naim, "Latin America the Morning After," *Foreign Affairs* (July/August 1995): 57.

14. Cited in ibid., p. 57.

15. See "Unity Cracking as American Nations Meet on Economic Zone," *New York Times*, 24 March 1996.

16. Weintraub, "Western Hemisphere Free Trade: Getting from Here to There," p. 338.

17. Robert Pastor, "The North American Free Trade Agreement: Hemisphere and Geopolitical Implications," in IDB/ECLAC, *Trade Liberalization in the Western Hemisphere*, p. 70.

18. Isaac Cohen Orantes, *Regional Integration in Central America* (Lexington, Mass., Toronto, and London: Lexington Books, 1972).

19. For an explanation of Costa Rica's uniqueness, see my *Underdevelopment Is a State of Mind—The Latin American Case* (Lanham, Md., and London: Center for International Affairs, Harvard University, and University Press of America, 1985), chap. 3.

20. World Bank, *World Development Report 1995*, table 1. *World Development Report 1980*, table 1, shows Costa Rica's per capita GNP as twice that of Nicaragua in 1978, one year before the Sandinistas took power.

21. World Bank, *World Development Report 1995*, table 1. No literacy data are reported for Nicaragua.

22. See Teodoro Moscoso, "The Will to Economic Development," in L. Ronald Scheman, *The Alliance for Progress—A Retrospective* (New York, Westport, Conn., London: Praeger, 1988), p. 86. Moscoso goes on to say, "Well, I have lived a little longer [twenty-two years] since saying those words, and I feel even more strongly today than I did then about this fundamental truth."

23. Weintraub, "Western Hemisphere Free Trade," p. 335.

24. Pastor, "The North America Free Trade Agreement," p. 63.

25. Ibid., p. 83.

26. In IDB/ECLAC *Trade Liberalization in the Western Hemisphere*, Rudiger Dornbusch (p. 42) leaves an erroneous impression in asserting that the purpose of EU's acceptance of Spain, Portugal, and Greece "was to spread irreversibly democratic institutions and progress." He should have used the word *consolidate* in lieu of *spread*. Spain, for example, had experienced more than a decade of democracy—and a quarter-century of open economic policies—when it joined the EC in 1986.

27. Dornbusch, in "North-South Trade Relations in the Americas: The Case for Free Trade," in IDB/ECLAC, *Trade Liberalization in the Western Hemisphere*, p. 42, predicts prosperity for Mexico through the 1990s.

28. Sidney Weintraub, *NAFTA—What Comes Next?* (Westport, Conn., and London: Praeger, 1994), pp. 74–75. Italics added.

29. This assertion is based on a speaking trip I made to Mexico City, Monterrey, Guadalajara, Ciudad Juárez, and Tijuana late in 1995.

30. See Weintraub, "Western Hemisphere Free Trade," p. 356.

10. NARCOTICS

1. The source for these estimates is the Office of National Drug Control Policy, *National Drug Control Strategy* (Washington D.C.: U.S. Government Printing Office, February 1995), pp. 20, 139. As Peter H. Smith points out in "The Political Economy of Drugs," in Peter H. Smith, ed., *Drug Policy in the Americas* (Boulder, Colo., San Francisco, and London: Westview Press, 1992), chapter 1, estimates are likely to be understated because, for example, survey respondents are not candid or because significant user groups (for example, the incarcerated) are omitted.

2. Cited by Smith in "The Political Economy of Drugs," p. 1.

3. Office of National Drug Control Policy, "National Drug Control Strategy 1995," pp. 144, 145.

4. Statement of Kathleen M. Hawk, Director, Federal Bureau of Prisons to House Judiciary Committee on International Law, Immigration and Refugees, 23 February 1994, cited by Peter Brimelow in *Alien Nation* (New York: Random House, 1995), pp. 183–84.

5. "Prosperity in New Chile Nourishes Drug Trade," *New York Times*, 27 March 1996.

6. Rensselaer Lee III, cited by Smith in "The Political Economy of Drugs," p. 9.

7. Francisco E. Thoumi, "The Economic Impact of Narcotics in Colombia," in Smith, *Drug Policy in the Americas*, p. 70.

8. "A Mission to Nowhere," *Newsweek*, 19 February 1990, p. 33; cited by Smith, "The Political Economy of Drugs," p. 10.

9. Smith, "The Political Economy of Drugs," p. 9.

10. Elena Alvarez, "Coca Production in Peru," in Smith, *Drug Policy in the Americas*, p. 81.

11. John Irving, *The Cider House Rules* (New York: Bantam Books, 1985).

12. David F. Musto, "Patterns in U.S. Drug Abuse and Response," in Smith, *Drug Policy in the Americas*, p. 30.

13. Ibid., p. 36.

14. Ibid., pp. 39–40.

15. In *Culture Shift in Advanced Industrial Society* (Princeton, N.J.: Princeton University Press, 1990, p. 438), Ronald Inglehart presents a table that shows the percentage of American respondents agreeing that "most people can be trusted" dropped from 58 percent in 1959 to 41 percent in 1981.

16. Douglas W. Payne, "Narcodemocracia," *El Comercio* (Lima, Peru), 16 February 1995, p. 2. My translation.

17. "Colombia: Guerrilla Economics," *The Economist*, 13 January 1996, p. 40.

18. The certification requirement appears in section 490 (b) (1) (A) of the Foreign Assistance Act of 1961.

19. U.S. Department of State Publication 10246, *International Narcotics Control Strategy Report*, March 1995, p. xxiii.

20. "An Offering to the U.S.: The Head of a Mexican," *New York Times*, 17 January 1996, p. A5.

21. "Mexico's Larger Drug War," *Christian Science Monitor*, 5 February 1996.

22. *New York Times*, 18 February 1996.

23. José Guillermo Justiniano, "The Power of Coca Producers," in Smith, *Drug Policy in the Americas*, pp. 100, 102.

24. In Smith, *Drug Policy in the Americas*, p. 17.

11. IMMIGRATION

1. U.S. Census Bureau, Pub. CPH-L–98 (1990 U.S. Census). The data appear in Center for Immigration Studies, "Immigration-Related Statistics–1995," p. 7.

2. "Mexico Woos U.S. Mexicans, Proposing Dual Nationality," *New York Times*, 10 December 1995.

3. Bouvier produced the estimate at my request.

4. U.S. Census Bureau P25–1104, October 1995; P25–111, March 1994.

5. "The Impact of International Migration on Sending Countries," pre-

pared for the Conference on Latin American Migration, Meridian House, Washington, D.C., 17 March 1995.

6. U.S. Embassy San Salvador message 003629, 23 May 1995.

7. "Migration Grows, Heads South as Well as North," *Washington Post*, 18 September 1995.

8. George J. Borjas, "Know the Flow," *National Review*, 17 April 1995, pp. 44–50. The article derives from a more detailed article, "The Economics of Immigration," *Journal of Economic Literature* (December 1994).

9. Borjas, "Know the Flow," p. 44.

10. Ibid., p. 47.

11. *World Development Report 1995*, table 1.

12. In a 1988 study of 1,114,800 amnestied immigrants (806,800—72 percent—of whom were from Mexico), one-third of the Mexicans had less than five years of education (presumably self-reported). See "To Import a Poverty Class: Data on the Characteristics of Recent Alien Amnesty Applicants," *Federation for American Immigration Reform* (February 1988).

13. See George J. Borjas, *Friends or Strangers* (New York: Basic Books, 1990).

14. Borjas, "Know the Flow," p. 49. This estimate will surely be debated by other analysts.

15. Ibid., p. 50.

16. See John Kenneth Galbraith, *The Nature of Mass Poverty* (Cambridge, Mass., and London: Harvard University Press, 1979).

17. Peter Skerry notes in *Mexican Americans* (Cambridge, Mass., and London: Harvard University Press, 1995—paperback), p. 190, that 5 percent of Mexican-Americans in San Antonio and Los Angeles were Protestants. In the early 1980s, the percentage had increased to 10. Skerry notes (p. 410, note 21) that Andrew Greeley's study, "Defections Among Hispanics" (*America*, 30 July 1988), suggests that defections are higher than the San Antonio and Los Angeles numbers he cites.

18. Consistent with the theories of Weber, the Harvard historian Stephan Thernstrom has found, in *The Other Bostonians*, that, at least in Boston, "the Irish and the Italians moved ahead economically only sluggishly and erratically; the English and the Jews, on the other hand, found their way into the higher occupational strata with exceptional speed. . . . [T]here is some reason for believing . . . that the cultures the immigrants brought with them had some effect" (Cambridge, Mass.: Harvard University Press, 1973), pp. 250–51.

19. U.S. Commission on Civil Rights, "The Economic Status of Americans of Asian Descent" (Washington, D.C.: Commission on Civil Rights, 1988).

20. Alfred N. Garwood, ed., *Hispanic Americans: A Statistical Sourcebook*

(Boulder, Colo.: Numbers and Concepts, 1993), pp. 101–2. The prime source is U.S. Bureau of the Census, *The Hispanic Population in the United States, 1991.*

21. Robert F. Schoeni, Kevin F. McCarthy, and Georges Vernez, *Pursuing the American Dream: The Progress of Immigrant Men in California and the United States* (Santa Monica, Cal.: RAND Corporation, June 1996), table 12.

22. U.S. Department of Education, National Center for Education Statistics, "Dropout Rates in the United States: 1993" (Document 94–669)

23. Linda Chavez, *Out of the Barrio* (New York: Basic Books, 1991).

24. Ibid., p. 114.

25. Ralph Rivera and Sonia Nieto, eds., *The Education of Latino Students in Massachusetts: Issues, Research, and Policy Implications* (Amherst: University of Massachusetts Press, 1993), p. 148.

26. Joan W. Moore, *Mexican Americans* (Englewood Cliffs N.J.: Prentice Hall, 1970), p. 97. The similarity of the Jewish and Japanese immigration experiences in the United States is the subject of a section in Alejandro Portes and Robert L. Bach's *Latin Journey* (Berkeley and Los Angeles: University of California Press, 1985), pp. 38–48.

27. *Hispanic Americans: A Statistical Sourcebook*, table 8, passim.

28. Ibid.

29. Joe L. Martinez, Jr., and Richard H. Mendoza, eds., *Chicano Sociology* (Orlando, Fla.: Academic Press, 1984), pp. 103, 104.

30. Kevin F. McCarthy and R. Burciaga Valdez, *Current and Future Effects of Mexican Immigration in California* (Santa Monica, Calif.: RAND, R–3365-CR, 1985).

31. Susan E. Keefe and Amado M. Padilla, *Chicano Ethnicity* (Albuquerque: University of New Mexico Press, 1987), pp. 7–8. For a comprehensive study of intergenerational dynamics, see George J. Borjas, "Long-Run Convergence of Ethnic Skill Differentials: The Children and Grandchildren of the Great Migration," *Industrial and Labor Relations Review* 47, no. 4 (July 1994): 553–72.

32. Leo Grebler, Joan W. Moore, and Ralph C. Guzman, *The Mexican-American People* (New York: Free Press, 1970); see esp. chap. 8.

33. RAND Corporation, "Annotated Briefing on the Effects of Large-Scale Immigration on California," p. 70 (draft of one section of Schoeni, McCarthy, and Vernez, *Pursuing the American Dream*).

34. Ibid., p. 84.

35. RAND Corporation, "Pursuing the American Dream," p. 23 (draft of a second section of Schoeni, McCarthy, and Vernez, *Pursuing the American Dream*).

36. Ibid., p. 27.

37. George J. Borjas and Stephen J. Trejo, "Immigrant Participation in the Welfare System," *Industrial and Labor Relations Review* 44, no. 2 (January 1991).

38. Borjas, "Know the Flow," p. 45.

39. Borjas and Trejo, "Immigrant Participation in the Welfare System."

40. RAND Corporation, "Annotated Briefing on the Effects of Large-Scale Immigration on California," p. 27.

41. Garwood, *Hispanic Americans*, p. 191.

42. Borjas, *Friends or Strangers*, pp. 150, 153.

43. "Single Motherhood: Stereotypes vs. Statistics," *New York Times*, 11 February 1996, p. E4. The source of the data is the National Center for Health Statistics.

44. "Advertising—A Campaign in California Aims to Reduce Sex and Pregnancies Among Teen-agers," *New York Times*, 8 February 1996.

45. "Mexico Woos U.S. Mexicans, Proposing Dual Nationality."

46. Sidney Verba, Kay Lehman Schlozman, and Henry E. Brady, *Voice and Equality: Civic Voluntarism in American Politics* (Cambridge, Mass., and London: Harvard University Press, 1995). The authors believe that participation in church activities is an important promoter of the idea of participation and the skills necessary to engage in it. The hierarchical, paternalistic traditions of the Catholic Church thus become an impediment to participation.

47. Skerry, *Mexican Americans*, p. 375.

48. Ibid., p. 378.

49. Peter Brimelow, *Alien Nation* (New York: Random House, 1995), p. 182.

50. Ibid., pp. 182–83.

51. *The Social Contract* (Summer 1995): 287.

52. Richard Lamm and John Love, "Apartheid: American Style," *Rocky Mountain News*, 18 September 1988.

53. National Narcotics Intelligence Consumers Committee, *The Supply of Illicit Drugs to the United States—1995*, p. 7.

54. Derrick Thomas, "The Foreign Born in the Federal Prison Population," presented at the Canadian Law and Society Association Conference, Carleton University, Ottawa, 8 June 1993. The quote is from page 16.

55. James S. Robb, *Affirmative Action for Immigrants—The Entitlement Nobody Wanted* (Petoskey, Mich.: Social Contract Press, 1995).

56. Chavez, *Out of the Barrio*, p. 20.

57. Rosalie Pedalino Porter, *Forked Tongue: The Politics of Bilingual Education* (New York: Basic Books, 1990).

58. Personal correspondence, 13 January 1991.

59. See, for example, Porter, *Forked Tongue.*

60. See Skerry, *Mexican Americans,* p. 283.

61. Interview with the author, 9 October 1995.

62. Michael E. Porter, *The Competitive Advantage of Nations* (New York: Free Press, 1990), pp. 3–7 passim.

63. In a coversation on 7 October 1995, Reyes made it clear to me that "Hold the Line" was a local initiative that got little support from INS until after its success.

64. Michael S. Teitelbaum and Myron Weiner, eds., *Threatened Peoples, Threatened Borders—World Migration and U.S. Policy* (New York and London: Norton, 1995), pp. 24–25. Reyes retired from the Border Patrol in the fall of 1995 to run for Congress as a Democrat.

65. Interview with the author, 7 October 1995.

66. I was advised of the existence of such a Mexican law by the Border Patrol's Marco Ramírez.

67. CNN reported on 18 February 1996 the results of a poll in which 80 percent of the respondents wanted to reduce immigration and 20 percent wanted to stop it altogether.

12. CONCLUSION

1. "Ferocious Differences," *The Atlantic Monthly,* July 1995.

2. The book appeared first in French as *Du Bon Sauvage au Bon Révolutionnaire* (1976), then in Spanish (*Del Buen Salvaje al Buen Revolucionario*) and in English as *The Latin Americans—Their Love-Hate Relationship with the United States* (New York and London: Harcourt Brace Jovanovich, 1977).

3. Rangel, *The Latin Americans,* p. 182.

4. Ibid., pp. 144, 145.

5. Teodoro Moscoso, "The Will to Economic Development," in Ronald Scheman, ed., *The Alliance for Progress—A Retrospective* (New York and Westport, Conn.: Praeger, 1988), p. 84.

6. Douglas Payne, "Ballots, Neo-Strongmen, Narcos, and Impunity," *Freedom Review* (January-February 1995).

7. *World Development Report 1995,* table 1.

8. *World Development Report 1981,* table 1.

9. Angus Maddison, *The World Economy in the Twentieth Century* (Paris: OECD, 1989), table 1.2.

10. Personal correspondence, 1 April 1996.

11. José Ortega y Gasset, *Invertebrate Spain* (New York: Norton, 1937), pp. 152–53.

12. Carlos Alberto Montaner, *Libertad—La Clave de la Prosperidad* (Madrid: Fundación Liberal José Martí, 1994), pp. 133, 135. My translation.

13. See, for example, "Lo que necesitan los paises pobres para que sus mercados funcionen" (What the poor countries need in order that their markets function) in *Revista INCAE* (Alajuela, Costa Rica: INCAE, 1996), pp. 76–80.

14. Montaner, *Libertad—La Clave de la Prosperidad*, p. 140.

15. Joan W. Moore, *Mexican Americans* (Englewood Cliffs, N.J.: Prentice Hall, 1970), p. 97.

16. Tomás Roberto Fillol, *Social Factors in Economic Development* (Cambridge, Mass.: MIT Press, 1961), p. 55.

17. Ibid., p. 97.

18. Ibid., pp. 98–99.

19. Michael Novak, *Will It Liberate? Questions About Liberation Theology* (Mahwah, N.J.: Paulist Press, 1986).

20. Michael Novak, *The Spirit of Democratic Capitalism* (New York: American Enterprise Institute and Simon and Schuster, 1982).

21. Michael Novak, *This Hemisphere of Liberty—A Philosophy of the Americas* (Washington, D.C.: AEI Press, 1990).

22. Michael Novak, *The Catholic Ethic and the Spirit of Capitalism* (New York: Free Press, 1993).

23. Bernice Martin, "New Mutations of the Protestant Ethic Among Latin American Pentecostals," *Religion* 25 (1995): 101.

24. Ibid., p. 108.

Index